Is Higher Education Fair to Women?

Is Higher Education Fair to Women?

Edited by
Sandra Acker &
David Warren Piper

SRHE & NFER-NELSON

Published by SRHE & NFER-NELSON
At the University, Guildford, Surrey GU2 5XH

First published 1984
© Sandra Acker and David Warren Piper

ISBN 1-85059-002-8
Code 8937 02 1

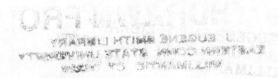

Printed and bound in Great Britain
by Billing & Sons Limited, Worcester.

Contents

The Authors

SANDRA ACKER is a lecturer in the School of Education, University of Bristol, where she teaches courses on the sociology of education and on education and social divisions and is convenor for the Centre for the Study of Women and Education. Her PhD dissertation was a study of sex differences in career ambition among postgraduate students and she has since published a number of articles on women and education. Recently she was guest editor for the 1984 *World Yearbook of Education* (Kogan Page) and is now writing about the careers of women teachers.

PETER BURNHILL heads the Data Library Services and leads the Scottish Data Centre Initiative at the University of Edinburgh, where he was the Scottish Educational Department's research fellow at the Centre for Educational Sociology. Formerly on the staff of the Social Science Research Council, he has research interests in educational inequality and the projection of higher education participation.

JOAN BURSTYN is Professor of Education at Rutgers, the State University of New Jersey, and directs the Women's Studies Program there. She is the author of *Victorian Education and the Ideal of Womanhood* (Croom Helm, 1980), and of chapters in anthologies and articles in journals on the history of women's education in both England and the United States. She is a member of the editorial boards of *Signs: Journal of Women in Culture and Society*, of *History of Education Quarterly* and of *History of Higher Education Annual*.

RENATE DUELLI KLEIN is a Swiss biologist who is now in Women's Studies. After two years in the USA at Berkeley, she now lives in London and does research on the theory and practice of Women's Studies. With Gloria Bowles she has edited *Theories of Women's Studies* (Routledge & Kegan Paul, 1983) and she is co-editor of *Feministische Wissenschaft und Frauenstudium* (1982). She is one of the editors of the *Athene Series* and European editor of the *Women's Studies International Forum*.

CAROL DYHOUSE is a feminist social historian who teaches courses in history and education at the University of Sussex. She has published a number of articles on the history of middle and working-class girls' education and her book *Girls Growing Up in Late Victorian and Edwardian England* was published by Routledge & Kegan Paul in 1981.

ANDREW MCPHERSON is director of the Centre for Educational Sociology, Edinburgh University. His previous publications include *The Scottish Sixth* (with Guy Neave) (NFER, 1976); *Tell Them From Me* edited with Lesley Gow (Aberdeen University Press, 1980) and *Reconstructions of Secondary Education* (with John Gray and David Raffe) (Routledge & Kegan Paul, 1983).

MARY PORTER is currently living in Seattle, USA. She was formerly a research associate in the Department of Sociology, University of Lancaster, and co-worker on the Postgraduate Research project. Her research interests are in methodology and in Asian women in Britain.

MARGHERITA RENDEL is Senior Lecturer in Human Rights and Education at the University of London Institute of Education, and directs the interdisciplinary MA in Rights in Education (including Women's Studies). She was the founding chairperson of the Research Committees on Sex Roles and Politics of the International Political Science Association. Her publications include: evidence to official bodies; works on Women's Studies, women in politics, law; and books on: *The Administrative Functions of the French Conseil d'Etat* (Weidenfeld & Nicholson, 1970); and, as editor, *Women, Power and Political Systems* (Croom Helm, 1981).

HELEN ROBERTS is a feminist and sociologist who has studied at the Universities of Reading, Sussex and Aix-Marseille and is currently senior researcher at Bradford and Ilkley Community College. She works and publishes largely in the areas of health care for women and the methodology of the social sciences. She is the editor of *Doing Feminist Research* (Routledge & Kegan Paul, 1981) and *Women, Health and Reproduction* (Routledge & Kegan Paul, 1981).

SUE SCOTT is currently a research officer for Nottingham County Council working in the field of community health. She was formerly a research associate and honorary research fellow in the Department of Sociology, University of Lancaster, and co-worker on the Postgraduate Research project. Her research interests are women in sociology, methodology and the sociology of health and illness.

DALE SPENDER is editor of *Women's Studies International Forum* and the *Athene Monograph Series*. She is the author of books and articles on feminism in relation to language, education and philosophy. She wrote the chapter on 'Sex Bias' in *Is Higher Education Fair?* (SRHE, 1981).

LIZ STANLEY is a feminist and sociologist who lives and works in Manchester. She spent all her secondary education in the bottom stream of a girl's grammar school, leaving at sixteen to work in Woolworths, as a groom, as a filing clerk, as a wages clerk and as a children's nanny before taking 'O' and 'A' levels part-time. Her first degree was in economics and politics, taken as an external London degree at her local technical college. Her main academic interests currently include the theory and practice of 'research' in the social sciences, changing academic ideas about sex and sexuality and women's perceptions of their own lives from the nineteenth century onwards. Her publications include (with S.Wise) *Breaking Out: Feminist Consciousness and Feminist Research* (Routledge & Kegan Paul, 1983).

DAPHNE TAYLORSON is a lecturer in the sociology of education in the Department of Education, University of Manchester. She has previously lectured at the University of London Institute of Education and at the University of Leeds. Her current research is on women at the University of Manchester in the late nineteenth century.

DAVID WARREN PIPER is head of the Centre for Staff Development in Higher Education, University of London Institute of Education, and at the time of preparing this book, was chairman of the Society for Research into Higher Education. Previous publications include: as editor, *Women in Higher Education* (UTMU, 1973); *The Changing University* (with Ron Glatter, NFER, 1977); and again as editor, *Is Higher Education Fair?* (SRHE, 1981).

HELEN WEINREICH-HASTE is a lecturer in psychology at the University of Bath. She has researched and published in several fields of adolescence, including moral development, and the effect of sex role on motivation and aspirations of adolescents. She is currently working on a book which assesses the extent to which sex roles have really changed over the last decade.

Introduction

Sandra Acker and David Warren Piper

Why is it that comparatively little concern has been expressed about women's participation in British higher education? In the United States, analyses abound of the difficulties and discrimination experienced by women students and staff (eg Astin 1969; Carnegie Commission 1973; Fox 1981; Furniss and Graham (Eds) 1974; Kilson 1976; Rossi and Calderwood (Eds) 1973; Vartuli (Ed.) 1982). In Britain, we have hardly a handful of such studies (Blackstone and Fulton 1975; Rendel 1975; Warren Piper (Ed.) 1975). Even feminist educationalists have largely avoided the topic, concentrating instead on primary and secondary schooling (eg Sharpe 1976; Spender and Sarah (Eds) 1980). Contributors to *Is Higher Education Fair to Women?* believe that 'women and higher education' is a 'problem' worth serious consideration. The book's origins are in the 1981 annual conference of the Society for Research into Higher Education, 'Biases in Higher Education', keynote papers from which were published in *Is Higher Education Fair?* (Warren Piper (Ed.) 1982). Revised versions of four more papers from that conference are included in this new volume (Taylorson; Rendel; Stanley; Duelli Klein). All others have been specially commissioned. As editors, we had the following intentions: a) to cover as many levels of higher education as possible; b) to present a variety of perspectives, methods, and disciplinary approaches; c) to set the present situation of women in higher education in a theoretical and historical context; and d) to consider reforms.

The tone and weight of the papers vary and consequently so may their appeal to the reader. Some are abstract, some statistical, some anecdotal, and some polemical.

The book opens with chapters by the editors giving a theoretical context for the contributed papers. David Warren Piper (Ch.1) raises fundamental questions about 'fairness' in the higher education system generally. Different models of the system produce differential support for arguments about equity. He considers what distinctions among people are appropriately made in arguments about fairness. He presents a list of criteria with which we might judge fairness. Complexities emerge, both in considering why people do or do not aspire to higher education and in discovering why they are sometimes inequitably treated when they do. Finally his argument focuses on the issue of discrimination against women and the possible use, abuse, or misuse of separate provision and separate treatment for the sexes within higher education.

Sandra Acker (Ch.2) locates her chapter more firmly in the literature on women in higher education and on gender relations. She identifies a series of ways in which a 'woman question' has surfaced in discussions of higher education. Do women lack sufficient confidence to aim for higher levels of education and occupation? Are they victims of sex discrimination in educational institutions? Are highly educated women best seen as an oft-neglected source of talent? Do the requirements of a capitalist and patriarchal economic and social order require restrictions on women's educational participation? Do women feel ill at ease in a culture which elevates knowledge based mainly on male experience to the status of knowledge representing all human beings? Or are our efforts to analyse the position of women in higher education simply a diversion from a concentration on other, perhaps more important, forms of inequity?

Looking Back

The two chapters in Part II provide an historical framework for present-day events. Carol Dyhouse (Ch.3) questions the optimistic version of women's educational history which imagines a clear path from Victorian 'revolutions' to late twentieth-century 'equality'. There were contradictions in the effects of higher education on women: for whilst it seemed in the beginning (as now) to secure valuable space for women to think and experiment, it operated at the same time to constrain and control them. The 'hidden curriculum' of women's early higher education is especially significant in this respect and featured male dominance of the governing structure of the colleges, claustrophobic surveillance of students, and contrast between dowdy female dons and glamorous staff wives.

The surveillance of students existed to protect not only their morals but their health for, as Joan Burstyn shows (Ch.4), there was no lack of late nineteenth-century scientific and medical books and articles warning against the dire consequences of women's participation in higher education. Although those seeking to expand educational opportunities for women rejected the more extreme arguments, they nevertheless fell into the trap of operating on their opponents' terms. They too ended up generalizing about 'women as a group', despite their own faith in individual differences, and they embarked on a vast amount of research into the health of educated women in order to prove the critics wrong. Meanwhile, to be on the safe side, educators guarded their women students against overwork, introduced extensive physical education programmes for them, and restricted their social lives.

Looking In and Out, Up and Down

Part III is a series of analyses of the present-day position of women in higher education. They 'look in and out', for they show how institutions of higher education mirror sexual divisions in the society outside.

In another sense the women themselves are looking in as they assess their talents and tailor their aspirations to suit their self-images and looking out at the structural and cultural barriers that serve to shape and mould these ambitions to gender-appropriate roles: in Daphne Taylorson's terms, they negotiate their 'academic' and 'gender' identities.

Contributors to Part III also 'look up and down', the hierarchical nature of higher education being omnipresent. Students and academic and academic-related staff are arranged in a progression from lowly first-year student to lofty professor, with their hierarchy superimposed on others: the hierarchies of cleaners, caterers, secretaries, porters, librarians, computing personnel, etc. (The presence of these groups is so taken for granted that research into higher education rarely, if ever, mentions it.) Women are not distributed through the hierarchies at random but are clustered in certain sectors and levels, looking up more often than down.

This book itself concentrates on students and academic staff. Peter Burnhill and Andrew McPherson (Ch.5) report findings from surveys investigating the values and plans of men and women students in Scotland. Burnhill and McPherson's sample includes degree students, students in other forms of education, and non-students, all from the ablest quarter of school-leavers. The authors are uniquely enabled to comment on social change, for their data, though cross-sectional, are collected from two similar groups ten years apart (1971 and 1981). They refer also to the history of Scottish higher education – the 'ambivalence of provision' (like the 'contradictions' identified by Carol Dyhouse) which gave women opportunities but also channelled them into the lower prestige college sector as trainee teachers. There are pronounced changes in orientation in the 1970s, perhaps because of contemporary changes in ideological climate and educational structure. Compared with the 1971 group, the women's occupational plans and the ideas of job satisfaction displayed in 1981 more closely resembled those of men: family plans had been deferred, desire to work with young people and children had declined and expectations of working full-time had increased. The decline in desire to work with children is especially interesting, suggesting that such a 'desire' may be a socially constructed response to opportunity structures as much as a matter of personality disposition. 'Qualified women have become more ambitious, educationally and occupationally, and more men and women are now prepared to accept such ambitions as legitimate,' say the authors. It is ironic, as they note, that such 'emancipation' coincides with a future where career opportunities seem to be sharply contracting.

Helen Weinreich-Haste's findings on undergraduates at seven English universities (Ch.6) are not inconsistent with the Scottish results. An additional dimension she considers is that of discipline (subject field). She finds strong disciplinary differences in attitudes and orientation among women (and among men) to career and politics. These variations pose an alternative to the 'women as a (homogeneous) group' framework that Joan Burstyn identifies in the attacks on and defences of women's higher education. Most of the students in Helen Weinreich-Haste's sample were relatively conservative politically. Women sociologists were the most 'radical': but even among this group only 37 per cent supported the Labour Party and an equal proportion supported the Liberal-SDP Alliance. Frequently 'discipline' outweighed sex − men and women in a given field gave similar answers to various questions. Among women, different types of orientation to feminism emerge from the data on career and family plans. One group is relatively work-orientated but politically conservative and individualistic (biologists/physicists/engineers); another is conservative across the board (economists/linguists); a third is, relatively, politically liberal and feminist (sociologists).

Those two papers focus on individuals making decisions in an historical and societal context. With Dale Spender (Ch.7), attention shifts to the institutional and political context and the question of who has policy-making power. She looks at teacher training, traditionally the choice of women in higher education (but curiously under-researched in this respect) and argues that there are few signs that teacher training is doing anything to reduce sexism among recruits to the teaching profession. Nor does the government take a significant lead in this direction. Her paper is angrier than the previous ones. She moves away from the considered optimism of Peter Burnhill and Andrew McPherson and stresses continuities rather than change: educational planning has been and still is dominated by men who do little to combat sexual inequality.

Daphne Taylorson's paper (Ch.8), returns to a concern with career orientations and questions about the context in which they develop. She reports a study of women doctoral students. As might be expected at this level, the women were highly motivated and quite clear about their occupational intentions. The tension between structure and identity is vividly demonstrated. While the women students − frequently lone women in otherwise all-male departments − appeared to be integrated into the academic life of their departments, this was not the case in informal social interaction.

Daphne Taylorson suggests that women postgraduates have a complex task, for not only must they participate in the process of professional socialization, they must do it always conscious of the fact they are women as well as physicists or historians or literary critics. They must cope with potential incompatibilities between academic, subject and gender identities. As Helen Weinreich-Haste found, disciplinary affiliation is important in differentiating <u>among</u> the student women. In Daphne Taylorson's sample, the arts students were least successful in negotiating the transition to an academic identity, the social science students most successful, and the scientists in between.

Women academics might be expected to have left such conflicts behind them and to be all but indistinguishable from their male counterparts. We have no information on the hopes and fears of such women, but statistics show where they are distributed in the academic hierarchy. Margherita Rendel analyses university statistics (Ch.9) and concludes not only that academic women are segregated by grade and subject but that their status has not significantly increased in the 1970s. Although the number of female professors increased from 61 to 105 between 1972 and 1979, proportions in senior posts overall declined (while markedly increasing for men). Margherita Rendel also singles out subject affiliation as strongly influencing the probability that women will progress to senior posts. Her concern is with upholding justice and fighting discrimination, an objective which she believes is as important for academic women as for any others.

The final paper in Part III is in deliberate contrast to most of the other papers in the section. Rather than report on the findings of research, Sue Scott and Mary Porter write about the experience of doing it. They give a personal testimony of what it feels like to be 'doubly marginal': women researchers working on someone else's project. Contract researchers have little security and few prospects − and many are women. Again, it is a question of how we construct an academic and personal identity within structural constraints, and again it is a contradictory situation, where marginality enforces limitations but brings with it certain insights and chances for creativeness.

Looking Forward

The three contributors in Part IV break away from documenting the position of women in higher education as it is (or was) and explore instead what it might become. Appropriately placed after Sue Scott's and Mary Porter's personal account, Liz Stanley's paper (Ch.11) argues that personal experience provides an essential base for feminist research in the social sciences. She points to the difficulties faced by people new to such research when they find disjunctions between' what they are supposed to experience and what they do experience, and how the conventional resolution requires novices to discard experience. Feminist experience may uncover a different reality (or several), and Liz Stanley aims for an alternative that starts from feminist axioms − including the understanding that women are oppressed, the insistence on the personal as political, and the practice of feminism in everyday life. The researcher researches her own experience. Some readers will disagree with the arguments made here, and most of our other contributors have chosen differing modes of inquiry which in their terms are also feminist research. Yet Liz Stanley's arguments are provocative and challenge us to go beyond simple critiques of sexism in social science.

Helen Roberts (Ch.12) examines affirmative action, a legal and political strategy used extensively in the United States, and speculates on its possible applications to Britain. Affirmative action is a means of remedying past injustices by requiring institutions (including universities) to make efforts to hire and promote qualified women (or minorities) who have hitherto been overlooked or excluded. The approach dovetails best with the type of feminism that perceives the problem of women in higher education as one of injustice and discrimination and aims toward sharing scarce rewards equally between the sexes rather than fundamentally altering the basis on which rewards are made. Affirmative action is not without its own problems and is unlikely to get far in Britain. Nevertheless, Helen Roberts argues that there are low-cost reforms, such as expanding child care provision in higher education, which could be introduced if only the will were found.

In the final paper (Ch.13), Renate Duelli Klein also writes of an innovation more widespread in the United States than in Britain: 'Women's Studies'. She restores our hope and optimism as she reports on the joy and energy realized in these programmes. There is the potential in Women's Studies, she believes, to transcend established disciplines, to develop new ideas about feminist research, and to mount an effective challenge to 'male-dominated, male orientated, male-defined education'.

The book concludes with an identification by the editors of four themes which emerge from this collection of essays and research papers: the double edged notion of women as an homogeneous group; the inter-relationships between the self-identity of women and institutional structures largely developed by and for men; the opportunities as well as the limitations implicit in the marginal positions occupied by women in the education system; and the interweaving of change and conservatism.

June 1983

REFERENCES

Astin, H.S. (1979) *The Woman Doctorate in America* New York: Russell Sage

Blackstone,T. and Fulton,O. (1975) Sex discrimination among university teachers: a British-American comparison *British Journal of Sociology* 26, 261-275

Carnegie Commission on Higher Education (1973) *Opportunities for Women in Higher Education* New York: McGraw-Hill

Fox,M.F. (1981) Sex, salary, and achievement: reward-dualism in academia *Sociology of Education* 54, 71-84

Furniss,W.T. and Graham,P.A. (Eds.)(1974) *Women in Higher Education* Washington, DC: American Council on Education

Kilson,M. (1979) The status of women in higher education *Signs* 1, 935-942

Rendel,M. (1975) Men and women in higher education *Educational Review* 27, 192-210

Rossi,A.S. and Calderwood,A. (Eds)(1973) *Academic Women on the Move* New York: Russell Sage

Sharpe,S. (1976) *Just Like a Girl* Harmondsworth: Penguin

Spender,D. and Sarah,E. (Eds)(1980) *Learning to Lose* London: The Women's Press

Vartuli,S. (Ed.)(1982) *The Ph.D Experience: A Woman's Point of View* New York: Praeger

Warren Piper,D. (Ed.)(1975) *Women in Higher Education* London: University of London Teaching Methods Unit

Warren Piper,D. (Ed.)(1981) *Is Higher Education Fair?* Guildford: Society for Research into Higher Education

The Society for Research into Higher Education

The Society exists to encourage research and development in all aspects of higher education: highlighting both the importance of this and the needs of the research community. Its corporate members are universities, polytechnics, institutes of higher education, research institutions and professional and governmental bodies. Its individual members are teachers and researchers, administrators and students. Membership is worldwide, and the Society regards its international work as amongst its most important activities.

The Society discusses and comments on policy, organizes conferences and sponsors research. Under the imprint SRHE & NFER-NELSON it is a specialist publisher of research, with over thirty titles currently in print. It also publishes Studies in Higher Education (SHE) *(twice a year),* Research into Higher Education Abstracts *(three times a year),* Evaluation Newsletter (EN) *(twice a year),* International Newsletter (IN) *(twice a year) and a* Bulletin *(six times a year).*

The Society's committees, groups and local branches are run by members with limited help from a small secretariat and provide a forum for discussion and a platform for ideas. Some of the groups, at present the Teacher Education Study Group and the Staff Development Group, have their own subscriptions and organization, as do some local branches. The Governing Council, elected by members, comments on current issues and discusses policies with leading figures in politics and education. The Society organizes seminars on current research for officials of the DES and other ministries, and is in constant touch with officials of bodies such as the CNAA, NAB, CVCP, CDP, UGC and the British Council. The Society's annual conferences take up central themes, viz. Education for the Professions (1984, with the help and support of DTI, UNESCO and many professional bodies), Continuing Education (1985, organized in collaboration with Goldsmiths' College, the Open University and the University of Surrey, with advice from the DES and the CBI) and Standards (1986). Special studies are being commissioned. Joint conferences are held, viz. Cognitive Processes (1985, with the Cognitive Psychology Section of the BPS). Members receive free of charge the Society's Abstracts, SHE *(corporate members only), annual conference proceedings,* Bulletin *and* IN, *and may buy SRHE & NFER-NELSON books at discount. They may also obtain* EN *(published jointly with CRITE),* SHE *and certain other journals at discount.*

Further information from the Society for Research into Higher Education, At the University, Guildford GU2 5XH, UK.

Part 1
Theoretical context

1 The question of fairness

David Warren Piper

This book questions whether higher education, as it is currently organized and conducted in this country, is fair to a defined section of the population – women. Each chapter presents argument and evidence on a different aspect of the question. The discussions in the book do not stand alone, unrelated to other social issues. On the one hand the treatment of women within the higher education system is but a small part of the wider issue of how women are treated in our society at large. On the other hand it is but a particular of more general questions of educational policy and of how all people are treated by the education system.

Most of the authors write from a feminist perspective, which implies that the issue of women's experience in society at large is integral to the argument. Although the focus of the discussion is higher education or some aspect of it, the frame of reference, implicit where it is not explicit, is the more general one of women in society. In her chapter, Sandra Acker reviews the literature and provides a framework within which to weave the various strands of the book.

Sandra Acker provides that framework, of feminist literature and the study of women. However, before embarking upon chapters addressing our central concern, it is worth setting them in the other context implied by the title of the book – the study of higher education. What follows cannot claim to be exhaustive, but is an attempt to highlight some of the implications of the question of fairness in education and a few of the conundrums to which it leads. Consider the following questions:

- Is fairness an appropriate criterion for evaluating an education system?
- How important is the comparison between men and women compared with other classifications which might be adopted to reveal inequity?

— What are the various ways in which unfairness might be reckoned?
— How might fairness be achieved; do, for instance, 'equal opportunity' and 'positive discrimination' provide an answer?

Is Fairness an Appropriate Criterion?

Taking 'fairness' as an important criterion for evaluating an education system presupposes a particular view about its main purpose. The point can be highlighted by describing three distinct views about the purpose of education, labelled for convenience; the 'functional', 'cultural' and 'social service' views (Table 1.1). Normally an education system is expected to fulfil all these purposes; but for clarity of argument let us suppose for a moment that only one purpose be adopted and allowed to override the other two. In each case what would the resulting education systems be like? Only higher education will be considered here.

A functional view of higher education takes the purpose to be the production of educated people. At its crudest it is the production of the right combination of trained person-power — technologists, engineers, teachers, doctors, lawyers — to meet the needs of the community. Such formulations can be more or less liberal, allowing for various proportions of, say, commentators, philosophers and artists whose contribution to the common good may be less certain and less open to quantification. Also goals may be specified with varying degrees of attempted exactitude. Nonetheless determination of the goals and the form of their specification is the province of government. Education becomes one of an administration's means of achieving its national development policy.

A system solely devoted to this end would rationally have the following characteristics. Its finances would be centrally controlled. Student numbers would be a matter of policy based on some appreciation of future needs. There would be central control over how many students entered each subject, either by directive or by a powerful system of inducement. The system would be selective and the aim of selection would be to admit those people most likely to meet the demands of their employment satisfactorily; a sophisticated approach would be some form of planned heterogeneity in various professions. Courses would be based on some analysis of the work or role for which students were being prepared. The result would most likely be many multi-disciplinary courses, as very few jobs indeed are identical in scope with an academic subject. Teachers' first identities would be as professionals; not professional teachers, but people working at the teaching end of their primary profession of engineering or acting or whatever. Many might well be part-time or teach for limited periods. Professional bodies would figure strongly in course validation and in the accreditation of students. The

Table 1.1 The implication of three views of higher education

	FUNCTIONAL	CULTURAL	SOCIAL SERVICE
Finance	Centrally provided and directed	Multiple sources of provision	Centrally provided but amount and distribution 'demand'-led
Student Numbers	Finance-led and reflecting employment projections	Dependent on 'pool of ability'	Dependent on demand
Distribution of Students	Dependent on 'national need'	Institutional policy	According to demand
Access	Selection according to suitability for employment	Selection on academic standards	Open entry
Courses	Based on 'job analysis'	Discipline-based	Contractual with students on their goals and personal development
Accreditation	Qualifications supervised by professional bodies	Academic degrees (protected by charter)	Descriptive rather than evaluative
Teaching Staff	Primarily practitioners, part-time or short contract	Primary identity with discipline	Primary identity teacher and 'facilitator'
Research	Policy or problem focused; r & d, consultancy	Pure; focused on theory building	Monitoring the education system

solving of practical problems would be a major focus of research if it appeared in the education system at all.

Where does 'fairness' figure in this view of education? The main criteria for judging the effectiveness of the system would be the success with which the desired numbers of trained (or educated) people were produced and how well they were prepared for the various jobs or roles they were to take up. In this system the supposed overall good of the community is given preference over the wishes of the individual. By some philosophies that is fair enough. In so far as fairness to the individual did appear, it might take the form of ensuring that selection was not corrupt and that every effort was made to see that discrimination was based as well as was humanly possible on suitability for the role in view and nothing else. The system would be a vocational meritocracy.

Such a system is discriminatory and élitist in the sense that only the most 'suitable' people will be admitted; suitability being based on some appreciation of the demands and goals of the profession (or role) in mind. However, despite its essential exclusiveness such a rationale can provide powerful arguments for representation of various groups of society in the education system. If a profession, for instance, is considered as a group of people, homogeneous in some respects but desirably heterogeneous in others, then some kind of quota system, or at least balance, is called for. If police officers, or general practitioners, or community lawyers are thought to be more effective as a whole if they include representatives of ethnic minorities, then the education system could admit and prepare appropriate numbers. There are countries where vigorous efforts are made to redress imbalances of ethnic groups among the highly educated − Malaysia for instance. A similar approach could be taken to ensure a higher proportion of women in any or all professions. This, however, is not an appeal to the fairness of the education system, which remains simply the instrument by which national policy is effected. Rather it is defining a desirable characteristic of the society − or at least part of its workforce − which is the intended end-product. So, although an appeal to equity could be invoked, it is not necessary: an argument for including more women in a profession could be based exclusively on a desire for increased effectiveness. If the admission of women is regarded as a sure path to ineffectiveness, the appropriate response is not an appeal to fairness but a forceful demonstration of the mistakenness of the view. (The matter of such stereotypes is taken up in the next section, pages 9-10.)

Still in the functional view a more general argument for the admission of women is that they represent a greatly under-used resource; economic necessity, rather than social equity, requires that more women should appear among the highly trained workforce. This differs from the earlier argument in that it is essentially expansionist: it is saying that modern society requires a large proportion of its population to be highly trained and that the inclusion of women is necessary to reach that proportion; women are needed as well as men. The earlier argument does not necessarily imply larger numbers; the ratio of the sexes can be adjusted by admitting women instead of men. The central point here is that appeals to equity and fairness are not a necessary part of a functional argument for the equal representation of the sexes in higher education.

The 'cultural view' of education sees its purpose as passing on a culture from one generation to the next. It also helps to fashion that culture through philosophic argument, research and artistic endeavour. Its aims are the induction of individuals into the ranks of 'the educated' and direct contributions to the progress of civilization. The main characteristics of a system which were exclusively devoted to these ends would seem very familiar in Europe because this view of education has been a powerful force in fashioning 'western' higher education. The sources of finance would be multiple, allowing the educational institutions the freedom and power to fashion their own destinies and pursue their own policies. Student numbers would be determined principally by the institutions, based on the importance they placed on various courses or subjects, no doubt tempered by an appreciation of available financial support and beliefs about the numbers of potentially suitable students. The system would be selective with the aim of admitting only those students likely to succeed on the courses offered. In turn those courses would reflect intellectual values rather than utility. In this form of meritocracy emphasis would be on academic standards and courses based on single academic disciplines. A departmental structure also based on disciplines would help to bolster the teachers' primary identity with their field of study rather than with the task of teaching. 'Academic freedom' and tenure would be mechanisms to ensure the rights of self-determination of staff together with their absolute control of course content and standards and of the accreditation of students. Research would tend to the fundamental, aimed at developing disciplines rather than solving practitioners' problems.

In this view of education the 'culture' is more important than the individual. The quality of thought and creative achievement are the overriding concerns. The achievement of heights of intellectual and artistic endeavour are seen to be of such general benefit to society that the disappointments or frustrations of individuals are prices well worth the paying. 'Fairness' is not an important criterion for judging the quality of the system. That being so, there is little potency in a charge of unfair practice. There are other grounds for criticism and for justifying changes in the population of students admitted. One might, for instance, argue that those running higher education were being inconsistent if they encouraged a school system, complete with national examinations designed to advance the academically most able, but then felt con-strained retrospectively to adjust the results because those coming forward contained a higher proportion of women than anticipated. Or one might point to tardiness in modifying a system which proved to advance the middle class rather more efficiently than it advanced the intellectually able. Again, one might argue that the tenets of academic stadards were themselves wrong headed, being over-dependent on a world view characteristic of only half the population at most. The first carries a charge of mendacity, the second of inefficiency, and the third of purblindness. All three imply the unwarranted use of power, certainly to the detriment of society at large, probably to the greater detriment of one section of the community. So again, an appeal to 'fairness' may have its place but it is not necessary when establishing a case for greater sexual equality within a system based on a 'cultural view'.

Both the functional and the cultural view of education provide justifications for educational policy with no need of recourse to an appeal for equity. Indeed it may be argued that they provide good reasons for policies which are manifestly unfair and that such unfairness is a price worth paying in meeting the prior claims of economic development or academic excellence.

It is in the 'social service' view of education that 'fairness' really comes into its own. This view assumes the primary purpose of the education system to be serving the ends of students. The system is there to facilitate the students' progress to their various chosen ends. Those ends may be long-term and they may be strictly vocational. They may be more diffuse, as in becoming more self-sufficient, less emotionally dependent, able to exercise greater choice of occupation and life-style. They may be short-term, as in providing the break from parents, or a few years with few worldly responsibilities. Now, it is quite true that the provision of such opportunities will be a matter of national policy and may be seen as generally contributing to national development in such ways as promoting social mobility, but it differs from the functional view in that the students' immediate opportunity for choice is the focus, rather than a pre-determined outcome.

A system devoted solely to these ends might have the following characteristics. Much of the distribution of finances throughout the system would be dependent upon student choice. Either the financing of institutions and departments would be 'demand-led', money being given out according to recruitment, or the principal income would be students' fees paid, nonetheless, from public funds. The principal source would be the public purse, in order to ensure that poverty was no bar, for social equity is the guiding principle of this view of education. There would be open entry into the system: that is, everybody would be offered some way in, although not necessarily the same way. However, each of the entry points would be equally accessible to those whom they suited, at comparable cost; and each would give equal opportunity of reaching one of a number of exit points. These exit points, giving different levels and types of accreditation, or implying different kinds of educational experience, would reflect the wishes and capacities of students. The system, being demand-led, would be self-correcting. The focus would be on the student body and adaptations would be made to the system to suit them, rather than, as in the cultural view, the focus being on the courses with the student population tailored to suit <u>them</u>. Thus we might expect very many different kinds of courses: some academic, some professional, some dedicated to the self-development of students. The teacher's first identity would be with that of teacher raher than with that of the subject taught. Accreditation might tend towards the descriptive rather than the classification of student qualities and achievements. One might also expect considerable emphasis on self and peer review. Research would contain a large element of reflectiveness – the system monitoring itself.

In such a view of education 'fairness' is the central concept, because the overall aim is social equity. Argument then centres on what constitutes such equity. A philosophical treatise on that subject is beyond the scope of this essay (and this author), but two issues require some attention as they are germaine to the whole book. The first concerns the categories used when comparing the relative fortunes of groups of people. The second concerns the various ways in which fairness might be manifest in an education system. The evidence requires scrutiny before the treatments are considered.

Categories for Comparison

How important is the comparison between men and women compared with other classifications which might reveal inequity? A fine but crucial distinction is necessary when arguing grounds for including or excluding members of groups from a profession or course. It concerns the relevance of the categories used to group people. To illustrate: a strong argument for having more West Indian police officers is that their very membership of the one ethnic group is the crucial factor affecting how well they fulfil their role in policing a predominantly West Indian community. Similarly, it is the very fact of being women which enables women doctors or counsellors to relate to their women clients in a way a man cannot. In these cases ethnic origin and sex <u>are</u> the relevant categories. That is not to say they are relevant for all peoples for all time because they are socially determined. If the argument holds one way, it also holds the other way. Thus sex may legitimately be claimed as a relevant factor for total exclusion; although instances are increasingly difficult to think of: even in modelling clothes the sex of the model must become increasingly irrelevant once clothes lose their potency as both the symbols and the physical means of subjugation (but there is still a long way to go; for the shirts that 'look even better on a man' belong with the hobble skirts rather than with the jeans). Very often, however, the category per se is not the primary factor which determines a person's suitability. Rather the category is taken to imply the existence of some other factor. Examples would be when 'womanhood' is taken as implying, say, physical frailty, or emotional instability or weakness in mathematics. Such factors may be legitimate grounds for exclusion, but in such cases the factors themselves should be evaluated, rather than sex (or race, or class) being taken as a sure indicator of their existence. Such a direct approach avoids the dangers of the stereotype, which is not only an unwarranted generalization but may be an expression of prejudice (see, for example, Richards 1980).

The categories chosen to reveal the existence of inequity may not be the most helpful when explaining the mechanisms by which an education system is discriminating and the exact nature of the biases that result. When the purpose is to demonstrate that education has an inequitable outcome the categories will be drawn to reflect the interests of the investigator, perhaps by class or ethnicity or sex. The origin of the inequity and just how it comes about make no difference either to the fact or the injustice of its existence. Discrimination may be an incidental outcome of educational procedures adopted for quite other purposes but that is of no relevance to the task of measuring its extent. Nor does it matter one jot how the categories of class, ethnicity or sex interact if the purpose is to show that an identified and defined group is under-represented or benefits less from education. By treating 'women' or 'the working class' or 'West Indians' as an homogenous group the arithmetical 'facts' of the matter can be revealed. In an earlier volume (Warren Piper 1981) such facts were presented and discussed. It is true that people from working-class homes and that people from West Indian and Asian communities are under-represented among students and staff in higher education. It is a 'fact' that roughly forty per cent of undergraduates, thirty per cent of postgraduates and thirteen per cent of academic staff are women. By assembling such data over time, trends can be detected − 'facts' of another kind. These facts are given meaning only by the political significance of the category system used; they have no other existence. 'Women' do not constitute an homogenous group on any other basis than the one defining factor; even introducing two factors, as with 'middle-class women', does not do much to reduce the heterogeneity. But the presentation of such data as the percentages above, coupled with a presumption that the chosen basis of categorizing people has no relevance to either their need or their suitability for education, can establish a case of equity or of incidental unfairness. Thus to argue that anything other than equal numbers of men and women in the education system is inequitable carries the presumption that gender is irrelevant to educational need and suitability. (Such a presumption, of course, cannot be taken for granted. As later chapters in this book relate, there have been times in recent history when general beliefs were explicitly to the contrary. Even today such contrary beliefs are smuggled into policy decisions, perhaps unconsciously, for they are less frequently espoused or defended openly than the case for equality.)

Adopting some refined categories can reveal information of particular significance. Thus the categories of those in and those out of education can be subdivided to reveal, for instance, that where women are employed in the higher education system they predominantly occupy junior positions (Rendel, this volume) and are disproportionately found in some (low status) subject areas. Should the current cuts be most heavily applied to the low status parts of the system it may be inferred that they would affect the employment of women more than men. Similarly the assumption that the demand for higher education will mirror (some eighteen years later) fluctuations in the birthrate, may be successfully challenged by establishing that the fecundity of that section of the population from which most students are drawn does not follow national trends (see, for example, Williams 1983).

The number of births recorded of people with fathers in white collar occupations has not been falling as fast as those with fathers in non-white collar occupations. This is entirely accounted for by an increase in the births in social class two (teachers, professional people). However, there has also been an increase in the people joining that group. What is not known is whether the new members of that group will have the same birth pattern as the old members. If they do, the number of eighteen-year-olds offering themselves for higher education will probably not drop in line with the general decline in the birthrate.The position is further complicated when considering the figures produced by the Royal Society because there has been a considerable increase in the 'illegitimate' birthrates. In the Royal Society figures these 'illegitimate' births have been distributed across the social classes in proportion to total numbers. One might suppose, however, that one parent families, and extended families with no formal marriage, are found disproportionately amongst the poorer and the immigrant sections of the community (The Royal Society 1983 and Figure 5.3 in this volume).

Fairness Manifest

What are the various ways in which 'unfairness' might be reckoned? In the previous section it was assumed that an investigator started with an interest in a particular group of people and set out to demonstrate that, compared with other groups, they were or were not disadvantaged. Such an approach does not reveal how it comes about that there are fewer women, or Asians, or working-class children in higher education – only that it is so. Such comparisons map the correlates of an educational policy in terms of the effects on a section of the population, they do not necessarily establish any direct connection between the policy and the effect. A category system which apparently revealed some form of unfair discrimination could in fact be quite irrelevant. Suppose, for instance, that there were (as there seems to be) a causal connection between some defining characteristic of social class and the probability of entering higher education. Suppose too that nearly all members of an ethnic group were working class, as may well be the case with first-generation immigrants. Then, is it their ethnic background or their working class-ness which accounts for their under-representation in higher education? The answer has practical implications for correcting the imbalance. A successful policy of increasing working-class participation rates might incidentally improve the position of the ethnic minority. Yet a campaign to increase the value placed on education by the ethnic group would not affect their representation in higher education if there were class mechanisms which effectively hindered their entry. Similarly, if the representation of various social classes is different among men students than among women students, a shifting of the balance between men and women would have an incidental effect on overall class representation. More middle-class girls might mean fewer working-class boys (Fulton 1982). Such observations simply support the old adage that correlations do not reveal cause and effect. Even less do they establish intent, either overt or covert, deliberate or subconscious, to discriminate unfairly.

If the discriminatory processes are to be changed then more needs to be known about those processes. List 1 shows possible origins of unequal representation: five possible reasons why people do not join or successfully complete a course of higher education.

List 1

1 They do not apply because they put a low value on the education offered.
2 They do not apply because they put a low value on themselves.
3 They do not qualify for entry. (This may be taken to include those who, although qualified for entry, fail to present all their strengths during selection.)
4 They fail to be selected. (Perhaps because the selection system is insensitive to relevant or sensitive to irrelevant characteristics of candidates.)
5 Their work is judged as below the required standard during or at the end of their course.

A tendency towards any one of these among a given section of the population can account for their under-representation.

Being admitted to an education system, even successfully completing it, does not guarantee that the experience has been equally beneficial to all. List 2 shows some ways in which some people might be comparatively disadvantaged.

List 2

1 They are treated differently.
2 The choices offered are more restricted.
3 What is offered is less suited to their needs or interests.
4 The education results in fewer subsequent advantages.

Inequality, then, may take many different forms, and it follows that remedies will be equally multifarious.

Achieving Fairness

How might fairness be achieved? Even such simple lists as those above reveal nine different ways in which inequity can show itself. Each requires different remedies. So the solution often advanced of 'positive discrimination' could take several different forms, each relating to different items in the lists. For example, one possibility is to predetermine quotas for final qualification and adjust the pass marks for each group so that the desired result is achieved. A disadvantage of this system is that initial inequalities are allowed to persist so that standards are quite likely to be lower in one group than in another. On the assumption that educational grades actually reflect professional competence, the result would be that one group (on the average) would be poorer practitioners than the other, a result which is settling for less than parity. It might be argued, however, that such effects would be short-term in vocational education, as professional norms would eventually assert themselves and pressure for the required standards filter back through the education system until an acceptable uniformity were attained.

However, with non-vocational education, pressures towards uniformity exerted by a profession do not exist and the danger is that differing levels of examination institutionalize (and so perpetuate) inequality. Such an argument was advanced in the early days of Girton (Dyhouse, this volume) in favour of women following the same curricula and examinations as men. Even to acknowledge the need for differing treatments, however temporary, was to connive in their being and so prolong their existence; best to stomach the inequality in the short-run, the better to ensure greater equity in the long-run. The option of special examinations for women led to the decorative but useless womens' Diploma (Burstyn, this volume). However, it might be noted that when nominal equity in courses and examinations was achieved, it largely took the form of women being given opportunities to adapt to the provisions made for and suited to men.

Another form of positive discrimination is to leave the accreditation system as even-handed but invest more educational resources in the disadvantaged groups. Such an approach requires a quota system at the point of entry. Alternatively, the extra investment may be made at a stage before higher education, with the aim of ensuring equal proportions apply and qualify for entry.

The last two approaches imply that the education on offer is basically sound. If the diagnosis of the problem is that the very nature of the education offered is suited to the interests, needs and style of one group but not another, then a change in the quality of education offered is required, either to embrace greater variety or to take a more nearly middle line.

An interesting example of this latter approach is provided by the integrated humanities, social-science and medical programme at the University of Michigan. It cannot be said that the primary goal of the innovation was to redress an extreme imbalance of the sexes, but it did have that effect incidentally. Indeed, it did more than simply increase the proportion of women graduates. The main goals were to produce physicians as competent technically and scientifically as those from more traditional courses, yet with a greater sensitivity to traditional and community health needs and a more holistic approach to medical care. To achieve this, a liberal arts course, which would normally precede entry to a professional medical school, was integrated with the medical programme to make a coherent whole. This new approach seemed to suit the women better than the traditional course had done which it replaced. Not only were fewer eliminated by failing intermediate tests but those who did succeed were able to retain many of their initial attitudes to medicine. Under the previous scheme women who qualified as physicians had by then adjusted their 'professional' attitudes to those typical of the men (Brown and Sloan 1982).

In the body of this book most if not all the forms of inequality in Lists 1 and 2 (pp.12-13) make their appearance. For some, various remedies are urged. In considering correctives, a number of complexities emerge. Some take the form of dilemmas which allow for no obviously fair resolution. The point can be amply demonstrated by taking the first item from each of the two lists: one will show the complexities of trying to correct aspiration levels, the other the complexities in trying to offer differing educational treatment.

Complexities in Aspiration

List 1 (p.12) gave reasons why people might not enter higher education. The first being that they did not aspire to it because they gave it no great value. There is an immediate dilemma here, when it comes to finding a corrective. The whole purpose of education is to introduce people to knowledge and values they would not otherwise have. The 'uneducated' person may not share the values that are being espoused and cannot have an adequate knowledge to evaluate fully the education being offered. It is very commonly the case that a key component of an educational course is the questioning of the beliefs and values which caused a student to choose or reject the course in the first place. Further, a central idea in education necessarily concerns just what 'education' is (even though it is often submerged in the 'hidden curriculum'). Almost by definition, people without a particular educational experience cannot know what they are missing. It is logically impossible for someone to choose to learn something of which they cannot conceive or to value something which finds no context within their current lives.

The implication of this dilemma is a heavy responsibility for the educator. There is no escape from the responsibility of holding and acting on a belief that they know better than their potential students what is good for them, at least in part. That holds true even for the most liberal teachers seeking to negotiate each step with their students; they still have a negotiating position. Given that an educator has come to terms with the responsibility and accepts this mission, there seem to be four recourses when people do not spontaneously choose the education offered. They are consciousness-raising, compulsion, compensation, and camouflage.

Consciousness-raising is an attempt to influence attitudes which govern choices. The problem is not just fear of flying but also conceiving of and valuing flying. The motive may be purely altruistic, but the educator must take an initiative in intervening uninvited in other people's lives; in logic no-one can know they need their consciousness raised, even if it is for their own good. For educators to take such responsibility upon themselves may be an imposition on others, but its justification is that a system which offers equal opportunity, and only equal opportunity, will not eradicate social division. The relevance of this point to the education of women is clear and its force is underlined when feminism is described as entailing a dramatic and fundamental change of perception (Stanley, this volume).

Recourse to compulsion, compensation or camouflage raises possibilities and, as ever, problems. Higher education is 'post-compulsory' education (and curiously that applies to staff as well as students: the reason why school teachers are trained and university teachers are not must largely be the matter of compulsion). Nonetheless there are effectively ways in which parts of courses become compulsory for those admitted to them (in American terms that may be compulsory courses within a 'program'). The insistance in some universities and in the art

colleges on a foundation year may be seen as a kind of enforced period
when educational choices can become more informed. For the most part,
however, (that is leaving aside 'mature students') the decision of what
course of higher education, if any, to take is made during the period of
compulsory schooling. Should girls be obliged to take science subjects at
school, so that their chances of being able and wanting to become, say,
engineers is enhanced? From the pupils (or social service) point of view it
is trading in one freedom of choice to gain another. From a functional
view the decision would be justified if sufficient value were placed on
having more women engineers. A more direct assault on the value girls
put on higher education might be possible in schools, but more to the
point might be compulsory classes on 'contemporary society' organized
on rather the same basis as religious instruction is today and aimed,
among other things, at giving children insights into the nature of social
discrimination and their own complicity in it.

In a crude sense the higher earning power, and perhaps even the
other apparent correlates of higher education (at least in America), such
as greater health, longevity, later marriage, more rational family
planning, lower divorce rate (Bowen 1977), are compensations for
suffering an education which in itself may not seem attractive to the
potential student. Yet the same problem exists: is education the cause of
those benefits; do possible applicants perceive those benefits as related to
higher education and do they value them against the more immediate
rewards of, say, a weekly wage, or leaving parents, or setting up home. It
would also be interesting to know whether the margin of these benefits
between the 'educated' and the 'uneducated' were greater or less for
women than men, for ethnic minority than majority, or for working class
than middle class.

The possibility of more immediate compensation, such as larger grants
to women students than to men, is not a political reality and in any case
the effects of grants on the elasticity of demand is little understood. One
of the more colourful arguments against student loans, thankfully less
often heard now than ten years ago, is that women would be particularly
disadvantaged by loans because, on graduation, they would come to their
potential husbands with negative dowries. This handicap in the marriage
stakes would, it was confidently predicted, prove a powerful disincentive
for women to enter higher education.

There remains the possibility of camouflage. In fact, part of this book
is devoted to exposing the hidden curriculum of a male dominated
education system. However, the problems being wrestled with in this
discussion are almost the opposite: those of introducing into a course
matters which would not have appealed to people at the time they
applied to join, but which are good for them and will, at the appropriate
time, come to be appreciated by them. Such things happen all the time in

education and perhaps an example for the current context would be an introduction of an equal rights discussion into a course for teaching staff that was advertised as 'Policy Making in Higher Education'.

The discussion above has assumed that the potential student, in not aspiring to higher education, was acting against her own self-interest. However, there is always the possibility that a person is making a quite rational decision to stay out, on the grounds that the education offered is less valuable to them than some alternative. The worst possible case would be that all the choices open to women are on the whole less valued by them than the choices open to men are valued, in turn, by them. Such an argument could be advanced on behalf of any disadvantaged group. The remedy is better options. There are a number of possibilities; an alternative to the dominant education could be offered especially for the disadvantaged group. Either within existing institutions or within custom built institutions. Another possibility would be to offer a new form of education equally valued by all. This brings the discussion to List 2 (p.13) and the issue of differing treatments.

Complexities in Differing Treatments

The next group of complexities is drawn from the first item of List 2 – differing treatment. The case for differing educational treatments for different sub-groups of the same society hinges on the distinction between 'equity' and 'equality' or, perhaps, more clearly between 'formal' and 'substantive' equality (O'Neill 1978). If identical treatment (formal equality) results in some inequity then variations of treatment may be introduced in order to achieve parity of outcome (substantive equality). Why may identical treatment lead to inequity? At least four reasons might be posited:

1 That what purports to be identical treatment in reality is not.
2 That sub-groups have different starting points which need to be taken into account.
3 That different sub-groups respond differently to the treatment, to the disadvantage of one or more of them.
4 That the educational goals of sub-groups are different and so require different experiences.

Is truly identical treatment possible in our current society? Perhaps the most frequent reason advanced in favour of single sex education is that the disadvantaging of women is so integral to our society that any treatment, any rules, any procedures, conducted in a mixed sex community will be inequitable. Whatever their good intentions, it follows that if men and women steeped in our culture co-operate in an educational venture, the men will dominate, and, just as inevitably, the women (staff and students alike) will have their confidence undermined, be constantly presented with inequitable role models, will be under-valued, ridiculed and harassed. The products of such education simply contribute to the perpetuity of a sexist society.

There are, of course, difficulties in reaching satisfactory integration of the sexes through completely segregated education. First, each group has no opportunity of learning to interact with the other, with the attendant danger that subsequent relations will be informed more by mythology than reality, more by romance than life. Secondly, segrega-tion may not be equally beneficial to the groups involved. If in single sex colleges women more easily learn self-esteem but men's assumptions of their superiority go unchallenged then we have the conundrum that segregation is good for women but not for men. Thirdly, role models offered by single sex staff may work against the successful integration of the sexes. Regardless of the truth of the matter, staff may be seen by their students as temperamentally disinclined to integrate with members of the other sex. Such a precept has educational implications whether it creates a model for emulation or opens a gulf between the identities of teacher and taught:

> Miss Buss and Miss Beale
> Cupid's darts do not feel,
> Miss Beale and Miss Buss
> Are not like us.

These difficulties lend weight to the argument that a segregated education produces a divided society. That, in turn, can only enhance the possibility of oppression.

Within a mixed sex institution inequity resulting from identical treatment can be quite simple to fathom, such as the expenses for conferences not including any element for looking after children in the parents' absence. The assumption in the regulation is that there is always a partner at home to look after the children. Sometimes it can be intractable and hugely complex, as when a woman gives as a reason for her absence the need to care for a sick child rather than report her own illness. Although this may seem to be the precise reverse of what would be expected, it is not unknown. The implication is that the woman feels that any admission of her own illness is more likely to be taken as a general indication of her inability to cope with the job (or the whole of her sex to cope with such jobs) than would be the case for a man. Somehow it feels safer for her to suggest that her role of mother may occasionally interfere with her work, rather than that her own constitution may limit her capacity. The further implication is an affirmation of the convention that motherhood brings greater responsibility for the children than does fatherhood. The complexities of such a tangle are immense and illustrate the emotional tensions inherent in working in a deeply inequitable society. However, it would be necessary to discover whether men have equivalent or related knots into which they tie themselves.

Another way in which identical treatments can have differing impacts devolves from the content of the syllabus. If, for instance, the only history taught is white mens' history, the message may have a quite different impact on black than on white, on women than on men. Although such biases come close to the third form of inequity listed on page 13 they arise directly out of the fact that the nature of the education offered is inherently cast within the conceptual world of one group rather than another. It is inequitable, however the groups may differentially react.

If the sexes are reckoned to have different starting points and are being educated to reduce these differences, it suggests that the higher education system is being required to compensate for earlier shortcomings. Other remedies are therefore at hand and the need for differing treatments may be temporary.

A third possible form of inequity which could also give reason for differing treatments, would be that sexes react to and therefore benefit differently from their educational experience. Here is a very rich field concerning sexual characteristics. It would include differences in temperament and physiology, not all of which have lost credibility along with the more bizarre views held in Victorian times (Burstyn, this volume). There is the matter of differing life-cycle patterns (Bernard 1981) and how education fits into them. There is a large literature which reports sex differences in various areas of cognition which could conceivably suggest the need to accommodate differing learning strategies. For instance, women have been reported as exceeding men in vocabulary, verbal fluency and memory, and falling short in mathematical reasoning, spacial judgement and mechanical aptitude (Maccoby and Jacklin 1975; Wittig and Petersen 1979). Distinguishing inherent from acquired characteristics is technically difficult and has long been a central issue in psychology. Deciding which differences are desirable and to be developed and which undesirable and to be masked gives scope for perpetual argument. On both counts we may be assured the issues will continue to be contested.

The fourth source of inequity and a justification for differing treatments is the desire for differing outcomes. This touches on the idea of 'women's culture' (eg Ås 1975; Acker 1980) and the question of whether 'Women's Studies' are exclusively <u>for</u> women as well as <u>about</u>

women (Duelli Klein, this volume). One central question is the reason for wanting women to learn different things from men. A distinction might be made between, on the one hand, an immediate wish of women to escape from the presumptions of a male dominated society and, on the other, the best path to an eventual egalitarian and integrated society. The two goals, one perhaps shorter term than the other, may need to be balanced one against the other if the education systems required for each prove incompatible. That will depend partly on the precise nature of the society which forms the goal: there are many Utopias.

The Misuse of Discrimination

The dangers of a separate-but-equal policy are only too evident in a world aware of the worst excesses of apartheid. The principle is misused to make irrelevant discriminations and abused when applied so as to disadvantage one group to the benefit of another. Abuse is always possible and Lists 1 and 2 (pp.12–13) identified nine possible sources of inequity – each an opportunity for discrimination. To guard against misuse four questions might be posed:

1 How significant are the distinctions between groups?
2 How relevant to education are the categories used to classify people?
3 Are the differences between groups permanent or temporary?
4 How can such differences be accommodated?

In categorizing the population into 'men' and 'women' the danger is that each group is considered homogeneous. It is easy to simplify and then distort an argument by reference to 'women's needs' or 'men's attitudes'. There is no absolute cut-off point between men and women; no characteristic (including the physiological) is totally exclusive to one sex. In some ways the distinction is quite artificial: no more than a set of correlations, and not very high ones at that. The humanity the sexes share outweighs their differences.

Is sex a relevant discrimination to make in higher education? Partly that is a political matter, and the ways in which it is politically relevant are detailed throughout this book. Partly it is a technical matter to do with measurement of the validity of certain educational procedures, although, as with all measures of efficiency and effectiveness, they eventually link back to philosophical questions, especially social values. Certainly the exploration of this question would entail further break-down: Is sex relevant to what aspect of higher education precisely? Discrimination by whom? What is implied by 'sex'?

The question of relevance is closely bound up with the matter of permanence of any difference between the sexes. The distinction of 'sex' (biological) from 'gender' (cultural) is useful here. Are there any irreducible differences between the sexes, and if there are, do they require special accommodation in all forms of education? Of the differences that are culturally determined, which ones are to be nurtured, and which ones eliminated? The first question is foremost a matter for psychological inquiry; the second for political debate. Both issues weave their way through this book and in so doing lead to a conundrum. Education is both a product of current society and a prime means of producing a society for the immediate future (in which most of us will continue to live). If it is a product of our current society, it is also a part of it. An inevitable tension between the conservative and the progressive functions of an education system can at times cause it to lose cohesion. Yet both functions are totally necessary. That tension is quite aside from any disagreement there might be about the nature of the society we are trying to produce and the way in which education might contribute to its development. The feminist argument is for a society radically different from that in which we currently live. There may be different Utopias but they all have in common an absence of the disadvantaging and oppression of women. Such a society, once attained, would naturally have an education system to provide an induction into its more egalitarian ways, helping to preserve essential features; just as today's education helps to bolster sexism and yesterday's sought to protect women from the harmful effects of cerebration.

This leads to yet another conundrum. In an egalitarian society both sexes would share the same perceptions. Are those insights, arising from that fundamental shift of perception which marks the feminist, available to men? If there is some element of those insights which is for ever exclusive to women, then to include them on the agenda for a universal education is as oppressive in that particular as is the current curriculum founded in the perceptions of men. The point is more than academic because it indicates the border between what we share and what we should accommodate. It makes a difference, for instance, to the eventual development of Women's Studies (Duelli Klein, this volume) and to the very nature of any connection between sex and mentality implicit in research processes (Stanley, this volume), and therefore to the resolution of problems which may arise therein.

The final question is whether the necessary differences of treatment can be accommodated within the same institution, or the same courses, or the same classroom, or the same teaching or assessment methods. Of course, there is a sense in which no two people get the same education: each individual's experience is unique, even of shared occasions, and each individual reacts differently and learns differently from similar experiences. Such differences might relate to ethnic background, or social class, or gender. If there are gender-related differences, which call for accommodation in the name of substantive equality, then further questions arise. Are the appropriate treatments mutually exclusive? Can they be accommodated within the same class? If not, can separate classes be arranged within the same course? If not, parallel courses in the same institution? There has never been a woman's university in this country, but until recently women's colleges were common enough. Of course their existence was certainly due to reasons other than the incompatibility of their activities with those of men's colleges, although that may have been part of it. However, such reasoning might figure strongly in an argument for women's courses, as they do for women's groups.

Whatever the niceties of these arguments their practical use may be limited. In order to offer different treatments to different groups successfully, a number of conditions are necessary. The differences of needs between groups must be significant compared with the differences of needs within groups. Doubt has already been cast on that assumption in relation to men and women. Secondly, the effects of educational treatment must be precise and predictable. In fact they are not so. The factors which determine success in education are legion and so capricious that it could well be that chance variations would completely mask all but the grossest effects of difference in treatment. Luck plays a considerable part in education. The teacher needs to be sensitive and insightful but more often able to detect and recover from first efforts than to plan ahead. Whatever the intent to treat one group differently from another, in the social interaction between teacher and taught, which still lies at the heart of higher education in our society, the largest variations are going to result from unforeseen events — when the teacher's first approach draws a blank or misses its mark or proves infelicitous or turns out to be a monumental blunder. On such occasions the successful teacher is the one who notices the mistake and has the emotional and technical resources to try something different. Such variations to accommodate the individual may easily mask any planned variation to accommodate groups; and, well and sensitively accomplished, may eliminate the need for them. Would that the training of lecturers and professors ensured they were up to it.

Conclusion

This essay began with a description of three views of education, 'functional', 'cultural' and 'social service', each related to a different educational purpose. They were treated as discrete entities and three fundamentally different education systems were derived from them.

The discussion of fairness – the forms it might take, the problems it presented and their possible solutions – was largely associated with one of these views: the social service view. In reality all educational systems try to encompass all three purposes and usually contain a mixture of elements reflecting all three views. However, the description of three hypothetical systems has some practical uses. First it helps to expose the fact that arguments over educational procedures and structures often conceal differing assumptions about the primary aim of education. Such arguments remain irresolvable until agreement on the more fundamental issue is reached. Secondly, it helps to reveal inconsistencies in the structure and procedures of given systems, for usually they are not designed as a coherent whole but grow piecemeal and different educational purposes will fashion their various characteristics. Thirdly, it allows a shift in philosophy to be detected behind a new proposal. For instance the Robbins Report dictum that places were to be available for all who wanted them and who were qualified was informed principally by a 'social service' view of education. Of such a system it is wholly appropriate to inquire whether or not it is fair and try to make it more so. More recent moves towards 'finance-led planning', the establishment of the National Advisory Body under the chairmanship of a Minister, the questioning of tenure, interest in the factors which affect the demand for education, all denote a shift away from the social service to the functional view of education. Not spelled out maybe, not always consciously formulated but a zeitgeist when not a government policy. The impact of an appeal to fairness may be waning and the politically attractive arguments, those that will attract the interests of the politicians and civil servants, are those which chime with a functional tone.

That is not to say that justice is irrelevant; it remains the fundamental consideration. The pertinent argument is found in Rawls' description of the 'private society' and the 'social union' (Rawls 1972):

'Only in the social union is the individual complete.'
'When men are secure in the enjoyment of the exercise of their own powers, they are disposed to appreciate the perfections of others, especially when their several excellences have an agreed place in a form of life the aims of which all accept.'
'Thus we may say...that it is through social union founded upon the needs and potentialities of its members that each person can participate in the total sum of the realised natural assets of the others.'

References

Acker,S. (1980) Women, the other academics *British Journal of Sociology of Education* I (I) 91-92

Ås,B. (1975) On female culture: an attempt to formulate a theory of women's solidarity and action *Acta Sociologica* 18 (2-3) 142-161

Bernard,J. (1981) Women's educational needs. In Chickering, A.(Ed.) *The Modern American College* San Francisco: Jossey-Bass

Bowen,H.R. (1977) *Investment in Learning* San Francisco: Jossey-Bass

Brown,D. and Sloan,H. (1982) *The Improvement of Professional Educators Through Specialized Curriculum Development and the Education within the Context of a Personality-Developmental Model* University of Michigan

Fulton,O. (Ed.) (1982) *Access to Higher Education* Guildford: SRHE

Maccoby,E.E. and Jacklin,C.M. (1974) *The Psychology of Sex Differences* Oxford: OUP

O'Neill,O. (1978) How do we know when opportunities are equal? In Vetterling-Braggin,M., Elliston,F. and English,J. (Eds) *Feminism and Philosophy* New Jersey: Littlefield, Adams & Co.

Rawls,J. (1972) *A Theory of Justice* Section 79,p.253. Oxford: Clarendon Press

Richards,J.R. (1980) *The Sceptical Feminist* London: Routledge and Kegan Paul.

The Royal Society (1983) *Demographic Trends and Future University Candidates* A working paper. Royal Society

Warren Piper,D. (1981) *Is Higher Education Fair?* Guildford: SRHE

Williams,G. (1983) The Leverhulme Programme of Study into the Future of Higher Education: Future prospects. In Philipson,N. (Ed.) *Universities, Society and the Future* University of Edinburgh Press

Wittig,M.A. and Petersen,A.C. (Eds)(1979) *Sex Related Differences in Cognitive Functioning* New York: Academic Press

2 Women in higher education: what is the problem?

Sandra Acker

Should we be more concerned about the dilemmas women present for higher education or the difficulties higher education presents for women? There is a range of approaches to such questions in the literature and the purpose of this chapter is to make these approaches explicit and assess their contributions to the debate. In the previous chapter, David Warren Piper gives us a starting point with his distinction among functional, cultural and social service views of higher education. The <u>functional</u> view stresses the production of appropriately qualified and motivated people to meet the needs of the economy. It is compatible either with a relatively conservative approach that advocates increased access for women to higher education and training in cases where society's 'manpower' needs are not otherwise met, or with a relatively radical one that points to higher education's pivotal role in the reproduction of the social and sexual division of labour. The <u>cultural</u> model emphasizes conservation and transmission of received wisdom and an approved culture. It can be usefully juxtaposed with the view that the problem for women in higher education is the exclusion of women's experiences and contributions from the definition and production of knowledge. The <u>social service</u> model sees higher education as aiming to serve equitably the interests of individuals. It has obvious connections with charges that higher education is in fact <u>in</u>equitable and participates in perpetuating discrimination and injustice towards women. Finally there are the additional possibilities of seeing the problem as stemming from women's inadequate aspirations or simply denying that a non-trivial problem exists.

It might be said that, unlike Friedan's (1963) 'problem that has no name' (a reference to the distress felt by well-educated suburban women whose American dream was becoming a nightmare), our problem has too many names. Is 'women in higher education' a problem of inadequate individual achievement, of social injustice, of under-investment in talent, of reproduction of the division of labour, of bias in the production of knowledge – or no problem at all? Let us consider each possibility.

Individual Achievement

Women in higher education (as well as those out of it) are sometimes thought to be at a disadvantage so long as their aspirations and achievements differ from those of men. Although such statements refer to women as a group, the group in this view is a collection of individuals making choices: taking up or refusing options, seizing or missing chances, seeking or foregoing opportunities. Whilst a few commentators believe such choices are biologically based, most blame sex-specific socialization through family, school and media for producing women orientated to arts rather than sciences, altruism rather than acquisitiveness, co-operation rather than competition. When compared with men, women are said to 'under-achieve', to 'under-aspire', or even to 'under-apply'.

Many studies have sought the determinants of 'career commitment' in the background and the social-psychological characteristics of student women. Sex-typed socialization experiences of women are thought to instil personality traits such as affiliative desires and dependency needs that hamper attainment of educational or career goals, especially when such achievements might cause loss of male approval (Bardwick 1971; Hoffman 1972). Beliefs that marriage will provide a prime source of identity push young women into keeping career plans vague and flexible (Epstein 1970, p.65). Student women find themselves in a double bind due to contradictory cultural pressures towards scholastic superiority and feminine inferiority (Komarovsky 1946; Zinberg 1973). Married women students, especially those with children, are thought to suffer from impossible demands on their time and energy and from the expectation that the husband's career will have priority in case of conflict (Feldman 1973; Fogarty et al.1971)

Those who have written about the university from such a viewpoint present an image of a fairly neutral institution, the source of the problem being located outside its compass. There is at least a hope that the university is fundamentally a meritocratic institution that will recognize and reward ambition and talent in women once they can be persuaded to display it. This is not to say that feminists operating within this model have not criticized higher education for its complacency and its greater suitability for the life cycle of the typical male rather than the typical female. Nonetheless, for those feminists the major task is one of encouraging young women to make full use of their talents, not to settle for second best, to recognize that they will spend most of their adult life in the workforce. It becomes necessary to persuade girls and women that science isn't 'really' masculine, that men don't 'really' dislike brainy women, that childcare isn't 'really' incompatible with career – in short, that the barriers to public achievement are in the mind, not the marketplace. As Lady Platt, head of the Equal Opportunities Commission, says:

> If a girl is well qualified and prepared to do her homework, then the world is her oyster. (Wilce 1983)

Reform is sought partly through education. Schools are charged with the task of reversing tradition through countering stereotypes (Guttentag and Bray 1976; Smail et al. 1982), while university and college women are encouraged through exhortation, assertiveness training or consciousness-raising to overcome such handicaps as lack of self-confidence, 'fear of success' (Horner 1972), need for approval (Hoffman 1972), and desire for dependency (Dowling 1982).

Justice and Discrimination

The problem of women in higher education can be conceptualized as a moral (or political or legal) one. The very question of whether higher education is 'fair' or 'just' reflects this approach. Concepts such as 'fairness', 'justice', 'discrimination', 'equality' and 'opportunity' admit of a range of meanings. They are the subject of philosophical disputation and the stuff of political rhetoric. In the educational literature a phrase such as 'equality of educational opportunity' has been shown to have multiple meanings (Tyler 1977). In America there are not only pitched legal battles but extended academic debates about the justice and morality of discrimination against women and minorities in higher education and about the appropriateness of affirmative action as an antidote (Dworkin 1977; Glazer 1975; Little and Robbins 1981; Roberts, this volume). Relatively little of this debate has been rehearsed in Britain (but see Richards 1982 and Robarts 1981), perhaps because our sex discrimination legislation only accords 'positive action' a minor role.

Those who stress discrimination and injustice have no difficulty in producing figures to show that women students and staff are not randomly distributed throughout the higher education system (Tables 2.1 and 2.2).

Women university students are likely to study French, English or sociology, but unlikely to do physics and engineering (Table 2.1)[1]. Even today they are far more likely than men to study education, despite the massive cuts in recent years in teacher training places available. Of the

Table 2.1   Percentages of students in selected categories of higher and advanced further education who are women

Women as a percentage of full-time:	
*University undergraduates	39.8
*University postgraduates	35.3
**Advanced further education students	35.8
**Initial teacher training students (all sectors)	69.2
*University first degree recipients	38.1
*University higher degree recipients	26.0
*University undergraduates studying:	
French	79.7
English	65.6
Sociology	64.2
Biology	46.4
Medicine	38.6
Mathematics	27.9
Chemistry	23.9
Physics	13.2
Electrical engineering	3.7

* Calculated from University Grants Committee (1982) *University Statistics 1980 Vol. 1: Students and Staff* pp. 7, 18, 19, 40-43. Figures are for 1980-81 'UK domiciled' students in universities in Great Britain. Figures for higher degrees do not include higher diplomas or professional teaching qualifications.
** Calculated from DES (1981a) *Statistics of Education Further Education Nov 1981* pp. 3, 71. Figures are for England 1981.

Table 2.2   Percentages of selected categories of staff in universities who are women

Women as a percentage of:	
*Full-time university academic staff	13.9
Professors	2.7
Senior lecturers/readers	6.4
Lecturers/assistant lecturers	15.6
Others	34.3
**Full-time non-clinical university researchers	26.0
On lowest grade	35.0
**Part-time university academic-related staff	41.0

* Calculated from University Grants Committee (1982) *University Statistics 1980 Vol. 1 Students and Staff* p. 51. Figures are for Great Britain 1980-81.
** Equal Opportunities Commission (1982) *Women in Universities* pp. 9, 20. Figures are for universities in Great Britain, end of 1979.

32,450 students in initial teacher training in England in 1981, 69.2% were female (DES 1981a, pp.71-72). Nearly a third of women university full-time postgraduates study education (UGC 1982, pp.12-13). Women were 35.8% of students in advanced further education (including polytechnics) in England in 1981. The sexes differed in their typical modes of attendance: women made up 50.5% of full-time students, 33.1% of evening-only students, 24.7% of sandwich-course students, and 23.4% of part-time day students (including those on day release) (DES 1981a, p.3).

Table 2.2 shows that women constitute only a small minority of full-time university staff (13.9%) and are especially scarce at the higher levels. There are no women vice-chancellors (EOC 1982). In 1980-81 there were 119 women professors (2.7% of the total professoriate). All but sixteen of these women were found in four of the nine subject areas used in the UGC statistics: forty-three were in administration/business/ social studies, twenty-nine in medicine/dentistry/health, seventeen in language/literature/area studies, and fourteen in other arts subjects (UGC 1982, p.51). (See also Rendel, this volume.) As Table 2.3 shows, women are slightly better represented in non-university sectors of higher and further education − 14.3% of full-time polytechnic staff and 22.4% of full-time staff at 'other major institutions'. Here again, women are missing from senior ranks. In polytechnics, for example, there are 897 men and forty-nine women vice-principals or other heads of departments. Women hold 6.8% of posts at the level of principal lecturer or above. There are no women principals (DES 1981b, p.35).

Table 2.3 Percentages of full-time teaching staff in polytechnics and other major further education establishments who are women: by grade

	Polytechnics	Other major further education establishments
	%	%
Principals	0.0	2.9
Vice-principals and heads of department	5.5	8.9
Principal lecturers and readers	7.2	10.3
Senior lecturers	14.5	14.9
Lecturer Grade 2	29.3	22.0
Lecturer Grade 1	37.1	31.7
All staff	14.3	22.4

Source Calculated from DES 1981b, pp. 35-36.

Women are better represented in the less secure posts in universities. Women are fully 41% of academic-related part-time staff, and 26% of non-clinical contract research staff (Table 2.2). It is likely that some of these relatively marginal research and part-time positions will disappear with the contraction of the university sector starting in 1983.

Discrimination, as defined by the Race Relations and Sex Discrimination Acts, basically consists of less favourable treatment for a member of one sex or ethnic group than is or would be accorded to a person of another sex or ethnic group whose relevant circumstances are the same or not materially different. Built into the legislation in Britain is a concern with the fate of individuals rather than the welfare of groups: in most cases a complainant must claim discrimination <u>in comparison with another individual</u>. It is not sufficient to give evidence that a particular group in a firm or institution is under-represented in top positions but over-represented in bottom ones. Such a demonstration may be grounds for permission to provide special training to the disadvantaged group to improve their (individual) achievement potential. Special training, however, is all that is permitted. Preferential hiring or promotion is not. So even if we can show that women students and academics are not distributed through the system in the same way as men are, we have not <u>legally</u> established the presence of discrimination. Feminists operating from within the 'justice and discrimination' framework, however, are more likely to agree with Margherita Rendel in this volume when she argues (pp.163–75) that there is no reason to believe that women academics are less able than men, and therefore no reason, other than sex discrimination, to account for their inferior status within the university.

The application of remedies for discrimination such as affirmative action is fraught with difficulties even for those dedicated to liberal reform. There are tensions between the rights of the individual and the group (Little and Robbins 1981) and between short and long-term gains. 'Reform' may merely involve giving further rewards to the most-advantaged individuals of a generally disadvantaged group (Wilson 1978). Moreover, attempts to equalize opportunities within education take on a paradoxical quality in light of the differentiation and difference (if not discrimination) at the very heart of an education system that participates in the sorting, selection and allocation of individuals to the various segments of the labour market.

Higher education serves only a fraction of the population, and in that sense discriminates against nearly everyone. Resources used to improve conditions for women in higher education will not be available for the less able. Nagel (1977) usefully reminds us that a system which allocates rewards on the basis of intelligence can itself be labelled unjust even if we do not conventionally regard it as such.

The reply by defenders of higher education to charges of élitism will stress the benefits to the entire nation of educating the most-talented individuals and the crucial role of the university in conserving the culture and furthering scholarship (Parsons and Platt 1973). Feminists whose main concern is the injustice suffered by women who occupy a subordinate position within universities (and within higher education generally) may not wholly accept the above defence, but they too generally write 'as if' the university is – or with minor adjustments could be – a meritocracy. They believe that within this system greater priority should be given to equalizing access, opportunities and outcomes between the sexes. They are critical of the age-graded academic career structure, which works to the disadvantage of women who take time out to have children. They have called for curricular reform, arguing that the neglect of women and distortion of their contributions to scholarship is unjust and discriminatory. Finally, they have argued in favour of a range of alterations to university practice such as improvements in maternity leave provision, childcare facilities, and grant allocation criteria, and they have asked for more support and less sexism from male staff and students.

These feminists put their faith variously in rational argument, economic and legal sanctions, and good will. Bringing to public notice the fact that women receive unequal shares of academic rewards or the existence of sexism in the curriculum <u>might</u> result in those who control higher education taking steps to ensure that 'merit' becomes a sex-neutral category and that the curriculum is reformed; but equally, it might not. Not everyone agrees that such discrimination exists (Cole 1979) or that it is inevitably unfair (Shaw 1979). Some commentators argue that the observed patterns are due to sex-differentiated personality characteristics or domestic responsibilities, rather than to bias in higher education. Currently, our sex discrimination legislation appears to give feminists insufficient ammunition with which to fight effectively for the rights of women academics (Rendel, this volume). And it is difficult to imagine universities and colleges, on the basis of moral arguments alone, altering the very basis of their career structures for the benefit of what is a minority group within their walls.

Investment in Talent

It is possible to appreciate that the 'problem' contains a moral dimension, but to prefer explanations for its existence couched in socio-economic terms. One such perspective is the 'womanpower' approach. Herein it is claimed that society cannot afford to ignore talent regardless of from whence it comes. It must invest in its brilliant women as well as its brilliant men.

The 'womanpower' approach was especially popular in the 1950s and 1960s when it meshed well with functionalist and human capital theories dominant in social sciences at the time (Karabel and Halsey 1977, p.13). In Britain and in America, technological change was thought to demand concomitant expansion of the education system, if the nation were to 'keep pace' and provide sufficient skilled 'manpower' to compete effectively with the Soviet Union. Through enlarging their lifetime options, individuals would also benefit from investing in their own education, provided society continued to reward materially those who engaged in extended study (Karabel and Halsey 1977, p.13). These arguments could be used not only to support increased investment in education but also to produce a rationale for efforts to reduce 'inequality of educational opportunity' and thereby avoid 'wastage of talent'. Studies in the British political arithmetic tradition did exactly this, though mainly confining their attention to the inefficiency (as well as the immorality) of allowing social class background to override ability in determining educational outcomes (Karabel and Halsey 1977, pp.10-11). As is still the case today, arguments about sex inequality in the 1950s and 1960s were found mostly in books about women rather than books about economics or the labour force or social class and education. But in spirit the discussions of equality for women were much the same as those concerned with 'manpower' more generally. The womanpower approach requires a fairly uncritical view of institutions of higher education. If education is a good thing for men (helping them individually to achieve a better standard of living and collectively to contribute to 'society'), then too must it be a good thing for women.

Such arguments were (and are) found in both Britain and America. In Britain, Arregger (1966), writing of graduate women, claimed that 'the country needs them. . . their knowledge, their experience, their skills' (p.xvii). 'Manpower shortages', especially in the professions, are 'one of the most intractable problems' (p.xv). 'There is no untapped reserve of men, but what of the women?' (p.xv). And Fogarty et al. state:

> . . . it is clear there are good economic grounds − apart from any question of personal interest and satisfaction or of civil rights − for enlarging the field so as to give women too their chance of selection for the top. Top jobs need the best available talent . . . it is in employers' and the economy's interest that women with great ability should have the chance to replace men of less ability. (Fogarty et al. 1971, p.483)

In the United States, the Carnegie report on women in higher education adds this:

> The supply of superior intelligence is limited, and the demand for it in society is ever greater. The largest unused supply is found among women. (Carnegie Commission 1973, p.1)

Since women in the United States with higher degrees have very high rates of labour force participation (Astin 1979; Carnegie Commission 1973, p.21) and are thought to give better care to children and greater services to the community (Carnegie Commission 1973, p.8) 'social gains' could be expected from investing in higher education for women (Carnegie Commission 1973, p.21).

Most succinctly, the author of a 1967 book on American women pleads: 'America needs its womanpower, and the American woman needs to be needed' (Harbeson 1967, p.122). Harbeson goes on to urge American women to provide a good example for women in 'underdeveloped' countries (p.123).

Today, human capital and functionalist arguments have lost much of their appeal. For feminists, who probably used womanpower arguments as much as a tactic as anything else, given the difficulty the opposition had in rejecting offers of 'talent', the argument has proved to be uncomfortably double-edged. (See Burstyn, this volume, on the consequences of arguing on one's opponent's terms.) Because it was essentially an élitist argument, it could not be used to help the great mass of women with 'average' talent or less; indeed the consequences would be that some of these 'average' women would be required as domestic servants and childcarers to release the talented ones for their career pursuits. Even the point made by Fogarty et al. (1971) about the importance of highly placed women as role models for the others does not completely deal with the problem. Even more damning was the way in which the womanpower argument could be turned on its head: if women were needed to alleviate labour shortages in professional fields, then presumably when there were no labour shortages their services could be dispensed with. No occupation illustrates this as well as teaching. In the 1960s pleas abounded for (especially graduate) married women teachers to return to work and some incentives were provided toward this end. Currently many women in Britain who left teaching to raise a family find it difficult or impossible to re-enter the profession through the traditional 'part-time route' (Trown and Needham 1980) while others still in service are returning shortly after childbirth and maternity leave despite their personal preferences otherwise (Thurston 1981). In Canada, Watson and Quazi (1981-82) advise authorities to reduce numbers of re-entrants in order to achieve a better age distribution across the profession. In Britain ACSET (Advisory Committee for the Supply and Education of Teachers), the committee set up to advise the Secretary of State for Education and Science in England and Wales, has recently set the maximum percentage of entrants to teaching who are returnees at 40% for primary and 20% for secondary education, and has strongly urged that preference be given to new entrants, who have better qualifications and more up-to-date knowledge (Blackstone and Crispin 1982, p.44).

It is arguable that human capital theory has been used more effectively against the interests of women than for them. It has been extended, for example, to provide a rationale for women's subordinate labour market position in terms of their expected time out for child-rearing, which is thought to lead to their lesser investment in education (due to lesser expected market return) and greater choice of occupations that permit interruption and do not require more than initial training (Ram 1980, pp.S60-61). Fitzpatrick (1976, p.126) shows how a high-prestige university using rational economic criteria alone would necessarily seek to minimize female enrolment. And finally there is cross-cultural evidence that the expansion of education per se does not necessarily increase and may decrease opportunities for women and girls (Smock 1981, p.260). Nor does educational expansion always reduce occupational sex segregation (Ram 1980, pp.S74-75). In many countries parents who act as human capitalists have good reasons for not investing in the education of their daughters, especially when school places are limited and those for girls are more abundant in the private (fee-paying) sector. The 'opportunity costs' are simply too great (Smock 1981, p.92)[2]. It may be true that our rate of return measures do not accurately measure returns on women's education, especially as they leave out indirect benefits, discount the value of unpaid work in the home (Woodhall 1973) and use the individual rather than the married couple as the unit of analysis – but presumably most of the 'investors' go by cruder criteria.

The Reproduction of Inequality

A quite different approach that also relies on socio-economic theories regards higher education as playing an integral part in schooling's complicity in the reproduction over the generations of an unequal and hierarchical social and sexual division of labour. Women in higher education are found in restricted numbers and in limited subject fields because this is what capitalist (and patriarchal) society expects, even 'needs'.

In recent years sociologists of education have concentrated on developing their understanding of social and cultural reproduction and the role of schooling in such processes (Althusser 1971; Apple 1982; Bourdieu 1977; Bowles and Gintis 1976). There are numerous debates among advocates of alternative postions that I cannot deal with here. But all these approaches suggest that schools play some part in perpetuating the role of schooling in such processes (Althusser 1971; Apple 1982; economies. For Bowles and Gintis (1976), to take one example, workers must be equipped with character traits that will encourage their allegiance to an economic system that operates fundamentally to their disadvantage. Largely through its characteristic rules and relationships, the school, in concert with the family, encourages differential personality dispositions for students at various levels of the structure, and from various social groupings, in line with their probable level of entry to the labour market. The popular American view of education as a strictly meritocratic sorting ground is an illusion, they argue: schools perpetuate, not mitigate, inequality and stratification. According to Bourdieu (1976, 1977) what schools applaud and reward as 'talent' may be mostly the possession of 'cultural capital' derived from the family. Families with economic capital are more likely to have cultural capital as well (Bourdieu 1977). (Such theories are discussed in greater detail in MacDonald 1977, 1981b and Apple 1982.)

What role has higher education in all this? Relatively little attention has been paid in these works to higher education as a separate sector. We can make some extensions: for example, the role of Oxbridge in Britain in confirming élite status is almost self-evident even to those not sharing these radical views. It is well known that students in the university sector as a whole are disproportionately drawn from upper social groups (Williamson 1981). Compared to Britain, Americans seem to cling tenaciously to the image of higher education as a meritocracy, even today. Perhaps this reflects the greater actual availability of higher education to a large proportion of the population. However, the higher education system in the United States is actually highly stratified and the most prestigeful institutions, with fees out of reach of most of the population, can be seen as catering for a socially as well as an academically select clientele. Some writers in the United States argue that expansion in higher education, especially at the Community College level, despite its rhetoric about extension of opportunities for 'new students' (Cross 1971), operates mainly as a mechanism of social control and social selection (Karabel 1972; Nasaw 1979, Ch.15). There remains only the wistful hope that the masses of students in higher education will be in a better position than most to analyse and expose their own situation (Bowles and Gintis 1976; Nasaw 1979, pp.237-8). Judging from the conservative attitudes that university students are reported to hold (see Freeman 1976; Weinreich-Haste, this volume) this does not seem likely in the near future.

Most of the 'reproduction theories' pay no more than passing attention to gender. In recent years feminist theorists have tried to rework and reshape these approaches to permit their extension to the analysis of schooling's role in the reproduction of gender relations as well as (or together with) class relations (Arnot 1981; Barrett 1980; Branson and Miller 1979; David 1980; Kelly and Nihlen 1982; MacDonald 1980, 1981 a and b; Wolpe 1978). They point, for example, to the inability of most reproduction theories to account for the sexual division of labour and the reluctance to expand their concern to include the reproduction of women's responsibility for household and children in the domestic division of labour.

Such arguments arise from a broadly socialist-feminist standpoint. Relatively few empirical studies of girls and women in schools and colleges have emerged from a socialist-feminist approach, which tends to be theoretical and macrosociological. With a few exceptions (Anyon 1983; Gaskell 1983; Sharp 1976) empirical material within this tradition relies on historical and/or documentary analysis (eg Blunden 1982; David 1980; Deem 1981; Purvis 1981a, b; Wolpe 1976). Studies of access, achievements and experiences of girls in school such as those found in Spender and Sarah (1980) and Stacey et al. (1974) more often draw upon feminist perspectives which emphasize socialization, discrimination, inequality, and sometimes male dominance, rather than the relations of production under capitalism (cf Arnot's, 1981, contrast between 'cultural' and 'political economy' perspectives).

Historians writing of women's struggle for access to university are frequently aware of the middle-class bias in the arguments of the pioneers and the élite-reinforcing nature of their appeal to bourgeois self-interests (see Dyhouse, this volume). But when we turn to questions of contemporary higher education, we find a virtual silence about its role in reproduction of sexual inequality. The absence of papers in the present collection that tackle contemporary higher education from an explicit 'reproduction' perspective reflects the gaps in the field. Nor can we develop a suitable account of higher education from this perspective in this chapter. However, we can make a few suggestions about the direction in which such an analysis might proceed.

The conventional profile of 'where women are' within higher education (see my earlier discussion of Tables 2.1 to 2.3) might be a starting point for discussion of why they are there. Women are less frequently represented than men among the higher degree students, in the senior and influential levels of the university hierarchy (both professional and administrative), in the research realm (except as low-level, short-term 'assistants'), and in the scientific and technological spheres. (See Weinreich-Haste, Spender, Taylorson, Rendel, Scott and Porter, all in this volume.) Women are 'visible' in certain arts-based subjects and in the subjects linked with the 'helping professions'. A follow-up study of 1960 women graduates found that most ended up as teachers, if not straight away, after a period of time in another occupation (Chisholm and Woodward 1980, p.164). A few writers have suggested that the disproportionate recruitment of women into school-teaching plays an important part in perpetuating the sexual division of labour, for example by reducing competition for other occupations, by institutionalizing a pattern whereby women adjust their labour force participation to school hours and child care (thus losing bargaining power in the marketplace), and by providing an unspoken message for the younger generation about appropriate feminine pursuits (David 1980; Deem 1978).

Another promising approach would draw upon the Weberian concept of social closure,[3] of increasing interest to writers on the professions (Saks 1983). Closure...

> broadly refers to the process by which given social collectivities seek to regulate market conditions in their favour, in face of actual or potential competition from outsiders, by restricting access to specific opportunities to a limited group of eligibles. (Saks 1983, pp.5-6)

Such monopolization can rest on 'virtually any group attribute' (Parkin 1979, p.44). Parkin (1979) extends the concept to include both strategies of exclusion used by insiders and strategies of usurpation used by outsiders. An example of an exclusionary strategy is the requirement for formal credentials for entry into privileged occupations, since economically well-endowed families can ensure their children are in line for these credentials. Usurpationary forms of social closure include mobilization of trade union power against management or, outside the class context, movements such as Women's Liberation. One of the ways in which this approach differs from traditional Marxist analysis is in its greater attention to intraclass divisions along lines such as race or sex and its acknowledgement of the use of exclusionary strategies by more powerful segments of the working class against less powerful ones (Parkin 1979, pp.89-90). Parkin uses the term 'dual closure' to refer to the simultaneous employment of usurpationary and exclusionary strategies, for example the use by male workers of usurpationary strategies against management and exclusionary ones against all women and against ethnic minority males. Another example of dual closure comes from the further education sector, where the complex system linking promotion chances to grading of courses has been said to favour men, who tend to teach those courses with higher grades (Whyld 1982). In such a system male lecturers may fight as usurpationary unionists for more privileges while guarding those they already have against would-be (female?) intruders.

Professional occupations are frequently thought to practise exclusionary closure; this includes closure against women, most complete in the case of the clergy but remarkably successful in the case of university teachers also, if the sparse representation of women in British universities can be taken as evidence. It was only in the 1970s that the quota restricting the proportion of medical school entrants who are female − a blatant example of exclusionary closure − was removed (followed by a sharp increase in female enrolment). Occupations such as teaching and nursing have been far less successful than medicine in gaining full acceptance as professions. These are occupations which are bureaucratically organized and closely supervised by the state; they also have high proportions of women workers. Parkin (1979, p.104) suggests we might see these as occupations which have not been especially appealing to men and therefore which have not been able successfully to operate exclusionary devices against women (except at the highest levels). At least in the case of teaching there are numerous historical examples of attempts by men to restrict women's participation, including unequal pay and marriage bars.

We might usefully look at aspects of higher education in much the same light. Those segments with lower prestige within the system (advanced further education vs. the universities; contract research staff vs. tenured researchers; lecturers vs. professors and senior administrators; arts specialists and social scientists vs. physical scientists) have in each case been less able to restrict women's entry (although within each less privileged sector, men dominate the top ranks). Future researchers might advance our analysis by identifying the strategies of exclusion and usurpation used (overtly or covertly) by groups in different structural positions within higher education. Saks (1983) criticizes closure theories for advancing exaggerated claims with insufficient empirical support; to my knowledge no empirical work on contemporary women and higher education has yet been conducted using this promising framework.

Correspondences between sex-differentiated subjects and the sexual division of labour in the labour force are not difficult to find, but the links with domestic labour also need elucidating. There is an apparent contradiction between the concept of higher education as a venue for reproduction of an élite and any representation of women. Why should anyone encourage women to aspire to occupational areas where they are hardly welcome? The answer may lie in the class origins and destinations of these women. Especially among the professional middle classes, their future role is likely to be as 'domestic pedagogues' (MacDonald 1980), ensuring their children have a good stock of cultural capital with which to face their school years. So too will they be companions to their husbands, whose professional or business careers frequently depend absolutely on 'domestic capital' − the altruistic services of a wife (Finch 1983; Papanek 1973). In a brilliant article, Hochschild (1975) shows that the clockwork of university careers is built on the life cycle of a traditional married man. She turns our attention, though not in an explicitly socialist-feminist way, to 'the system' rather than the individuals within it. Perhaps in time others will build on her insights. Clearly the image of the university from this standpoint will not be one of meritocracy, or as a collection of individuals acting for good or for evil.

The segregation of women within and among institutions of higher education will be seen as an integral not an accidental feature of their societal role. It is not surprising if women 'under-aspire' and the university does little to counter it, if such under-aspirations mean that the university is producing well-educated wives and mothers for the bourgeoisie. The direction for feminist reform within education is, however, cloudy — if capitalism is at the root of things there are limits on what one can accomplish by challenging the education system. Perhaps 'a little learning' will deepen discontent — and ultimately be 'a dangerous thing'.

Culture and Knowledge

The question whether higher education serves capitalism logically leads to the question whether it also serves patriarchy (or capitalist patriarchy, or simply the interests of men and male dominance). Men not only dominate women, they preside over the creation and distribution of knowledge. It is often accepted (or advocated) that women and men in effect inhabit two different cultures. It is argued that knowledge generated by the women's culture has been 'muted' while that produced by the men's culture is universalized and recognized (Spender 1981). Interest in the possibility of 'two cultures' stems from empirical studies that produce differing 'his' and 'her' versions of 'reality' (Bernard 1972), from anthropological observations of 'dominant' and 'muted' groups and the socially-determined 'inarticulateness' of the latter (Ardener,E. 1975; Ardener,S. 1975); from extensions of the Marxist concept of 'hegemony', used to describe the ways in which ideas derived from the ruling class and serving their interests are accepted as commonsense knowledge by society in general (MacDonald 1977, pp.68-69); and finally, from attempts by feminist sociologists to understand and conceptualize the gap between their own experiences and what they have learned about society through their studies (Smith 1974; Stanley, this volume.)

The notion of separate cultures remains problematic, for several reasons. It is unclear whether women share a culture on the basis of common biology, common social experience, or both. If it is the former, arguments sail close to those historically used to condemn all women (seen as an undifferentiated group) to inferior status and opportunities (see Burstyn, this volume). To argue that, say, women are more co-operative or sensitive or peace-loving than men — whilst it may be empirically true ('on the average') — may be to give ammunition to those (with more power) who will wish to restrict women to spheres where co-operation, sensitivity and peace are the only options. If the argument is based on sex-differentiated social experiences, in a given case the divisions among women (according to class, ethnicity, country, religion, region, sexual orientation, motherhood) often appear to outweigh the similarities.

Ivan Illich (1983), using both the biological and social approaches, has recently argued that the pre-industrial practice of organizing society around separate gender groups, with a clear demarcation of labour between them (the exact collection of tasks reserved for each sex varying from society to society), has now given way to a 'genderless individual-ism', where female individuals compete with male individuals for scarce rewards — and almost inevitably lose the competition. Whilst there are provocative, illuminating facets to his argument, it nevertheless seems to leave only a depressing choice between accepting subordination as a group or subordination as individuals.

Even if we cannot resolve the difficulties of defending the concept of women's culture, we can turn to one outcome of such conceptualizations, the assault on what is seen as men's knowledge, in its masquerade as human knowledge. Much of the effort that has gone into 'Women's Studies' in recent years is an attempt to transcend what is argued to be arbitrary disciplinary boundaries and to create new forms of knowledge free from the distortions introduced by men's power to create knowledge in their own image (see Duelli Klein, this volume).

Critiques of numerous disciplines have appeared in recent years (eg Acker 1981; Spender (Ed.) 1981). To some extent Women's Studies can be produced within the 'discrimination' framework, for there is a central concern with fairness. Some feminists (those Liz Stanley in this volume criticizes for retaining conventional academic approaches) attempt to contribute to fairness by remedial work in their disciplines: adding studies of women, filling gaps within the existing literature. Others insist that the disciplines are so distorted that 'we cannot trust what we know'; that if sexism were removed from the curriculum little would remain (Spender 1982, pp.2-3). Socialist feminists tend to be somewhat suspicious of the more sweeping statements. Barrett (1980), for example, criticizes relativist arguments, which she sees reflected in some forms of Women's Studies, ie those that deny all claims to objective knowledge and locate truth in the pens of its producers and the eyes of its consumers. 'There are dangers attached to such a wholesale rejection of the possibility of objective knowledge: it is a high price to pay for the demystification of existing bodies of knowledge' (Barrett 1980, p.150). Defenders might reply that the aim is not to relativize knowledge but ultimately to replace pseudo-objective knowledge with a more truthful version that reflects human experience (Spender 1982, p.17).

The claim that women and men occupy separate cultures is easier to conceptualize within a specific setting such as an institution of higher education. As we have seen, women tend to be clustered in certain departments and relatively junior positions, which might well contribute to a sense of common consciousness among them, especially when this is seen as a consequence of common experiences of marginality within the institution. Those who are promoted to senior positions, or who study atypical subjects to doctoral level, are isolated from a 'women's culture' and instead exist on sufferance as individual anomalies in man's daily world. Carol Dyhouse (this volume) tells of the horror in the Senior Common Room in the 1920s when the Egyptologist Margaret Murray dared to intrude − and one suspects that the few professonial women in Margherita Rendel's statistics, and the 25 per cent of Daphne Taylor-son's doctoral student sample who were the only women in their departments would recognize the continuities between their experiences and Margaret Murray's. The difficulty of negotiating between a gender identity and an academic identity, to use Daphne Taylorson's terms, though no doubt experienced largely as an individual problem, may be the defining characteristic of much of women's experience in higher education. Higher education in this view is the quintessential male preserve, where decision-making power is concentrated almost exclusively in the hands of men (Spender 1981, p.106). Women will inevitably be the aliens in this scenario − either uncomfortable as individual representatives of womanhood (though flawed, by definition, for being 'like men') or ghettoized in departments accorded low status and little influence because they are 'dominated' by women (DiNitto et al.1982).

One feminist solution to this situation is to build upon separateness and make of it a virtue. An approach to the concentration of power is to encourage women-controlled institutions, where women can determine priorities (Rich 1975; Spender 1981, p.127). Where this is not realistic, the emphasis is on the production of ideas, namely the elaboration of Women's Studies within established institutions. This strategy has been most successful in the United States, as the appendix to Renate Duelli Klein's chapter in this volume shows, where programmes are welcomed provided they attract students and thus money. It is more difficult to initiate Women's Studies in the framework of British higher education where innovativeness is controlled not so much by the market as by the vetting by the CNAA and by Faculty Boards, often traditional in their view of higher education and its functions. In both countries the possibilities remain that 'ghettoization' of Women's Studies will simply remove the responsibility of the traditional disciplines to tackle reform (a point made by Liz Stanley in this volume) and that whenever economies are demanded, the institutional tolerance for Women's Studies will diminish.

No Problem?

Finally, we must consider the view that the problem of women in higher education is 'no problem'. In this perspective we may include arguments that the battles for access to higher education are safely in the past and that opportunities are now there for those who want them. It has been suggested that this popular view among academics has been responsible for the AUT (the university lecturers' union) placing little emphasis on women's rights until very recently (Jobbins 1983). Others arrive at the 'no problem' perspective from the difficulty of making decisions about where one's priorities for reform are most urgently required. It is not uncommon for left wing ideologues to argue that the women's movement divides the working class, diverts the energies of women, and sets back the struggle for socialism. Socialist feminists might reply that socialism cannot be attained without justice for women while radical feminists point out that violence practised systematically against women worldwide (rape, pornography, genital mutilation) is hardly an insignificant instance of oppression.

Even within feminist ranks, many believe that the position of 'women in higher education' is relatively unproblematic. In the British context, Eileen Byrne (1978) argues that feminist concern is more properly turned toward girls who are multiply disadvantaged by factors such as class, region, and level of ability, rather than academic women who are an élite among women (if not among academics).

In a worldwide context, it is clear that higher education is unavailable to the masses of the world's population (especially the women); even universal literacy is beyond the reach of many countries. In many developing countries, the extent of education provided is not great for either sex. However, the disadvantage to girls is often more pronounced. Unesco figures for the educational enrolment of the population aged six to twenty-nine in thirty-nine countries show a higher enrolment rate for girls than boys in only five countries (Deblé 1980,p.19). In the developed world and most of Latin America, there is parity of enrolment at primary level (Bowman and Anderson 1980, p.S20). But 1977 World Bank figures for thirty-eight low income countries reported 90 per cent of males but only 64 per cent of females were receiving primary education (Smock 1981, p.13). When children move from primary to secondary levels in the developing world, boys almost always receive preferential treatment according to Deblé (1980, p.21). It is difficult to find clear country-based factors that systematically account for variations in provision for women's education. For example it is not simply the extent of expansion of the education system overall that makes a difference — sometimes this works for, sometimes against, opportunities for women. In a study of five developing countries, Smock (1981, p.256) finds that structural considerations (eg provision of science facilities and teachers at girls' schools) appear more significant than cultural ones.

In a world where large proportions of the female population are illiterate or have minimal education, how can we justify lavishing great concern on women in higher education in Britain and America? Janet Radcliffe Richards (Richards 1982, p.335) provides us with one possible way out of this dilemma. Compared with instances of brutality and torture across the world, and perhaps even with cruelty toward animals, women in the West may be seen to suffer injustice but their treatment is not atrocious. There is no point in claiming priority of oppression for Western women. However, it does not follow that this is a reason to ignore the claims of women until after another cause has had priority (Richards 1982, p.337).

The contributors to *Is Higher Education Fair to Women?* believe that it makes sense to try to understand what makes even apparently highly advantaged women in developed countries still disadvantaged in comparison with male counterparts. If Illich is right this is an inevitable consequence of the demise of separate gender spheres. But others argue that we have hardly begun to provide a fair chance for women to compete. If some of the barriers could be removed this 'academic élite' might be in a better position to help others oppose oppression and injustice.

Notes

1   A recent study (Vellins 1982) reports data on first-year UK university students showing that women born in South Asia or East Africa (but classified as home students) are more likely to study science (especially the South Asians) and much less likely to study arts and languages than the UK-born women students.

2   Kelly (1984) points out, however, that the likelihood of parental investment in daughters' or sons' education varies according to economic considerations that differ from area to area. In some parts of the world where their labour is not needed in the fields girls are more likely than boys to be sent to school.

3   I owe this suggestion to Sheila Miles.

References

Acker,S. (1981) No-woman's-land: British sociology of education 1960-1979 *The Sociological Review* 29(1) 77-104

Althusser,L. (1971) Ideology and ideological state apparatuses. In *Lenin and Philosophy and Other Essays* London: New Left Books

Anyon,J. (1983) Intersections of gender and class: accommodation and resistance by working-class and affluent females to contradictory sex-role ideologies. In Walker,S. and Barton,L. (Editors) *Gender, Class and Education* Lewes: Falmer

Apple,M. (Editor) (1982) *Cultural and Economic Reproduction in Education* London: Routledge and Kegan Paul

Ardener,E. (1975) Belief and the problem of women. In Ardener,S. (Editor) *Perceiving Women* London: Dent

Ardener,S. (1975) Introduction. In Ardener,S. (Editor) *Perceiving Women* London: Dent

Arnot,M. (1981) Culture and political economy: dual perspectives in the sociology of women's education *Educational Analysis* 3(1) 97-116

Arregger,C. (1966) *Graduate Women at Work* Newcastle upon Tyne: Oriel

Astin,H.S. (1979) *The Woman Doctorate in America* New York: Russell Sage

Bardwick,J. (1971) *Psychology of Women* New York: Harper

Barrett,M. (1980) *Women's Oppression Today: Problems in Marxist Feminist Analysis* London: Verso

Bernard,J. (1972) *The Future of Marriage* London: Souvenir

Blackstone,T. and Crispin,A. (1982) *How Many Teachers? Issues of Policy, Planning and Demography* (Bedford Way Paper No.10) London: University of London Institute of Education

Blunden,G.P. (1982) *Women's Place in Non-Advanced Further Education: The Early Development of Three Colleges in Southwest England* Unpublished PhD dissertation, University of Bristol

Bourdieu,P. (1976) The school as a conservative force. In Dale,R., Esland,G. and MacDonald,M. (Editors) *Schooling and Capitalism* London: Routledge and Kegan Paul

Bourdieu,P. (1977) Cultural reproduction and social reproduction. In Karabel,J. and Halsey,A.H. (Editors) *Power and Ideology in Education* New York: Oxford University Press

Bowles,S. and Gintis,H. (1976) *Schooling in Capitalist America* London: Routledge and Kegan Paul

Bowman,M.T. and Anderson,C.A. (1980) The participation of women in education in the Third World *Comparative Education Review* 24(2,2) S13-S32

Branson,J. and Miller,D.B. (1979) *Class, Sex and Education in Capitalist Society: Culture Ideology and the Reproduction of Inequality in Australia* Melbourne: Sorrett

Byrne,E. (1978) *Women and Education* London: Tavistock

Carnegie Commission on Higher Education (1973) *Opportunities for Women in Higher Education* New York: McGraw-Hill

Chisholm,L. and Woodward,D. (1980) The experiences of women graduates in the labour market. In Deem,R. (Editor) *Schooling for Women's Work* London: Routledge and Kegan Paul

Cole,J.R. (1979) *Fair Science: Women in the Scientific Community* New York: Free Press

Cross,K.P. (1971) *Beyond the Open Door: New Students to Higher Education* San Francisco: Jossey-Bass

David,M.E. (1980) *The State, the Family and Education* London: Routledge and Kegan Paul

Deblé,I. (1980) *The School Education of Girls* Paris: Unesco

Deem,R. (1978) *Women and Schooling* London: Routledge and Kegan Paul

Deem,R. (1981) State policy and ideology in the education of women, 1944-1980 *British Journal of Sociology of Education* 2(2) 131-143

Department of Education and Science (1981a) *Statistics of Education: Further Education. November 1981* London: DES

Department of Education and Science (1981b) *Statistics of Teachers in Service in England and Wales 1981* London: DES

DiNitto,D., Martin,P.Y. and Harrison,D.F. (1982) Sexual discrimination in higher education *Higher Education Review* 14(2) 33-54

Dowling,C. (1981) *The Cinderella Complex: Women's Hidden Fear of Independence* London: Tavistock

Dworkin,R. (1977) *Taking Rights Seriously* London: Duckworth

Epstein,C.F. (1970) *Women's Place: Options and Limits in Professional Careers* Berkeley: University of California Press

Equal Opportunities Commission (1982) *Women in Universities 1982: A Statistical Description* Manchester: EOC

Feldman,S. (1973) Impediment or stimulant? Marital status and graduate education. In Huber,J. (Editor) *Changing Women in a Changing Society* Chicago: University of Chicago Press

Finch,J. (1983) *Married to the Job* London: Allen and Unwin

Fitzpatrick,B. (1976) *Women's Inferior Education: An Economic Analysis* New York: Praeger

Fogarty,M., Rapoport,R. and Rapoport,R. (1971) *Sex, Career and Family* London: Allen and Unwin

Freeman,R. (1976) *The Over-Educated American* New York: Academic Press

Friedan,B. (1963) *The Feminine Mystique* New York: Dell

Gaskell,J. (1983) The reproduction of family life: perspectives of male and female adolescents *British Journal of Sociology of Education* 4(1) 19-38

Glazer,N. (1975) *Affirmative Discrimination: Ethnic Inequality and Public Policy* New York: Basic Books

Guttentag,M. and Bray,H. (1976) *Undoing Sex Stereotypes: Research and Resources for Educators* New York: McGraw-Hill

Harbeson,G. (1967) *Choice and Challenge for the American Woman* Cambridge, Mass: Schenkman

Hochschild,A.R. (1975) Inside the clockwork of male careers. In Howe,F. (Editor) *Women and the Power to Change* New York: McGraw-Hill

Hoffman,L.N. (1972) Early childhood experiences and women's achievement motives *Journal of Social Issues* 28, 129-156

Horner,M.S. (1972) Toward an understanding of achievement-related conflicts in women *Journal of Social Issues* 28, 157-176

Illich,I. (1983) *Gender* London: Marion Boyars

Jobbins,D. (1983) Breaking down the barriers of academic machismo *The Times Higher Education Supplement* 29 April 1983

Karabel,J. (1972) Community colleges and social stratification: submerged class conflict in American higher education *Harvard Educational Review* 42, 521-562

Karabel,J. and Halsey,A.H. (1977) Educational research: a review and an interpretation. In Karabel,J. and Halsey,A.H. (Editors) *Power and Ideology in Education* New York: Oxford University Press

Kelly,G.P. (1984) Factors influencing women's access to education in the Third World: myths and realities. In Acker,S., Megarry,J., Nisbet,S. and Hoyle,E. (Editors) *World Yearbook of Education 1984: Women and Education* London: Kogan Page

Kelly,G.P. and Nihlen,A. (1982) Schooling and the reproduction of patriarchy: unequal workloads, unequal rewards. In Apple,M. (Editor) *Cultural and Economic Reproduction in Education* London: Routledge and Kegan Paul

Komarovsky,M. (1946) Cultural contradictions and sex roles *American Journal of Sociology* 52, 184-189

Little,A. and Robbins,D. (1981) Race bias. In Warren Piper,D. (Editor) *Is Higher Education Fair?* Guildford: SRHE

MacDonald,M. (1977) *The Curriculum and Cultural Reproduction I and II* (Open University Course E 202 Block III Units 18-19) Milton Keynes: The Open University Press

MacDonald,M. (1980) Socio-cultural reproduction and women's education. In Deem,R. (Editor) *Schooling for Women's Work* London: Routledge and Kegan Paul

MacDonald,M. (1981a) *Class, Gender and Education* (Open University Course E 353 Block 4 Units 10-11) Milton Keynes: The Open University Press

MacDonald,M. (1981b) Schooling and the reproduction of class and gender relations. In Dale,R., Esland,G., Fergusson,R. and MacDonald,M. (Editors) *Education and the State: Politics Patriarchy and Practice* Vol.2. Lewes: Falmer

Nagel,T. (1977) Equal treatment and compensatory discrimination. In Cohen,M., Nagel,T. and Scanlon,T. (Editors) *Equality and Preferential Treatment* Princeton, NJ: Princeton University Press

Nasaw,D. (1979) *Schooled to Order: a Social History of Public Schooling in the United States* New York: Oxford University Press

Papanek,H. (1973) Men, women, and work: reflections on the two-person career. In Huber,J. (Editor) *Changing Women in a Changing Society* Chicago: University of Chicago Press

Parkin,F. (1979) *Marxism and Class Theory: A Bourgeois Critique* London: Tavistock

Parsons,T. and Platt,G.M. (with the collaboration of N.J. Smelser) (1973) *The American University* Cambridge, Mass: Harvard University Press

Purvis,J. (1981a) The double burden of class and gender in the schooling of working class girls in nineteenth century England 1800-1870. In Barton,L. and Walker,S. (Editors) *Schools, Teachers and Teaching* Lewes: Falmer

Purvis,J. (1981b) Women and teaching in the nineteenth century. In Dale,R., Esland,G. Fergusson,R. and MacDonald,M. (Editors) *Education and the State Vol.2 Politics Patriarchy and Practice* Lewes: Falmer

Ram,R. (1980) Sex differences in the labour market outcomes of education *Comparative Education Review* 24 (2,2) S53-S77

Rich,A. (1975) Toward a women-centered university. In Howe,F. (Editor) *Women and the Power to Change* New York: McGraw-Hill

Richards,J.R. (1982) *The Sceptical Feminist* Harmondsworth: Penguin

Robarts,S. (1981) *Positive Action for Women: the Next Step* London: National Council for Civil Liberties

Saks,M. (1983) Removing the blinkers? A critique of recent contributions to the sociology of professions *The Sociological Review* 31(1) 2 – 21

Shaw,B. (1979) Sex discrimination in education: theory and practice *Journal of Philosophy of Education* 13, 33-40

Smail,B., Whyte,J. and Kelly,A. (1982) Girls into science and technology: the first two years *School Science Review* 63, 620-630

Smith,D.E. (1974) Women's perspective as a radical critique of sociology *Sociological Inquiry* 44, 7-13

Smock,A.C. (1981) *Women's Education in Developing Countries* New York: Praeger

Spender,D. (1981) Sex bias. In Warren Piper,D. (Editor) *Is Higher Education Fair?* Guildford: SRHE

Spender,D. (Editor) (1981) *Men's Studies Modified* Oxford: Pergamon

Spender,D. (1982) *Invisible Women: The Schooling Scandal* London: Writers and Readers

Spender,D. and Sarah,E. (Editors) (1980) *Learning to Lose* London: The Women's Press

Stacey,J., Bereaud,S. and Daniels,J. (Editors) (1974) *And Jill Came Tumbling After: Sexism in American Education* New York: Dell

Thurston,G.J. (1981) *Women Teachers and Maternity Leave* Unpublished MEd dissertation, University College Cardiff

Trown,E.A. and Needham,G. (1980) *Reduction in Part-time Teaching: Implications for Schools and Women Teachers* Manchester: Equal Opportunities Commission

Tyler,W. (1977) *The Sociology of Educational Inequality* London: Methuen

University Grants Committee (1982) *University Statistics 1980 Vol.1 Students and Staff* Cheltenham: Universities' Statistical Record

Vellins,S. (1982) South Asian students at British universities: a statistical note *New Community* 10(2) 206-212

Watson,C. and Quazi,S. (1981-82) The aging Ontario teacher force *Interchange* 12(1) 39-52

Whyld,J. (1982) Sexism in the college *Natfhe Journal* 7(1) 21-22

Wilce,H. (1983) Pursuing sexual equality in a ladylike manner *The Times Educational Supplement* 29 April 1983

Williamson,B. (1981) Class bias. In Warren Piper,D. (Editor) *Is Higher Education Fair?* Guildford: SRHE

Wilson,W.J. (1978) *The Declining Significance of Race* Chicago: University of Chicago Press

Wolpe,A.M. (1976) The official ideology of education for girls. In Flude,M. and Ahier,J. (Editors) *Educability, Schools and Ideology* London: Croom Helm

Wolpe,A.M. (1978) Education and the sexual division of labour. In Kuhn,A. and Wolpe,A.M. (Editors) *Feminism and Materialism* London: Routledge and Kegan Paul

Woodhall,M. (1973) Investment in women: a reappraisal of the concept of human capital *International Review of Education* 19(1) 9-29

Zinberg,D. (1973) College: when the future becomes the present *Annals of the New York Academy of Sciences* 208, 115-23

Part 2
Historical context

3 Storming the citadel or storm in a tea cup? The entry of women into higher education 1860-1920

Carol Dyhouse

Historians interested in the higher education of women in modern England have traditionally adopted a 'Whiggish' theoretical framework. They have commonly begun their accounts in the mid-nineteenth century, documenting the foundation of Queen's College (1848) and Bedford College (1849) for women. They have then depicted a gradual opening up of opportunities for women in the universities, from around the 1860s (when Emily Davies successfully campaigned for permission for girls to sit the Cambridge University Local Examinations) through the foundation of the separate women's colleges in Oxford and Cambridge; from London University's opening of its degrees to women by means of a Supplementary Charter in 1878 down to the (disgracefully tardy) decision on the part of the University of Cambridge finally to admit women as full members on the same terms as men in 1947. This historiographical tradition, with its implications of steady progress towards an eventual victory for 'equal opportunity' has involved a good deal of omission — sometimes wishful thinking, perhaps — and distortion. History does, after all, have a minimal obligation to explain the present, and universities in Britain scarcely present us with anything like a picture of equal opportunity today. It is a fact that the higher one looks up the higher education hierarchies — academic, administrative and political — the fewer women there are.

Why is it that conventional historical accounts have presented such an optimistic picture? Partly, it is a question of relative perception or standpoint. I may see a glass as nearly empty. Someone else who has tended to take its emptiness for granted and who watches it receive a few drops of water perceives it as filling up. That Agnata Frances Ramsay achieved a splendid First in the Cambridge Classical Tripos in 1887 (outstripping all her male rivals); and that only two per cent of professors in British universities in 1979 were female are both selected 'historical facts'. The pattern of facts that the historian chooses to emphasize will obviously depend greatly upon 'commonsense' assumptions and political and historical viewpoint. Historians have a vested occupational interest in <u>change</u>: in identifying and locating 'revolutions' or debating whether 'revolution' or 'evolution' supplies the best description of a given sequence of changes in this or that social institution.

Early histories of women's education — particularly when they were written by feminists — were sometimes intended to spur women on to greater effort in the battle for educational opportunities by emphasizing both the sum of achievements to date and the obstacles still to be overcome.[1] Change was seen as revolutionary because of the close involvement in struggle and it is hardly surprising that these accounts are full of the imagery of the battlefield, or of climbing mountains. Many later historians have retained this kind of imagery and continued to write of revolutions and to emphasize the scale of changes which took place in the period 1870-1900: indeed a recent study of the history of women's education in the last century by Margaret Bryant takes as its title *The Unexpected Revolution*.[2] It is only in the last few years that a new generation of historians — many of them feminists — have paused to take stock of the position of women in English society today and have begun to ask new questions. Instead of trying to explain a revolution whereby women successfully stormed the citadels of higher education in late Victorian England and hot-footed it down the road to a glorious twentieth-century field of sexual equality, they want to know <u>why</u>, in spite of one-hundred-and-fifty-odd years of struggle at all social levels, in which the <u>rhetoric</u> of equality emerged triumphant, women's situation remains what it is. Why, if the gates of the universities are theoretically open to girls on the same terms as boys, have women not been able to <u>use</u> education to alter the basic features of their social position? Why are women <u>still</u> so massively under-represented, so conspicuously lacking in power and status in the more exclusive areas of higher education today? In other words, if there was indeed a 'revolution' in the higher education of women over the last century and a half, why did it achieve so little?

In the short space which follows I shall look briefly at some of the most interesting recent work on the history of women's higher education in order to show how this has served to modify more traditional accounts.

New forms of provision for girls' education at the 'secondary' level developed in the second half of the nineteenth-century in Britain. Two schools were particularly important as models — these were Cheltenham Ladies' College during the reign of Dorothea Beale, and the North London Collegiate School, founded by Frances Mary Buss in 1850. Miss Buss's regime in North London was particularly influential, serving as a model for girls' 'High' schools all over the country: for example the schools established by the Girls' Public Day School Company (founded in 1872 and responsible for thirty-six schools by 1896), those of the Church

Schools Company (inaugurated in 1883, and with twenty-four schools by 1896), and a whole range of endowed High Schools and 'reformed' Grammar Schools. Progress for women in higher education went hand in hand with these reforms in secondary education between 1860 and 1900. The academic ethos of the new schools contrasted sharply with the tone of the small, homely 'Ladies' Seminary' or domestic 'academy': small numbers of the most determined and academically competent pupils began to penetrate the universities. There were pitifully few occupational niches open to women who had completed their studies in higher education. Most of those who needed to earn their own living either chose, or had no choice but to return to schoolteaching.[3]

It is often assumed that the new developments in girls' education — provision for more academic forms of schooling rather than a training in ladylike accomplishments and the widening scope for women to study at college or university level — were brought about largely or even exclusively by the reforming energy and pressure-group tactics of feminists bent upon removing barriers around women's education and employment. The older histories — with their somewhat hagiographical celebration of the work of pioneers like Miss Buss and Miss Beale — their tendency to portray a 'Great Woman' theory of history — have done little to dispel this impression. Recently, however, the work of two scholars in particular — American historian Joyce Senders Pedersen, and English sociologist Sara Delamont — have pointed out that the history of reform was rather more complex than this.[4]

Joyce Pedersen has analysed the origin and dynamics of the late nineteenth-century reform movement in women's education and looked closely at the values and aims of the individuals and social groups most involved. She has emphasized the contrasts between the newer girls' schools founded in the second half of the nineteenth century, with their commitment to scholarship and meritocratic values, and their predecessors — the small domestic academies. These earlier seminaries had often been run by the 'distressed gentlewoman' type of lady proprietress — often without any training or pretensions to scholarship of any kind. Headmistresses of the newer kinds of High School were sometimes scholars or public figures of some importance — they saw themselves as dignified professional workers involved in a new and important area of service to the community.[5] They were well paid and enjoyed comparative freedom from the pressures and demands of individual parents. Whereas the loss of a pupil might well have implied financial disaster to the proprietress of the older kind of school, the new institutions were large and the salaried headmistress enjoyed some security: if the whims of the occasional parent conflicted with her ideas about the conduct of the school then that parent might simply withdraw (or be asked to remove) the daughter from the school. It is very important to remember that this was only a <u>relative</u> immunity from parental pressure. The new schools had to attract pupils, they were still dependent on the market.

Where did support for the new schools come from? By the last quarter of the century there was no doubt that a section of the middle-class community was seeking a new kind of education for its daughters. Pedersen argues that support came mainly from professional groups and wealthy businessmen who were seeking to confirm their social position and differentiate themselves from the bulk of the middle class through aspiring to new standards of gentility. The lifestyle favoured by this group involved a rejection of purely commercial values and an emphasis on new codes of professional ethics and new forms of cultural idealism which particularly shaped their attitudes to education. Pedersen points out that women's education was perceived by this group as being important precisely <u>because</u> women were not expected to earn their own living − as dependent wives they were expected to use their leisure time to cultivate 'refinement', to indulge in aesthetic or social activities which would lend prestige or distinction to the family as a whole. This view was expressed time and time again by middle-class advocates of higher education for women in the later nineteenth century.

As Pedersen points out, seen like this the reforms in girls' secondary and higher education begin to appear in a distinctly conservative light. The new schools and colleges can be argued to have shared essentially the same kind of goals as their predecessors, aiming to turn out 'cultivated' ladies of leisure. There was indeed a revolt against super-ficiality and pretentious 'accomplishments'. But the new institutions were hardly aiming to turn out feminists bent on challenging the sexual division of labour or even inspired by any vision of reshaping the sex roles conventional in bourgeois family life. The reformers rejected any notion that ignorance was 'feminine' and emphasized the desirability of educating women to be cultivated wives and mothers. Very few of them queried the assumption that a married, middle-class woman − economi-cally dependent upon her husband and with servants to carry out domestic work − would enjoy a life of leisure: in the main they simply urged the responsible or community-minded use of this leisure-time. In other words, the reformers <u>redefined</u> the Victorian concepts of feminin-ity and 'woman's sphere': they did not (in the main) <u>reject</u> them.

Sara Delamont's work on women's education in the nineteenth century has similarly highlighted the contradictions rooted in the Victorian movement for reform. Like Pedersen, she points out that middle-class parents had as their main aim that of ensuring that their daughters grew up eligible for 'good' marriages. They simply would not have sent girls to schools which went too far in the direction of unconventionality or social radicalism. Delamont has found it useful to divide the pioneers of reform in women's education during the period into two groups, which she calls the 'separatists' and the 'uncompromising'.[6] The uncompromising group were as the name implies the more radical exponents of the need for change. Emily Davies, the founder of Girton College, was the best known of this group, which took the view that reform could only succeed if women insisted upon studying the same kinds of curricula and sitting the same examinations as men. The separatist reformers aroused much less opposition than the uncompromising party because they were prepared to countenance improvements in provision for women's education without demanding absolute comparability with men. The separatists were less likely to be seen as subversive or stigmatized as 'unreasonable', 'unladylike' or 'unfeminine' than were their uncompromising counterparts. However, Delamont shows clearly that all the reformers were to some extent trapped in a 'double-bind'. They were torn between on the one hand mollifying public opinion and proving their respectability by scrupulous adherence to the standards of 'proper' or 'decent' 'ladylike' behaviour, on the other by the need to assert themselves as intellectually confident and well able to mount an offensive on the bastions of the male academic establishment. These conflicts, albeit in a modified form, have left their mark on women's education down to the present day.

I want now to look at some of the conservative ways in which the new institutions for the higher education of women functioned in order to reinforce, through their structure and curricula, what girls had already learned about 'femininity' from their families, and from the society in which they had grown up.[7] I am not propounding a simple functionalist model of education-as-social-control: it would be ludicrous to suggest that the new schools and colleges for women functioned solely or primarily to reinforce conventional ideologies about the sexual division of labour or women's role. These institutions supplied women with valuable space for learning and self-expression and played a crucial role in the history of the feminist movement, as even the most casual reading on the subject will testify. To focus on the 'conservative face' of reform is essentially to modify or supply a corrective to traditional accounts. There are three areas I want to comment upon. These are firstly sponsorship, organization and control, secondly, social relationships within the new institutions of higher education, in particular women students' relationships with their tutors, both male and female, and thirdly, the lifestyles of women academics and the extent to which these women served as role models for their students. In all these areas I am concerned with what we might call the 'hidden curriculum' of the colleges and the social experiences of women who entered higher education — both of them areas which have until very recently received scant attention from historians.[8]

Late Victorian society was a deeply patriarchal society and no movement for reform of women's education could have succeeded without the support of the men in power. The women who worked for reform were well aware of this and set out to court the patronage of men of social standing or intellectual distinction, win for their projects the seal of respectability, and increase their chances of acceptance by the public. The standard histories of girls' education have not always made it clear perhaps just how much the new educational institutions for women depended upon male sponsorship, patronage, organization and control. In the arena of secondary education, for instance, most texts have discussed the work of the Shirreff sisters and other women centrally connected with the foundation of the Girls' Public Day School Company (GPDS).[9] But in the social climate of the late nineteenth century it would have been unthinkable for women to set up and run a Limited Liability Company on their own. Women had little or no experience of public administration and in the eyes of the majority of the public there was still something unusual (if not unseemly) in seeing women sitting on platforms and addressing meetings.

It is not surprising to find then, that the first four presidents of the GPDS Company were all peers of the realm. The first Council (1872-3) comprised twelve men and six women. Successive chairmen of Council from 1872 down to the 1960s were all male. It is a small fact but one of immense social significance that Laurie Magnus, sometime vice-chairman of the GPDS Council, and historian of the Trust, composed the preface to his history in that most gentlemanly of all patriarchal hidey-holes, the Athenaeum.[10] All over the country the initiative in the founding of girls' schools at the local level was likely to come from the clergy, doctors, or prominent local businessmen.[11] Men sat in large numbers on the governing bodies of girls' schools and women's colleges, they often dominated the platforms in the halls of these institutions on speechdays and at gala events. When girls' schools and colleges needed a public face, that face was almost invariably male.

In higher education a similar pattern was clear. Even in their own colleges, women were likely to be presented with images of male authority.[12] Professors and distinguished academics were (as nearly as made no difference) all male. The higher a girl aimed up the academic ladder, the more she would feel a trespasser in male preserves. Female students in Oxford or Cambridge at the turn of the century were not, of course, entitled to call themselves 'undergraduates' since they were not formally admitted to university membership. *Punch* may have jokingly coined the word 'undergraduettes', but their status was anomalous – they were only there on sufferance. Winifred Peck, whose autobiography *A Little Learning, or a Victorian Childhood* (1952) contains evocative memories of her student days in Oxford, notes that she and her fellow students looked upon male academics 'reverently, from a distance'.[13]

Going to university as a social experience <u>confirmed</u> their deference to the male intellect, <u>confirmed</u> their lowly sense of themselves as relatively insignificant females.

In trying to reconstruct something of the social experience of the women who first entered higher education, one finds that autobiographical accounts and memoirs often convey the exhilaration felt by some of the pioneers, from the uplifting feeling of 'making history' down to the small freedoms of late-night cocoa parties in one's own room away from the tyranny of family life. But the 'hidden curriculum' and social relationships experienced in college life often spelt out a very different set of messages. As Sara Delamont and others have emphasized, those responsible for the conduct of students in the new women's colleges were terrified of scandal. They meticulously supervised the appearance and behaviour of their charges, insisting on seemliness at all times. Girls' relationships with the male sex were sometimes policed to an extent which even at the time seemed laughable.[14] The early women's colleges contrived in many instances to continue the work of a bourgeois family upbringing in sheltering its daughters from the pollutions of the outside world.

The female principals of the new women's colleges often saw themselves as 'mothering' their charges and were solicitous about their health, diet and sleep. It should be remembered that there were good reasons for this. Many eminent medical men were unsympathetic to the idea of intellectual education for women. They were prepared to stake their reputations upon insisting that brainwork would wreak all kinds of havoc upon the female physiological system. Menstrual disorders, hysteria, atrophied breasts and ovaries could all, they claimed, be brought about by too much mental activity during puberty.[15] Women educators watched anxiously over the physical wellbeing of their pupils. Mrs. Sidgwick, at Newnham College, kept careful data on the health of students in Oxford and Cambridge and took pains to emphasize that their studies did not appear to prejudice their chances of mothering children successfully later in life.[16] Even given these considerations, though, some of the mistresses of the new colleges seem to have carried their maternal solicitude a little too far. Some of them appear to have tried to foster a sense of mother-daughter intimacy, which the more independent-minded amongst their students could find claustrophobic or intrusive.

The women responsible for the new institutions of higher education for girls were, of course, feeling their way, unsure, in many cases of the kind of role they were expected to play. They were generally chosen as mistresses of colleges precisely because they were unimpeachably respectable figures, high-minded, God-fearing women exemplifying in their own lives the quintessentially 'feminine' virtues of selflessness and service. These women were almost always unmarried because full-time salaried employment was still generally considered unacceptable for middle-class women after marriage. Women like Dorothea Beale, Constance Louisa Maynard (Mistress of Westfield College) and Alice Ottley (Headmistress of Worcester High School for Girls) were inspired by a religious sense of mission, moved by something very close to the conventual impulse. They all saw their own studies and careers very much in terms of service to God, a Divine Calling. Both Dorothea Beale and Alice Ottley cherished visions, at one time or another, of establishing holy teaching orders. They constantly exhorted their pupils to acts of self-renunciation. This outlook was wholly in keeping with conventional definitions of femininity as self-sacrifice. It was, however, an austere vision which might and did inspire disciples but was hardly calculated to appeal to the majority of girls who came into contact with it. Learning was <u>not</u> to be seen as a form of self-development, let alone a route to personal liberation, it was an act of discipline or a form of service.[17]

In the early days of establishing a female presence in higher education women of intellectual distinction available for employment were in short supply. This was one reason why those who sought to appoint mistresses of colleges, or lady principals of boarding houses tended to settle for respectable women with a sense of purpose, whether or not these women were scholars. As time went on, of course, the numbers of women with academic honours in the universities increased, and female students were more likely to come into contact with or to be taught by intellectuals of their own sex. It becomes important to consider the extent to which these women dons might have acted as more acceptable role models for their students.

Of course the popular image of what *Punch* tended to dub 'The Female Intellectual Type' was hardly an attractive one. Women intellectuals were caricatured in the popular press and novels of the 1890s as ugly, mannish and sexually deviant. As long as learning was considered of essence to be unfeminine this was likely to continue. Dorothy Sayers' detective novel *Gaudy Night*, first published in 1935, provides us with a rich portrait gallery of caricatured women dons. The descriptions stem from a mixture of prejudice and (one fears) sharp personal observation. Dorothy Sayers was herself an early student at Somerville. Vera Brittain, a contemporary of hers, remembers that Dorothy continually dissociated herself from and implicitly mocked the dowdiness of the women dons by wearing extravagant and vivid clothes. On one particularly noteworthy occasion she caused consternation by appearing at breakfast:

'Wearing a three-inch-wide scarlet riband round her head and in her ears a really remarkable pair of ear-rings: a scarlet and green parrot in a gilt cage pendant almost to each shoulder and visible right across the hall.'[18]

Women dons were in a very difficult position. They remained socially insecure vis à vis their male colleagues right through the early years of the twentieth century (some would argue that their social insecurities persist even today)[19] Conspicuously in the minority, their behaviour was held up for public scrutiny and comment much more often than was ever the case with their male colleagues. They were continually made to feel out of place. Margaret Murray, the distinguished Egyptologist, described how women lecturers in University College London in the 1920s were not even able to enter the men's common room to drink coffee and discuss research with colleagues. The sanctions were informal ones — the place was strongly characterized by the ethos of the gentleman's club. On one occasion Dr. Murray steeled herself to enter the common room. She was greeted by an embarrassed silence, and all hell was let loose as soon as she left.[20] Of course even today Oxford and Cambridge Colleges harbour misogynists steeped in patriarchal tradition who crawl out of the woodwork whenever they are given the opportunity to vote against co-residence or the appointment of a female 'fellow'. There are still — in the 1980s — common and combination rooms which a woman cannot (unless she is a domestic servant) comfortably enter.

Even — or perhaps especially — in matters of dress, personal appearance and lifestyle the late Victorian female don was trapped, again, in a double-bind. If she dressed with conventional 'feminine prettiness' she might feel herself to be lacking in dignity, in danger of attracting patronizing or compromising treatment from male colleagues. If she dressed austerely she was likely to be dismissed as mannish. Most women dons did elect to dress plainly — they probably did not want to make themselves any more conspicuous than they already were. Vera Brittain remembered that when she went up to Oxford as a young girl to find out about the entrance requirements for Somerville, she felt she had committed a social howler in the way of dress:

'Being quite ignorant of the plain-Jane-and-no-nonsense conventions of Oxford women dons, I had carefully changed, in accordance with the sartorial habits of Buxton, into evening dress, and was wearing a flimsy, lace frock under a pale blue and grey reversible satin cloak, and an unsubstantial little pair of high-heeled white suède shoes. So unlike the customary felt hat and mackintosh of the average 1913 woman student was this provincially modish attire that the Principal actually referred to it when she interviewed me during the Scholarship examinations in the following March. "I remember you", she said immediately, "you're the girl who came across the lawn in a blue evening cloak".'[21]

The lack of interest in fashion so often alleged to be characteristic of women dons did not always endear them to their students. Winifred Seebohm, a student at Newnham College in the 1880s, commented acidly, in letters home, on the personal appearance of her tutors:

> 'You <u>should</u> see Miss Gardner's get-up-droopy straw hat, Shetland shawl thrown on without any grace, and big heel-less felt slippers in which she shuffles along. Then she evidently uses no mirror for her toilet, for this morning she came down with the ends of her hair sticking straight out like a cow's tail — she drags it back tight, twists it, and sticks one hair pin through. The style of dress here is certainly <u>not</u> elegant.'[22]

Such recollections could be multiplied. Women dons who earned any reputation for dressing well were markedly in the minority. Jane Harrison at Newnham was generally considered to have style. Mrs. Toynbee was always 'elegant and diaphanous'.[23] And Winifred Seebohm was spellbound by the graceful pre-Raphaelite charm of the young Mrs. Marshall. She sent glowing descriptions home:

> 'But now I must tell you about Mrs. Marshall, from whom I have had two lectures. She <u>is</u> a Princess Ida. She wears a flowing dark-green cloth robe with dark brown fur round the bottom (not on the very edge) — she has dark brown hair which goes back in a great wave and is very usefully pinned up behind — very deep set large eyes, a straight nose — a face that one likes to watch. Then she is enthusiastic and simple. She speaks fluently and earnestly with her head thrown back a little and her hands generally clasped or resting on the desk. ...She looks at Political Economy from a philanthropic woman's point of view.'[24]

From the detailed observation here we can safely conclude that Mrs. Marshall served as something of a role model for the young Winnie Seebohm. Twenty years earlier Mary Arnold (later Mrs. Humphrey Ward) had confessed herself similarly captivated by the charm of Emilia Pattison, the young wife of the Rector of Lincoln.

> 'It was in '68 or '69 that I remember my first sight of a college garden, lying cool and shaded between grey college walls, and on the green a figure that held me fascinated — a lady in a green brocade dress, with a belt and chatelaine of Russian silver, who was playing croquet ... and seemed to me as I watched her a model of grace and vivacity.'[25]

Emilia Frances Strong's marriage to the Rector of Lincoln was popularly held to have been one of the sources of inspiration for George Eliot's description of the union between Dorothea Brooke and Casaubon in *Middlemarch*. Pattison himself was much older than his wife, grey and hoary although very scholarly, and it is generally supposed that Emilia was attracted to him as something of a father-figure.

Sara Delamont has argued that late Victorian reforms in women's education created two new female roles, on the one hand that of the unmarried 'career woman', on the other that of the cultured, well-educated wife who was an intellectual partner to, though still economically dependent upon, her husband. She points out quite rightly that the choice of celibacy was one way in which women could reject society's prescriptions about 'woman's sphere' whilst at the same time evading social censure.[26] Frances Mary Buss, Dorothea Beale, Constance Maynard and many other women educationalists deliberately rejected suitors. Women with a strong sense of their own autonomy often found it difficult if not impossible to reconcile themselves to the idea of dependency in marriage.

However, the idea of celibacy has never exerted any mass appeal. The majority of female students from the late nineteenth century down to the present have found the vision of a married life more congenial than the celibacy of the majority of women academic careerists. Emilia Pattison and Mary Paley Marshall were in many ways very unalike but they shared characteristics which made them attractive as role models to the younger women around them. They were both beautiful, well-dressed and intelligent and they both married men older and more eminent than themselves. In other words, they both managed to dovetail their intellectual energies and personal charms into fittingly 'feminine' lifestyles. Both women saw their husband's careers and social position as vastly more important than their own. And that was exactly why they earned the approval of their contemporaries.

Many of these issues are brought out in a novel by Alice Stronach, published in 1901. The novel is badly written but of a representative type, important because it spells out so many social assumptions of the period about higher education for women, and dramatizes conflicts with which many individual women would have been familiar. It is called *A Newnham Friendship*. Carol Martin, the heroine, is a student at Newnham in the 1880s. She is a young woman with an independent mind and socialist political convictions who achieves a First in political economy and leaves Cambridge to work in a settlement in the East End of London. She is committed to the idea of remaining single in order to live out a life of social purpose, and rejects the advances of a (wealthy) suitor, Ted Carew, whom she finds anyhow rather boyish and naive. Ted, broken-hearted, goes off to South Africa, where apparently, after a few near-miss episodes involving 'niggers and assegais' he manages 'to make a man of himself'. It is suggested that deep down, Ted has 'soul' — Stronach tells us that he took Carol's copy of Thomas à Kempis with him on his travels in order to wile away his leisure moments. The novel ends, not surprisingly, with Carol's conversion to the belief that women, to be whole people, need marriage and motherhood as well as Useful Work. The imagery is that of Botticelli madonnas and the shrivelled buds of Gloire-de-Dijon roses. (The latter representing the fate, of course, of professional careerist spinsters.) Carol's friend Elspeth (the brilliant classicist) tenders advice.

> 'It's no use shirking it, my friend: Our work, our latchkeys, our independence, our comradeships, even, are all very well for a time, but not for always.'

Carol comes to realize

> 'that a woman's destiny holds love as well as work, that, as Maeterlinck says, "we had far better leave behind us work unfinished than life itself incomplete".'

The theme and 'message' of the novel may seem close to those of Tennyson's poem about the higher education of women and 'femininity', *The Princess*. Women too earnestly bent upon the acquisition of learning or on the pursuit of Serious Work in life are — however splendid — unfeminine and basically deluded. If they are attractive a strong man should be able to appeal to 'their feminine instincts' and sort them out. The inescapable truth that intelligent women could be seduced by this idea, suitably gift-wrapped, with romantic trappings (we remember that Winnie Seebohm saw Mrs.Marshall as Princess Ida) is testimony to the extent to which Victorian prescriptions about sexual and gender identity were so deeply internalized by young women of the period.

Stronach's novel has more feminist content than Tennyson's poem. Carol's enlightenment proceeds not from her rejecting work in favour of marriage, but from her determination to recognize both as the necessary ingredients of a fulfilled life. The novel ends on this note and alas we can but speculate on how she fared. As a social historian I would stake my money on the likelihood that ten years time would see her firmly ensconced in the home tied up with domestic routine and childcare whilst Ted commuted daily into the City on the 8.30 train. She may have managed to fit in a bit of voluntary, unpaid social work on the side. The 'real-life' Carol Martins in late Victorian Britain who actually managed to combine professional careers with marriage and family life were few and far between. Higher education altered the outlook of a small minority of middle-class women but the lifestyles of the majority registered little change.

Notes

1   See, for instance, Bremner,C.S. (1897) *The Education of Girls and Women in Great Britain* (London), also the sections on education in Strachey,R. (1928) *The Cause: a Short History of the Women's Movement in Great Britain* (London).

2   Bryant,M. (1979) *The Unexpected Revolution: A Study in the History of the Education of Women and Girls in the Nineteenth Century* (London).

3   Gordon,A. (1895) The after-careers of university educated women *The Nineteenth Century* XXXVII, June, 955-60; Purvis,J. (1981) Women and teaching in the nineteenth century. In Dale,R., Esland,G., Ferguson,R. and MacDonald,M. (Eds) *Education and the State* (Brighton) pp.359-375.

4   Pedersen,J.B.S. (1974) *The Reform of Women's Secondary and Higher Education in 19th Century England: A Study in Elite Groups* (University of California (Berkeley) DPhil thesis); Pedersen,J.B.S. (1979) The reform of women's secondary and higher education: Institutional change and social values in mid and late Victorian England *History of Education Quarterly* Spring; Delamont,S. (1978) The contradictions in ladies' education, and The domestic ideology and women's education. In Delamont,S., and Duffin,L. (Eds) *The Nineteenth Century Woman, Her Cultural and Physical World* (London).

5   Pedersen,J.S. (1975) Schoolmistresses and headmistresses: élites and education in 19th century England *Journal of British Studies* Autumn.

6   Delamont (1978) *op.cit* ., p.154 ff.

7   Dyhouse,C. (1981) *Girls Growing Up in Late Victorian and Edwardian England* (London) analyses girls' socialization in the family during the period.

8   Some of the points raised in the following pages are discussed in more detail in the second chapter of my book *Girls Growing Up...* *op.cit* .

9   The best account of the history of the GPDST is still Kamm,J. (1971) *Indicative Past: 100 years of the Girls' Public Day School Trust* (London).

10 Magnus,L. (1923) *The Jubilee Book of the Girls' Public Day School Trust, 1873-1923* (Cambridge).

11 Pederson,J.B.S. (1979) *op.cit* ., pp.114-5

12 See Dyhouse (1981) *op.cit* ., esp.pp.60-4

13 Peck,W. (1952) *A Little Learning, or a Victorian Childhood* (London) pp.170-1.

14 Delamont (1978) *op.cit* ., p.145 ff.

15 Burstyn,J.N. (1980) *Victorian Education and the Ideal of Womanhood* (London) esp. ch.5; Dyhouse (1981) *op.cit* ., p.154 ff.

16   Sidgwick,Mrs.H. (1890) *Health Statistics of Women Students of Cambridge and Oxford and of Their Sisters* (Cambridge).

17   Dyhouse (1981) *op.cit* ., pp.74-6.

18   Brittain,V. (1960) *The Women at Oxford, A Fragment of History* (London) p.123.

19   Acker,S. (1980) Women, the other academics *British Journal of Sociology of Education* 1(1) 81-91.

20   Murray,M. (1963) *My First Hundred Years* (London) pp.159-60.

21   Brittain,V. (1933) *Testament of Youth, An Autobiographical Study of the Years 1900-25* (London) p.66.

22   Glendinning,V. (1969) *A Suppressed Cry: Life and Death of a Quaker Daughter* (London) p.73.

23   *Ibid* ., p.181.

24   *Ibid* ., p.71.

25   Courtney,J. (1934) *The Women of My Time* (London) p.149.

26   Delamont (1978) *op.cit* ., p.184.

4 Educators' response to scientific and medical studies of women in England 1860-1900

Joan Burstyn

Scientific studies of women provided a serious challenge to educators in England during the last forty years of the nineteenth century. These studies claimed that prolonged education would lead to mental and physiological derangement in women students, especially those who attended college. Those who objected to women having the same education as men used these conclusions to buttress their belief that women's role was in the family and the home. Because scientific studies formed a basis for intellectual discourse, and because medical histories, in particular, were regarded with respect, lay persons found it difficult to refute scientific arguments even when they felt them to be inaccurate or irrelevant. While not accepting the conclusion that prolonged education was dangerous for women, educators nevertheless amended the curriculum and the social environment in schools and colleges to allay fears and forestall prophesied ill-effects. At the same time, educators themselves began to gather data with which to refute the claims that education was damaging to women's health. In this they were aided by some physicians who supported higher education for women, and who attributed the maladies of their women patients to causes other than their educational experiences.

Educational reformers felt obliged to defend their work for women's education in terms defined for them by their opponents. Ironically, by collecting data on a systematic basis, women educators themselves provided source material for further scientific studies of women. These educators also fell into their opponents' mode of discourse: they spoke of the value of higher education to women as a group. Thus, as they sought to defend their position, they abandoned their original emphasis on the need for a person to pursue that education which best served his or her individual needs.

Those who believed women should be accepted as university students and be encouraged to follow a profession were concerned with the importance of individual variation. They did not claim that all women should go to college, or that all women should become professionals. They expected few women to do so, but for them individual choice was paramount, and could be exercised only when all occupations were open to men and women alike. Those who opposed higher education for women thought of women as a separate scientific class or group whose aspirations had to be constrained by the characteristics of the group. Those individuals who differed from the norm were aberrations, and had to be treated as such. Women with manly characteristics, whether physical or mental, were abnormal women, not men. Scientific studies that purported to find general laws that applied to the scientific class of Woman were welcomed as grist for political and social arguments to support this view.

The first scientific studies used in arguments about the higher education of women in England were drawn from the work of comparative anatomists on the structure of the human brain. Carl Gegenbaur (1826-1903), a comparative anatomist working both on vertebrates and invertebrates, described comparative anatomy as critical anatomy. 'The critical approach... looks for factors outside of the object but connected to it and revealing new facets of it and, because it indicates a causal connection between these elements it contributes to an explanation of these phenomena.'[1] After the pioneering work of Georges Cuvier (1769-1832), several comparative anatomists turned particularly to comparing the brain structure of human beings. Skull measurements were made by Paul Broca using skulls from Parisian cemeteries; measurements were made in Germany by Welcker and Ecker, and in England by John Cleland. Comparisons of brain weights, including differences between males and females, were made by Robert Boyd, T. Peacock, and J.B. Davis in Britain. Davis calculated the volume of the brains of men and women from his collection of *exotic* skulls. He emphasized the need for caution in drawing conclusions:

> 'Attempts have been made by different observers to determine the proportion in weight by which the brains of men exceed those of women. This appears to be variable, and possibly the variation may be in relation to particular races; but to decide this question would require materials of a very exact nature. ... It may be said in our series to range from less than 10% to something more than 12½%.'[2]

In 1864, with the translation into English of Karl Vogt's *Lectures on Man*,[3] the work of European craniologists became widely known in the English speaking world. According to Vogt, the female brain, among Europeans, averaged from five to six ounces less than the male brain. This fact, together with the differing heights of the cranium and differing angles at which the skull was held on the spine, was used by some people to support the claim that women were innately less intelligent than men. It was even argued at a meeting of the London Anthropological Society that 'the inequality of the sexes increases with civilization' since differences between the skulls of the two sexes appeared more obvious among Europeans than among more primitive societies.[4]

The discussion of men's superiority to women was bound closely to discussions of racial superiority, first of Europeans to Africans and Australian Aborigines, and then of some European nationalities to others. Although Davis was careful to point out that his skulls had been collected specifically for their *exotic* nature, it was but a step to assume his data applied to all specimens.

The work of comparative anatomists was widely discussed in the anthropological literature of the 1860s and 1870s. Publication of Darwin's *Origin of Species* (London, 1859) had heightened interest in the data. With regard to differences between men and women, Darwin's theory of evolution could be used to indicate that the sexes were at different stages of evolution. Since anatomists wrote that women's brain size and skull structure were more akin to children's than were those of men, it was assumed by some that women had evolved less far than men, an idea that accorded well with traditional views of woman's subordinate role in society. People's *a priori* assumptions about the value of higher education for women clearly influenced, even determined, the conclusions they drew from scientific studies. While some argued that women had been left behind in the process of evolution, and therefore should not try intellectually to compete with men, others, like W.L. Distant, argued that by using their brains women could stem an evolutionary trend toward inferiority.[5] Distant cited Darwin's comments on the brain of domesticated rabbits as evidence that the brain decreases in size if it is not used.[6] Hence, the need to educate women was as great, if not greater, than the need to educate men, because women had to learn anew how to use their brains to the full in order to reverse a process of evolution that had already begun.

Distant's arguments were made at a time when the discussion of women's intellectual ability had become heated because a group of reformers, men and women led by Emily Davies, had succeeded in opening the Cambridge lower examinations to schoolgirls as well as boys, and had founded a college at Hitchin where women followed exactly the degree requirements of men at Cambridge University. These successes drew from the medical profession an argument against higher education based on the effect of women's physiology on her mental capacity. Replying to an address to the British Association by the reformer Lydia Becker 'On Some Supposed Differences in the Minds of Men and

Women with Regard to Educational Necessities', in which she argued that any differences between men and women were not innate but were the result of childhood training, *The Lancet*, in September 1868, claimed that men and women needed different forms of education because their physiologies, and hence their minds, differed. Data on brain size was not relevant — nor was it conclusive since 'woman might fairly urge that her sex has an amount of brain relatively equal to that of man'; however, there was 'a corresponding relation between the delicacy of the organization and character of woman's structures and that of her duties in life.' Woman's delicacy of organization was linked to her quickness of perception and her inability as far as sustained thought was concerned. Because woman's body and brain worked more rapidly than man's, she experienced a more rapid waste of tissue and hence needed more rest. Women, therefore, could never undertake the sustained physical and intellectual work performed by men. 'Imagination, memory, and quickness of perception' were not the same things as 'power of sustained thought, judgement, and creativeness' according to the article, which implied that while the former characteristics might belong to some women, the latter group belonged only to men.[7]

The arguments that women were innately less intelligent and physiologically less robust than men accorded so well with existing relationships between the sexes that many who wished to improve women's education felt bound to accept their validity. Consequently, pressure was put upon the universities to introduce less stringent examinations for women, or at least, to offer examinations of a different nature from those offered to men. In 1868 the first special examinations for women were held by the University of London, and in 1869 Cambridge University introduced a new examination for women over eighteen.[8]

Unlike the examinations for boys and men, on which they were modelled, the special examinations for women provided neither entry to the universities, nor, at higher level, the equivalent of a degree. They gave young women an outlet for their energies, and a measure of their intellectual competence, while leaving intact the male monopoly of universities and professions. Ladies' diplomas were solely consumer items, to be displayed like the latest fashions. They were loudly applauded by those who opposed women's entry into the professions.

Some women, however, were not to be bought off by an education designed solely for display. They needed to support themselves and resented being shunted into lesser jobs than their brothers. They persisted in studying subjects and taking examinations other than those prescribed for them. In part, it had been the growing number of girls applying to enter the University lower examinations during the 1860s that had persuaded the universities to establish special examinations for women at the end of the decade. Not that girls were unsuccessful in the lower examinations. To the contrary, their results during the 1860s showed that women were as capable as men at passing examinations. Not all young women passed them, but then neither did all young men. Enough girls did well on the examinations to challenge the validity of the theory that woman, as a scientific class, was innately inferior to man. Where girls failed their teachers assumed the reason was their inadequate preparation, not their innate lack of intelligence. As Joshua Fitch, one of Her Majesty's Inspectors of Schools, wrote to George Grote, Vice-Chancellor of the University of London, in opposition to that university's plan to establish special examinations for women:

'I am sure that the low state of girls' education in schools – its inexactness, its want of breadth, and its utterly unscientific character – would be in great measure corrected if the ordinary tests by which the education of boys is measured, were systematically applied to it.'[9]

And, in fact, under the influence of the examination results, girls' schools from the 1860s onwards made successful efforts to improve the instruction they offered. Women teachers pressured the universities to provide lecture series for women, and many teachers obtained through them their first opportunity to study at university level. As a consequence, over the years, the girls' results on the University lower examinations improved, more girls felt capable of taking them, and the universities were persuaded by the mid-1880s to abandon special examinations for women.[10]

With the discrediting of scientific studies on the innate inferiority of women's intelligence through the empirical evidence of examination results, there followed a series of studies to prove women's physiological danger in undertaking higher education.[11] Since college education for women was earlier established in the United States than in England, and the number of women's colleges in the United States far exceeded those in England, the first empirical evidence of the effects of higher education on women was gathered in the United States. In looking for the motivation for these studies, as for the motivation of the earlier ones, one is driven to the conclusion that a large component was fear by men of economic competition from women. As Emily Pfeiffer, author of *Women and Work* (London, 1888), wrote:

'Now it so happens that the callings which sentimentalists of the opposite sex are most earnest in tabooing to women, those against which they are most ready to affix the black mark of "unwomanly", are precisely such as offer the highest rewards in money and consideration.'[12]

The doctors who, after 1870, described the ill-effects of higher education on women knew that medicine was a profession women wanted to enter. By 1870 the census in the Unites States listed 525 women doctors; in England Elizabeth Garrett had qualified as a doctor, and, though the Society of Apothecaries had subsequently amended its regulations to exclude women, an indomitable handful of women from England were training as doctors abroad. In 1874 the London School of Medicine for Women opened, and during the next fifteen years 159 women qualified there as doctors.[13] As in the United States, there was a strong feeling at this time that women with gynaecological problems would do well to consult women doctors. Elizabeth Garrett found by 1870 that most of her practice was gynaecological.[14]

The medical case against women studying regularly during and after puberty claimed that mental effort halted or delayed the onset of puberty, caused malfunction of the reproductive system even when menstruation was firmly established, and led, possibly, to permanent sterility or inability to nurse one's babies.[15] Gynaecologists and neurologists used evidence from their own case studies to support their arguments. Some were supporters of women's demands for improved education, for they believed the nervous disorders of many women patients resulted from the vacuity of their minds; however, they made it clear that though they wanted better education for women, they did not want women to have the same education as men. As with earlier anatomical studies of the brain, the conclusions one drew from one's data depended on one's prior assumptions about women's roles in society. For several writers the role of woman as mother was supreme; they feared national disaster if the most intelligent women turned to education and careers rather than to marriage and childbearing. In the words of Robert Lawson Tait, sometime president of the British Gynaecological Society:

> 'To leave only the inferior women to perpetuate the species will do more to deteriorate the human race than all the individual victories at Girton will do to benefit it.'[16]

To protect women's reproductive functions, and to ensure the perpetuation of superior stock, John Thorburn, professor of obstetrics at Owens College Manchester urged women not to undertake such work as men did; women needed rest during menstruation. Education for women had to be non-competitive and discontinuous. His hope was:

> 'that some British University will ultimately found degrees and plan corresponding work for women alone, degrees which will recognize that higher "enthusiasm of humanity" in which women excel, and

work which will allow for their position as future mothers of our race.'[17]

Educational reformers responded to the arguments of physicians by making sure that women students did not overwork, and by gathering data on the health of women students in order to refute the arguments entirely. Some educators rejected the idea that women should take part in competitive sports, and urged instead that women should find relaxation from intellectual effort in accomplishments: needlepoint, piano playing, or drawing. They felt the 'will to win' was unnatural among women, and that women who played sports, if they were to remain womanly, would play only for enjoyment not mastery, and hence would 'destroy the integrity of the game'.[18] Most girls' schools, however, chose to protect the health of their students by introducing gymnastics and, later, competitive team sports. In doing so they followed the lead of boys' public schools which advocated physical exercise as an antidote to excessive study and as a necessity for character building. The first college for training women physical education teachers opened in 1885, and others followed during the next fifteen years.[19] By the 1890s gymnastics, field hockey, and tennis were offered in girls' schools.

Mental fatigue was a primary concern for the founders of women's colleges, as it was for school teachers. And, as in schools, competitive sports only gradually found acceptance as a valid counterbalance to studying. In the 1870s walking and rowing were thought to be suitable means of relaxation for women students. A majority of the women at Oxford and Cambridge colleges, as reported up to 1887, took between one and two hours exercise each day. For many this included games, riding, swimming, and calisthenics as well as walking.[20] In 1890 an American student at Newnham College, Cambridge, drew the following picture of daily life there:

'In the interval between 12.30 and 3.30 p.m. the students set off for long walks, or they crowd to the tennis and five courts; wet or fine everyone tries to go out somewhere. On wet days the gymnasium is a great resort. There are numbers of tennis courts, both grass and cinder. The latter dry so quickly that students are able to play all the year round.'[21]

The author was particularly struck by the health of the students during her four-year stay at Newnham. She felt that 'the arrangements at the large colleges provide such opportunities for recreation that it is only very exceptional students who are likely to overwork.'[22]

Educators protected the health of women students by closely supervising their social lives as well as by organizing their physical education. At

Newnham College doors were closed at 8 pm in summer and 6 pm in winter, although students could stay out until 11 pm merely by handing in their names. Only in special circumstances could they stay out beyond that time. (There was however no bedtime curfew, and late-night cocoa parties were a tradition.) At Oxford, women were no longer chaperoned to lectures after 1893, but chaperoning to social functions went on much longer.[23] Whether educators were most concerned to prevent sexual promiscuity, or whether they wished to guard against the ill-effects of too much party-going and dancing as doctors warned, they recognized that either would have proved fatal to their own aspirations and those of their students.

The medical arguments against higher education for women had been drawn from experience in the United States as well as in England. In both countries, therefore, educators were eager to gather data with which to refute them. Although English doctors who reported on the ailments of American women students did not emphasize this distinction, English educational practices differed markedly from American. In England there were no daily marks allotted for daily recitations. On the contrary, periods of intense effort followed by periods of relative relaxation have been hallmarks of English university education, and to some extent of education in schools as well. In the United States, however, the strain placed upon women students by daily recitations was claimed to be dangerous as early as 1873 by Edward Clarke in *Sex in Education*, and during the 1880s women as well as men felt that the physical condition of 'American women of the educated class is painfully low.'[24]

Then, to the surprise of many, in 1885 the Association of Collegiate Alumnae published evidence that educated women were NOT less healthy than other women.[25] The Association reported on an 1882 survey of 55 per cent of the women who had ever graduated from twelve colleges and universities in the United States, a total of 705 women. The questions asked, and the correlations studied in thirty-six pages of tables, were influenced by medical reports concerning the dangers of higher education to women's reproductive system. Graduates were asked to report on their individual life experience and health in childhood, college, and since graduation. Correlations were drawn for fourteen groups of items including: 'time of entering college after beginning of menstrual period as compared to present health,' 'outdoor exercise compared to present health,' 'college study and college worry as compared to health during college life,' and 'number of graduates who studied severely at college reporting disorders, as compared with present health.' Disorders were broken down by type, with the largest numbers being disorders of the nervous system (69), the generative organs (51), and the stomach (47). The authors also found out how far graduates felt their disorders were caused by heredity not environment.

The average age of the American respondents was 28.5 years, and approximately one quarter were married. While 74.9 per cent reported that their health during college had been excellent or good, 77.9 per cent reported that since college they had been in excellent or good health. The report cited a study of working girls in Boston carried out in 1883 to show that the health of women college students held up better than that of their age mates at work in industry. The statistics for the ACA study were collated by the Massachusetts Bureau of Statistics of Labor whose superintendent summed up the results:

'The female graduates of our colleges and universities do not seem to show as the result of their college studies and duties any marked difference in general health from the average health likely to be reported by an equal number of women engaged in other kinds of work.'[26]

Women educators in England were impressed with these results. When, in 1887, a committee from the women's colleges at Oxford and Cambridge decided to carry out a similar study, they obtained copies of the Association of Collegiate Alumnae questionnaire to use as a model. However, the committee felt Englishwomen would be reluctant to answer some of the questions asked; therefore they simplified the questionnaire, and merely invited information about the nature of any disorders a person had suffered. The committee decided to obtain information on a similar group of women who had not attended college, so they sent to each student a second questionnaire to be filled out for the sister closest in age to her so long as she had NOT attended college. (If no sister fitted this description, a female cousin closest in age was to be used.)

The results gathered from the second questionnaire were not necessarily reliable, however, since the sister or cousin was not required to fill it out herself; the student could do it for her.[27] Because of difficulty equating experiences at the University of London, or at Owens College Manchester with those of students at colleges in Oxford and Cambridge, only students from the latter two cities were included in the survey. In all, 566 students responded. Questionnaires were filled out for 382 sisters, and 68 cousins, making a total of 450 for the comparision group who had not attended college.

When asked to describe their health at various stages of their lives, students at all stages (before, during, and after college) showed better health than their sisters. While 63.08 per cent of students reported excellent or good health during college, only 58.45 per cent of sisters were reported to have excellent or good health from the age of 18 to 21; similarly, 68.02 per cent of students reported that their present health was excellent or good, but only 59.34 per cent of sisters were so reported.

Eleanor Sidgwick, the author of the report, speculated that it was possible that better health than average was 'implied in the desire to go to college.'[28]

The report then turned to family health, and in a series of tables an attempt was made, first, to see whether there was any correlation between the present state of health of the students and their family health, and, secondly, to see whether the actual distribution of numbers correlated with a statistical norm for that population. (The norm was referred to throughout the report as the Ideal.) 'A comparison of actual with ideal tables here shews us that among students whose parents are either both alive or lived beyond the age of 55, the number enjoying excellent or good health exceeds by about 4½ per cent. what we should expect by chance.'[29]

In a correlation with the health of brothers and sisters, it was noted that in the healthiest families 'the number of students in excellent or good health exceeds by about 10 per cent the number most probable by pure chance.'[30]

English medical writers had been most urgent in their fears that higher education would cause intelligent women to turn away from marriage, or that, if they did marry, the strain of studying would have left them sterile. The report showed that a surprisingly small proportion either of students or sisters had married: 10 per cent of students (or 12 per cent if one omitted those who had just left college at the time of the survey) and 19 per cent of sisters.[31] However, the rate of marriage for students and sisters between the ages of 20 and 30 was remarkably similar, and the average age of students at marriage was 26.70 as against 25.53 for the sisters. Most remarkable, however, from the point of view of refuting medical prognostications, were the statistics on childbearing. Students had a lower proportion of childless marriages than their sisters (28 per cent compared to 40 per cent), and the average number of children born per year of marriage was .36 for the students compared to .27 for the sisters. Eighty four per cent of the students' children were reported in excellent or good health, while only 59 per cent of the sisters' children were reported in the same categories.[32] These figures, though based on small numbers of families, contradicted the evidence previously offered by doctors who opposed higher education for women.

As had been the case in the earlier American study, the Sidgwick report showed a direct connection between anxiety and impairment of health. Those students who reported they had experienced little anxiety while at college tended to have been young at the time they entered college. The returns showed that women entering college at nineteen or younger enjoyed better health at college than those who were older. The report made an extensive investigation of those students who reported either that their health had improved in college, or that it had deteriorated. There appeared to be a tendency for students' health to deteriorate if their mothers became ill or died; failure of health in fathers did not have such a noticeable effect on the health of their student daughters. There was no marked difference in the improvement or deterioration of health between those students who read for Honours and those who did not. However, a difference in health did appear according to subjects read at college.

'Of those who read for the Mathematical, Moral Sciences and Natural Sciences Triposes, about as many improved as deteriorated in health at College, but of those who read for the Historical Tripos 9 deteriorated and only 3 ... improved, of those who read for the Classical Tripos 19 deteriorated and only 3 improved, while among the candidates in the new Mediaeval and Modern Languages Tripos none improved and several deteriorated.'[33]

These figures were all taken from Cambridge students. The numbers graduating from Oxford were too small to conceal individual identities in some cases, hence they were not used. However, at Oxford 'English Language and Literature, an important branch of study at Oxford, seems to be improving to the health.'[34] One can hypothesize from these figures that women reading the subjects most respected in each university found themselves buoyed up by the high morale of their environment. Possibly men were affected by the same phenomenon. However, it is also possible that men and women were differentially treated by faculty in those disciplines which were held in low esteem at their respective universities. Male faculty, whose contact with female students may not have been extensive, may still have felt more threatened by them if their own status vis à vis their colleagues in other disciplines was low.

There followed a brief comparison of the English and American statistics. A greater proportion of American students had married (27.8 per cent compared to 10 per cent), but the American figure was lower than for the female age group in the whole American population. Under the heading 'Present Health (English) and Health since Graduation (American)' the following percentages were given:

	Excellent or Good	Fair	Indifferent or Poor (Bad or Dead)*
American students	77.87	5.11	17.02
English students	68.02	22.08	9.90
English sisters	59.34	27.11	13.55

* The categories of Bad Health and Dead were included only in the English survey.

In both countries, the majority of those surveyed who had attended college claimed to be in excellent or good health. Of those who claimed to be less healthy, a larger proportion in the United States than in England felt their health was indifferent or poor.[35]

Although the method of collecting data for the control group was haphazard compared with that used for the two groups of students, the results suggested that a greater proportion of women students in England and the United States enjoyed better health than many of their female contemporaries.

Sidgwick's conclusion was muted, allowing the tables in the previous ninety pages of the report to speak for themselves. 'Summing up the results of our investigation,' she wrote, 'we may I think say with confidence that there is nothing in a university education at all specially injurious to the constitution of women, or involving any greater strain than they can ordinarily bear without injury.'[36]

Despite the evidence gathered by the two surveys, fears for the health of women students did not abate rapidly in either country. Women themselves were made fearful, even those women who had already attended colleges. So pervasive was the notion that each person had only a set amount of energy, and that to use it for intellectual pursuits was to deny it for other purposes, that women as well as men felt the need to restrain over-zealous women students.

It is intriguing to assess how far women's education in England was actually changed as the result of scientific and medical studies of women in the period 1860 to 1900. Clearly the so-called proofs that women's brains were inferior to men's added power to those who wished to set up or maintain separate courses for women. Those who provided girls with coaching for the University lower examinations or encouraged women college students to take the same courses as men seem to have believed that women's early education and socialization had handicapped them, not that women's brains were functionally inferior to men's. However, special examinations for women were introduced by the universities, and many women who would otherwise have completed the same courses as men were directed, in the period prior to 1885, into easier options, which did not provide those who took them with the same credentials for work as did the courses taken by men.

After the special examinations for women had been abandoned, those who felt women should not enjoy the same education as men suggested that a separate university be founded for women, that would allow for women's need to rest during menstruation. It is interesting in light of this move to note that the survey reported by Sidgwick had omitted all the questions relating to menstruation contained in the American survey. A majority, 55.46 per cent, of the American students had not answered those questions; however, of those responding, 239, or 33.90

per cent of the total sample said they abstained only from physical exercise during menstruation, two abstained from mental work only, and 73, or 10.35 per cent of the total sample abstained from both physical exercise and mental work at that time.[37] The scheme was first discussed at Cambridge in 1887, but it was not seriously canvassed until 1896 when it gained popularity at both Oxford and Cambridge Universities where women were agitating to be allowed full rights as students. A year later, the governors of the Royal Holloway College convened a conference of educators in London to discuss the founding of a women's university, according to the wishes of the founder of the college. The assembled educators argued that degrees would lose their value if the number of degree-granting institutions were increased, and that women's colleges could maintain their status only by attaching themselves to existing universities. Hence the scheme was abandoned. A women's university was never founded, and Royal Holloway College later became a constituent college of the University of London.

Although several hundred women took special examinations after 1865, pressure for women to have the same education as men did not diminish as a result of scientific studies of women's brains. The success of women hardy enough to take men's subjects and men's examinations was empirical evidence against the earlier interpretations of the scientific data.

The effect of physiological studies claiming to prove that higher education was dangerous to women's reproductive functions was more subtle, and more women were co-opted into believing the assertions made by doctors who opposed higher education for women. For one thing, doctors had an aura of authority that was difficult for a lay person to challenge. For another, the evidence doctors offered matched closely the conventional wisdom on women's place in society. Hence, women reformers and their male supporters were particularly susceptible to the arguments.

Educators did all they could to alleviate those conditions they feared might lead to ill-health in women. They introduced compulsory calisthenics, gymnastics, or team sports, and strict regulations for social behaviour. In these activities women educators, themselves products of the very education cautioned against by some doctors, played a crucial role. It was they who urged college authorities to improve their physical education facilities, and they who set up the administrative machinery to monitor the social life of women students.

In taking these actions educators abandoned their concern for individual free choice in order to ensure the survival of women students as a group. This change in their thinking was perhaps the most profound consequence of the scientific and medical studies of women during the last years of the nineteenth century.

Notes

1 Carl Gegenbaur (1967) The condition and significance of morphology. As translated by William Coleman in *The Interpretation of Animal Form* p.42 (New York).

2 Joseph Barnard Davis (1868) Contributions towards determining the weight of the brain in different races of man *Phil. Trans.* 158, 507.

3 Karl C. Vogt (1864) *Lectures on Man: His Place in Creation and in the History of the Earth* (James Hunt, ed.) (London).

4 R.S. Charnock reported in Emma Wallington (1874) The physical and intellectual capacities of woman equal to those of man *Anthropologia* 1, 563. Charnock, then President of the London Anthropological Society which published *Anthropologia*, repeated almost word for word the English translation of Vogt's *Lectures on Man*, page 81. Vogt, however, while pointing out that two other researchers, Huschke and Welcker, seemed to agree, cautioned that more observations were needed before generalizations could be made. However, Vogt's argument became less tentative as he developed it. As late as 1893, Emil Durkheim, in his treatise *The Division of Labour in Society*, repeated Vogt's theory, using Gustave Lebon's *Man and Societies* to support his views, rather than invoking Vogt, the great master of the earlier generation.

5 W.L. Distant (1875) On the mental differences between the sexes *Journal of the Anthropological Institute* 4, 78-85.

6 *Ibid* p.83. Vogt hinted at the possibility of such an interpretation in his *Lectures on Man*: 'If it be true that every organ is strengthened by exercise, increasing in size and weight, it must equally apply to the brain, which must become more developed by proper mental exercise.' (82).

7 Miss Becker on the mental characteristics of the sexes *The Lancet* (1868) 2, 321.

8 At the University of London, special examinations were designed at two levels, one equivalent to Matriculation (the qualification needed to enter university degree examinations), and the other equivalent to the university degree itself. At Oxford and Cambridge the University lower examinations were <u>not</u> qualifications for taking degree programmes, and therefore they were opened to women in 1870 and 1863 respectively. These universities instituted special examinations for women in lieu of undergraduate examinations for a degree.

9 Letter from J.G. Fitch to George Grote, July 23, 1866, University of London Archives.

10 Special examinations for women at the University of London

ended with the admission of women to all degrees at the university in 1878. The special examinations for women at Cambridge were transformed into the Higher Local Examination which was opened to men also. It was taken especially by those taking university extension courses. In 1881 Cambridge University allowed women to take the Previous and Tripos examinations, although they were not accepted as graduates of the university. At Oxford in 1884 a statute allowed women to take the first of the Honours examinations in Literae Humaniores, and the Final Honours Schools of Mathematics, Natural Science, and Modern History; it did not, however, allow women to sit for any intermediate examinations upon which one's degree depended; hence, at Oxford also women were not accepted as graduates of the university.

11 These studies included: Edward H. Clarke (1873) *Sex in Education* (Boston); Robert Lawson Tait (1883) *Diseases of the Ovaries* (London); John Thorburn (1884) *Female Education from a Physiological Point of View* (London). *The Lancet* published a number of articles on the subject during the 1870s and 1880s. Henry Maudsley, professor of medical jurisprudence at University College London, publicized Clarke's work in his article (1874) Sex in mind and in education *Fortnightly Review*, n.s.15, 466-83.

12 Emily Pfeiffer (1888) *Women and Work* (London) p.8.

13 Letter to the Editor from F. May Dickinson Berry, M.D. Lond., Assistant Physician, New Hospital for Women, February 28, 1894, *The Lancet* (1894) I, 651.

14 Jo Manton (1965) *Elizabeth Garrett Anderson* (London) p.73.

15 These arguments are described in detail in Joan N.Burstyn (1980) *Victorian Education and the Ideal of Womanhood* (London) ch.5.

16 Tait (1883) *Diseases of the Ovaries* as quoted in Thorburn (1884)*op.cit.*, p.11.

17 Thorburn (1884) *op.cit.*, p.18.

18 A detailed study of Victorian attitudes towards women and sports may be found in June A. Kennard (1974) *Woman, Sport and Society in Victorian England* EdD Dissertation, University of North Carolina, Greensboro, 1974.

19 *Ibid.*, p.78.

20 Mrs. Henry (Eleanor) Sidgwick (1890) *Health Statistics of Women Students of Cambridge and Oxford and of their Sisters* (Cambridge) pp.48-50.

21 Eleanor Field (1890) Women at an English university: Newnham College, Cambridge *Century Magazine* 42 (n.s.20) 290-91.

22 *Ibid.*, p.294.

23 Vera Brittain (1960) *The Women at Oxford* (New York) p.92.

24 This quotation is taken from the first printed circular of the Association of Collegiate Alumnae on Physical Education (Boston 1882).

25 American Association of University Women, *Health Statistics of Women College Graduates*. Report of a special committee of the Association of Collegiate Alumnae, Annie G. Howes, chairman, together with statistical tables collated by the Massachusetts Bureau of Statistics of Labor (Boston, 1885).

26 Mr. Carroll D. Wright in the Sixteenth Report of the Massachusetts Bureau of Statistics of Labor, as quoted by Catherine Baldwin (1890), Note on the Health of Women Students *Century Magazine* 42 (n.s.20) 294.

27 Sidgwick (1890) *op.cit.*, pp.7-8.

28 *Ibid.*, pp.20-21.

29 *Ibid.*, p.37.

30 *Ibid.*, p.43.

31 *Ibid.*, p.57.

32 *Ibid.*, Tables 25-29, pp.61-65.

33 *Ibid.*, p.87.

34 *Ibid.*, p.88.

35 *Ibid.*, p.90. The figures were taken from Table 41.

36 *Ibid.*, p.91.

37 American Association of University Women (1885) *op. cit.*, p.26.

Part 3

Current position

5 Careers and gender: the expectations of able Scottish school-leavers in 1971 and 1981

Peter Burnhill and Andrew McPherson

Introduction

Although demographic aspects of women's access to higher education in Britain can be described fairly systematically, accounts of the quality of their experience, and of its significance in relation to their plans for an occupational, marital and familial career, are inevitably more speculative and impressionistic. Nor is there much systematic evidence of how women differ from men in these respects; or on the extent to which attitudes and expectations may be changing, whether among those entering higher education or among their other age-peers. Our main purpose here is to offer such evidence in the form of a description of two nationally representative samples of academically well-qualified Scots, drawn from school-leavers in 1969/70 and in 1979/80. Apart from their date, the two target populations were identically defined and the data too were collected and analysed in a manner that was virtually identical.

We call the earlier survey 'the 1971 survey'. It was conducted in the Spring of 1971, about nine months after most of the target sample had left school. It was not designed to be the first point in a study of sex differences and change although it was subsequently to prove suitable for this purpose. Our main aim in 1971 had been to test two broad types of explanation of why certain female school-leavers went to colleges of education (mainly monotechnic colleges for the training of non-graduate teachers for primary schools) rather than to university. One type of explanation derived from developmental psychology and the other from sociological theories of the role of schooling in the selection and socialization of individuals to adult career roles. We had therefore collected, from all members of the sample, data on their occupational values, intentions and commitments; on their educational records and aspirations; on their intentions with respect to marriage, family building and paid employment; and on their beliefs about public attitudes to

83

women and marriage, and to familial and occupational careers. Happily most of these questions were asked of men as well as women.

The main conclusion from the 1971 analyses was that selection and socialization processes were playing a major part in channelling able teenage girls into a secondary school track characterized by academic under-achievement and the discontinuation of mathematics and science studies. This track, which has subsequently been studied by Kelly (1981), led on to non-graduating, liberal-arts courses in the colleges of education and thence to primary school teaching. Gender-related 'occupational values' (such as 'nurturance') and occupational intentions seemed as often to be formed in the light of educational tracking as to cause it (Flett, Jones and McPherson 1971 and 1972; Jones and McPherson 1972a).

What we call here 'the 1981 survey' was planned as a repeat of that of 1971, although it (1981) was in fact only one element in a much larger national sample survey of all Scottish school-leavers, including those with examination qualifications and those with none. The strength of the combined data for 1971 and 1981 lies in their potential to describe attitudes and behaviour in a pre-defined, national population at two time-points a decade apart. Moreover, sex-related trends within this population paralleled those elsewhere in Great Britain, as we explain in the next section. The changes that the data describe may also, therefore, characterize the situation in England and Wales.

We have provided an Addendum to this paper in which we outline the methods used to generate the data. The Addendum also contains comments and caveats which qualify the generalization of our findings.

Background

The tracking process mentioned earlier may be understood in the light of the historical development of the provision of higher education for women in Scotland, of which two aspects are pertinent. One is the link between educational provision and recruitment to particular occupations, especially school teaching. The other is the ambivalence with which provision was indeed made for women, but made on a basis that differentiated women's from men's opportunities, often in the latter's favour (Acker 1983; Corr 1983; Cruickshank 1970; Jones and McPherson 1972a). Over the period 1870 to 1970 the stability of this historical configuration was founded partly on the state's 'need' for more teachers than the market could supply and partly on the compliance of women with the expectation that they should not behave, educationally or economically, in too competitive a manner. Since Robbins (Robbins Committee 1963), and especially since 1970, both these foundations have weakened.

The nineteenth-century Scottish colleges of education offered women a liberal arts education that was considered inferior to the university arts curriculum. The colleges also provided a ladder of upward social mobility for many working-class men that extended to the university through male students' concurrent attendance at university classes (Cruickshank 1970). Women were not admitted to university until 1892. In the same year a new degree structure was imposed on the Scottish universities whereby students on non-professional courses would either graduate from a four-year, specialized, Honours course or from a three-year, general, Ordinary course. This course structure continued through to the 1960s by which time it was heavily sex-linked. In the faculties of art and science, two-thirds of women, but only one-third of men, took the Ordinary degree rather than an Honours degree. Among men and among women, Ordinary graduates tended to have markedly lower scholastic aptitude test scores than Honours graduates (McPherson 1972) and high proportions of Ordinary graduates (over half) subsequently trained as school teachers (McPherson and Atherton 1972). Non-graduating teacher-training courses in the colleges of education were almost wholly comprised of women.

By the time of Robbins, then, women were to be found in disproportionately large numbers in the academically inferior parts of the Scottish system of higher education (ie in Ordinary degree courses and non-graduating courses). This aspect of the inequality of provision for women was, at least until the early 1970s, reflected in, and dependent upon, their tendency to comply with expectations of inferior performance. For example, in an analysis of the 1971 survey data, Hutchison (1972) reported that women gave up more readily than men in their pursuit of university admission; and Jones (1972) found in the cohort entering Edinburgh University in 1969 that, *ceteris paribus*, women settled more readily for the Ordinary rather than the Honours degree.

Several more recent developments suggest at least a few changes at the surface of this configuration, if not a more fundamental subterranean shift. There has been retrenchment in school teacher recruitment and, more recently, in higher education provision generally. Also, since Robbins, the educational behaviour of women has steadily and increasingly refuted the assumption that they will accept second best, and confounded the deeper assumption of female compliance. Table 5.1 shows the post-school destinations of Scotland's school-leavers in 1970 and 1980. The dates given in the column headings correspond to the surveys of 1971 and 1981, the target populations for which were drawn from these two groups of leavers. The percentages refer to all school leavers, qualified or otherwise. In 1981 identical percentages of men and women left school with Highers and continued with full-time education (16.6 per cent) whereas, in 1971, more women than men had continued.

The effect of retrenchment on women's entry into non-degree courses in full-time, post-school education is apparent. However, the percentage of women entering degree courses increased from 7.2 to 10.3 per cent (a percentage that was, however, still below the 12.6 per cent for men in 1981). A consequence of this change has been that the percentage of first-time, first-degree, entrants to Scottish universities (including English entrants) who are women has increased from 33 per cent in 1968/9 to 42 per cent in 1979/80. The comparable figures in England and Wales are 29 and 38 per cent. Moreover, in Scotland this change has been

Table 5.1   Size and distribution of the 1971 and 1981 target populations: frequencies and percentages

	Population estimates				Percentaged distribution			
	Men		Women		Men		Women	
	1971	1981	1971	1981	1971	1981	1971	1981
Leavers with one or more pass at SCE H grade:								
Degree students	4100*	6000	2700*	4600	10.4	12.6	7.2	10.3
Non-degree full-time students	1400	1900	3200	2800	3.6	4.0	8.6	6.3
(Un)employed	4300	4200	3500	5500	10.9	8.9	9.4	12.4
SUB-TOTAL	(9800)	(12100)	(9400)	(12900)	(25.0)	(25.6)	(25.1)	(29.0)
Leavers without passes at SCE H grade	29500	35100	28000	31600	75.0	74.4	74.9	71.0
TOTAL NO. OF LEAVERS (N = 100%)	39400	47300	37500	44500	100	100	100	100

* These figures are approximations.

The populations referred to comprise leavers from the 1969/70 and the 1979/80 school sessions. The dates in the column headings refer to the years of the respective surveys. The estimates for the total number of leavers overall, and for those with one or more pass at the Scottish Certificate of Education H Grade, are taken from SED (1971) and were based on population returns. The estimated distribution across post-school destination categories for 1971 was kindly supplied by the Statistics Division of the SED and was based on the SED's own Qualified School Leavers Survey. The 1971 numbers and proportions on degree-level courses are approximations; the numbers at university (3900 men and 2600 women) have been increased to allow for the unknown, but small, number of degrees studied elsewhere. The 1981 estimates of the distribution are based on data from the CES/SED National School Leavers Survey (Burnhill 1983). Numbers of leavers are rounded to the nearest hundred. Percentages are rounded to the first decimal place. Consequently, totals may differ slightly from the sum of the individual components.

Table 5.2 Occupational intentions: percentages

'Which of the following statements is most applicable to you?'	All				Degree students				Non-degree students				Employed			
	Men		Women		Men		Women		Men		Women		Men		Women	
	1971	1981	1971	1981	1971	1981	1971	1981	1971	1981	1971	1981	1971	1981	1971	1981
I am fully commited to making a life-time career in one particular occupation	17	22	18	21	12	18	10	16	21	12	24	24	21	34	18	24
I have decided on a particular occupation, but thereafter I shall see how it goes	46	43	47	47	32	39	24	40	47	46	58	49	60	45	55	52
I have a particular occupation in mind, but I have not finally decided to enter it	18	19	18	16	28	24	31	17	17	19	9	14	8	11	15	17
I have thought a fair amount about occupations but have no particular one in mind	14	14	14	15	20	16	28	23	12	18	7	13	9	9	10	5
I have not thought much about my future occupation	4	3	3	3	8	3	6	4	2	6	2	0	2	2	3	2
PERCENTAGE TOTALS	99	101	100	102	100	100	99	100	99	101	100	100	100	101	101	100
Achieved sample size (= 100%)	1048	412	1318	505	533	250	455	217	212	45	545	74	393	117	318	184

accompanied by a move into Honours courses by women, though not by men (no table shown). In 1968/9, 35 per cent of women graduates of all faculties took Honours. By 1979 the percentage was 43. (Comparable figures for men were 52 and 53 per cent respectively (DES 1982, Tables 4(4) and 18(18)).)

Occupational Plans

Table 5.2 offers one perspective on how the sample members were thinking about jobs approximately nine months after they had left school. The overall picture (shown in the left-hand block of the table) is remarkably stable for men and for women between 1971 and 1981. About one-fifth said they were 'fully committed to making a life-time career in one particular occupation.' Just under a half ringed the response 'I have decided on a particular occupation, but thereafter I shall see how it goes.' The remainder, just over one-third, were still to some extent undecided (though very few said they had 'not thought much' about their future occupation). These responses may partly reflect orientations to the place of an occupational career in overall life plans, and we discuss this in later sections. In part, Table 5.2 is also a reflection of young persons' responses to a continuing process of educational and occupational selection. Thus, compared with the 'employed' (a significant minority of whom, as we explain in the Addendum, were in fact unemployed in 1981), smaller percentages of degree students were either 'fully committed to a particular occupation' (row 1) or had 'decided on a particular occupation' (row 2). A large minority of degree students had, of course, entered professional courses that implied particular occupations or types thereof; but other degree students were as yet not required to make occupational decisions (or to acknowledge the decisions that were implied by the process of educational selection).

One change between 1971 and 1981 merits a comment. Among both men and women degree students the percentages who had decided on a particular occupation (row 1 + row 2) increased: from 44 per cent to 57 per cent among men, and, more strongly, from 34 per cent to 56 per cent among women (the sex difference in this respect thereby disappearing between 1971 and 1981). Figure 5.1 illustrates this change.

We did not collect information on the particular occupations that the sample members were considering or had chosen, but we did ask them all to rate on a nine-point scale (described in the Addendum) the importance of nineteen attributes of their 'ideal job'. These nineteen items had mostly been taken from studies of occupational behaviour conducted within a developmental psychology tradition (Rosenberg

Figure 5.1　Occupational intentions

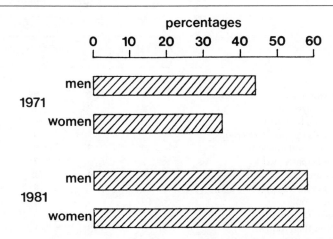

Percentage of degree students "fully committed to making a life-time career in one particular occupation" or "decided on a particular occupation, but thereafter . . . shall see how it goes"

1957). Using a multidimensional scaling technique, Coxon and Jones (1977) have reported on the 'dimensionality' of the 'values' that may be postulated to underlie responses to the individual items in the 1971 data. In unreported work we ourselves have used co-variance structure techniques to check that, over the sample as a whole, the latent factor structure of the items was unchanged (though we have not explored changes in structure within sub-groups). This work and the work of Coxon and Jones guided us in selecting from the nineteen items those which reflected constructs of interest. Eleven items were chosen. Their arrangement in Table 5.3 also, in part, reflects the inter-correlation of the individual items.

In Table 5.3 the eleven items have been assigned ranks according to the percentage of respondents indicating that they wanted each attribute as an aspect of their ideal job. Rank '1' indicates the highest percentage. (The percentages themselves, which contain more information than the ranks but which are less easily digested, are shown in Appendix Table 5.2, disaggregated by sub-group, whilst Appendix Table 5.1 shows the percentages ticking the mid-point meaning ' "can't say" or "neutral" '.)

It is evident that the vast majority were sure that their 'ideal job' would 'enable (them) to look forward to a stable secure future'. This item elicited the lowest percentages of mid-point responses (ie ' "can't say" or "neutral" ') and the highest percentages of 'positive' responses, approaching close to one hundred per cent (Appendix Tables 5.1 and

Table 5.3   Relative importance of the qualities sought in the 'ideal job': rank scores

	All			
	Men		Women	
	1971	1981	1971	1981
A stable secure future	1	1	2	1
Move up in the world	2	2	3	2
Senior position by age 30	3	4	10	6
Power to make important decisions	4	5	9	5
Absorb energy and interests	9	7	8	7
Original and creative work	7	6	7	8
Work full-time with ideas	8	9	11	9
Excitement or adventure	6	3	5	4
Help young people	10	10	4	9
Work with young children	11	11	6	11
People rather than things	5	8	1	3

Note The items are abbreviated here. The full text is given in Appendix Tables 1 and 2.

5.2). It is also clear that such security became more important for women between 1971 and 1981 both in relative (ie rank order terms (Table 5.3)) and in absolute (ie percentage) terms. (The percentages of men wanting such security has also increased but this increase could not, of course, be reflected in the ranking.

There follow in Table 5.3 three items that measure aspects of what might be called 'competitive individualism'. Among men, the ranking of these items remains fairly stable between 1971 and 1981 (to within one rank position). Among women, however, all three items become relatively more important in 1981. For example, the wish for a job that would offer 'the power to make important decisions' moved from ninth to fifth rank, reflecting an increase in the percentage of women who wanted this power from 46 per cent in 1971 to 66 per cent in 1981. The corresponding percentages for men were 69 per cent and 72 per cent. Thus the sex difference in the wish for such power has virtually disappeared over the decade.

The four items that follow measure aspects of intrinsic job satisfaction. The rankings are fairly stable between 1971 and 1981 though Appendix Table 5.2 shows that, in general, the percentages wanting these attributes in their ideal job have increased. For example, the wish for a job that would 'absorb...energy and interests both inside and outside working hours' moved from ninth to seventh rank among men (reflecting an increase in the percentage wanting this attribute fom 52 per cent to 61 per cent), and from eighth to seventh rank among women (reflecting an increase in the percentage wanting this attribute from 52 per cent to 61 per cent), and from eighth to seventh rank among women (refecting an increase from 51 per cent to 59 per cent). The generally increased wish for jobs that would provide 'excitement or adventure' might also be noted.

The next two items had been included in the 1971 study as potential predictors of entry to college of education (and thence to the occupation of school teaching). These items concerned 'an opportunity to help young people' and 'an opportunity to work with young children'. They were ranked towards the bottom by the men both in 1971 and in 1981. Among the women in 1981 they were also ranked towards the bottom but this position represents a fall from the middling ranking they had had in 1971. The fall of these items in the women's rank order reflects an absolute decline in the percentages wanting these satisfactions from their ideal job, from 64 per cent to 51 per cent in the case of 'helping young people', and from 56 per cent to 38 per cent in the case of working 'with young children' (Appendix Table 5.2). The decline in the wish to work with young people or with children was greatest in the non-degree student sector and clearly reflects the diminishing provision for teacher training. The wish for 'an opportunity to work with people rather than things' has also declined both in rank order and in absolute percentage terms among both men and women. However, the percentage of women wanting this attribute remains high and the item still discriminates women from men.

Whilst limitations of space require us to restrict extensive description of the sub-groups, it is worth commenting on one aspect of change among the women degree students. Inspection of Appendix Table 5.2 indicates that the magnitude of the changes we have discussed tends to be greater among women degree students than among their male counterparts. Among women degree students these changes include an increase (1971-1981) from 57 to 78 per cent in the percentage wanting to 'move up' in the world; from 37 to 57 per cent wanting 'the opportunity to hold a senior position by the age of thirty'; from 42 to 72 per cent wanting 'the power to make important decisions'; from 48 to 60 per cent wanting work that would 'absorb (their) energy and interests'; from 49 to 66 per cent wishing to be required 'to produce original and creative work'; and from 40 to 54 per cent wishing to 'work full-time with ideas and theories'. These are quite large changes. Other data on university degree women that we have reported in more detail elsewhere have indicated that, compared with 1971, they were much more likely to have come to university in order to seek the general occupational advantages that degree certification would bring them; that they were more likely to be planning careers in industry and commerce; and also that more were still, in the first year of their degree course, contemplating the possibility of doing doctoral work on graduation (Burnhill and McPherson 1983).

Two additional comments, which draw on calculations (not shown) based on the figures in Appendix Tables 5.1 and 5.2, can serve to introduce a brief summary of this section. First, respondents in 1981 were less likely to tick the mid-point of the scale (' "can't say" or "neutral" ') in response to the nineteen 'ideal job' items. We interpret this as a decline in uncertainty about the importance of the items and as an indication of an increased concern with future careers. This change was greater for women, 1971 to 1981, than for men. Second, more women ticked the 'positive' scale points (ie points six to nine, indicating that the job attribute was wanted) than had done so in 1971, but the men showed little change.

In sum, women in 1981 were more likely than in 1971 to have well-formed views about what they wanted from their 'ideal job'; and also to want more from it. Among degree students, and especially among women degree students, young people in 1981 were more often thinking about, and deciding upon, particular occupations than were their counterparts a decade earlier (Table 5.2). (The position of the employed, as we have called them, was more equivocal in this respect, possibly because they were already 'trading down', or experiencing actual unemployment.) Expecially among the women, more young people in 1981 gave indications of wanting careers which were demanding of time and energy, and had prospects. These changes in general have occurred, at least to some extent, across all women in the target population (the academically able) and not just across those who went on to be students. In general, the differences between the sexes in what young people wanted from their jobs have diminished markedly since 1971. This convergence has resulted mainly from an increased likelihood that women wanted qualities from an occupational career that a decade earlier had been sought more often by men than by women, qualities such as 'moving up in the world', 'having the power to make important decisions' and 'opportunities for promotion'. At the same time, however, 'the wish to work with people rather than things' was still in 1981 expressed by high percentages of women. In general, the young adults of 1981, and especially the women, wanted more from the world of work than their counterparts had wanted ten years earlier.

Marriage and Family-Building

We have already suggested in our comments on occupational choice and placement that many people make relatively firm occupational choices and commitments only when confronted with the expectation that they should do so. In such circumstances, giving thought to such choices is also influenced by the fact that a decision is becoming more pressing. Similar considerations apply to the life-events of marriage and family-building, events which will still have lain at some point in the future for the large majority in our samples of 18/19 year-olds, at the time they answered the questionnaires. It is not surprising, therefore, to find that larger proportions had thought 'a great deal' or 'a fair amount' about the age at which they would like to get married than had thought about the age at which they would like to start a family (Table 5.4). Nor is it surprising that relatively few had given a great deal of thought to either eventuality. The table also shows, first, that women had tended to think about these issues more than had men and, second, that fewer had thought about marriage and family in 1981 than ten years earlier. Among the three destination sub-groups, there was only one marked departure from the general pattern in Table 5.4 and this was among employed women in 1971 (not shown): 61 per cent of them said they had thought 'a great deal' or 'fair amount' about when they would like to marry, and 41 per cent had given this much thought to when they would like to start a family. The comparable percentages for this group of women in 1981, however, were 28 per cent and 20 per cent respectively, differing little from the percentages among their student peers.

Table 5.4   Thinking about marriage and about starting a family: percentages

| | 'Have you thought much about the age at which you would like to get married?' All | | | | 'Have you thought much about the age at which you would like to start a family?' All | | | |
| | Men | | Women | | Men | | Women | |
	1971	1981	1971	1981	1971	1981	1971	1981
A great deal	10	5	14	6	6	3	7	3
A fair amount	24	13	31	23	14	7	21	14
From time to time	34	39	40	46	29	26	35	33
Hardly at all	29	40	14	23	49	60	33	42
No wish to . . .*	3	4	1	2	3	4	4	7
PERCENTAGE TOTALS	100	101	100	100	101	100	100	99

* Respectively 'no wish to marry'/'no wish to have children'

We turn to the remaining evidence in this section bearing in mind that the responses relate mainly to non-immediate eventualities and may be presumed to express an admixture of intentions and values. Indeed, the two questions on the preferred ages of marriage and of starting a family (Figure 5.2) invited an expression of values through the use of the word 'ideally'. In neither of the two survey years did more than eight per cent of respondents in any destination category indicate that they had 'no wish to marry' or 'no wish to have children'. This in itself is perhaps an

Figure 5.2   Ideal ages of marriage and of starting a family: arithmetic means

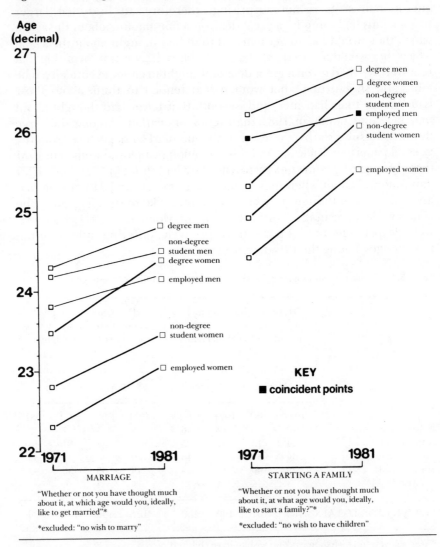

Age
(decimal)

degree men
degree women
non-degree
student men
employed men
non-degree
student women

employed women

degree men
non-degree
student men
degree women

employed men

non-degree
student women

employed women

KEY
■ **coincident points**

1971   1981   1971   1981

MARRIAGE   STARTING A FAMILY

"Whether or not you have thought much
about it, at which age would you, ideally,
like to get married"*

*excluded: "no wish to marry"

"Whether or not you have thought much
about it, at what age would you, ideally,
like to start a family?"*

*excluded: "no wish to have children"

interesting finding. It also led us to exclude these responses from Figure
5.2.

The most striking single conclusion to emerge from Figure 5.2 is that, by
comparison with 1971, there was in 1981 a tendency to prefer a later age
of marriage and a later start to family-building. Second, these changes
are more marked with respect to starting a family than with respect to
marriage. A third conclusion is that sex differences have narrowed
during the decade; only very slightly with respect to the preferred age of
marriage, but more markedly with respect to the preferred age for

starting a family. In 1971, with respect to both these preferences, the women in each sub-group intended on average to marry earlier than the men. By 1981, as far as marriage was concerned this was still true in general, but to a lesser extent. Of particular note is the small difference in 1981 between the average intended age of marriage of the degree women and that of the men in each destination category. A similar conclusion holds with respect to the age at which a first child was intended. In 1981 the age preferred by degree men was very close to that preferred by degree women; the preferences of non-degree men and women students were also close to each other. Although differences between the sexes diminished, particularly with respect to plans for starting a family, differences between those in the three post-school destination categories did not. Among both men and women, in 1971 as well as in 1981, postponement of marriage and child-rearing was greatest amongst degree students and smallest amongst the employed.

The distributions of the women's preferred age for starting a family in 1971 and 1981 were generally symmetric. But in 1981 there was evidence, amongst degree students, of a group of women who intended to postpone having their first child until they were 29 or older. These comprised 18 per cent of degree women. In 1971 the distributions had tailed off evenly as they approached thirty years and there was no indication of what, by 1981, seemed to be a small, but perhaps not insignificant, group of women whose preference for a considerably delayed start to their family-building distinguished them from the generality of their sex-peers. (We mentioned earlier that the proportions intending never to have children were low both in 1971 and 1981.)

We did not ask respondents whether they had 'thought much' about the size of family they planned but the decision about completed family size lay even further in the future than did that of starting a family. In 1971, when asked about the preferred size of family, seven per cent of the women indicated that they had 'no idea' and one per cent omitted to answer the question. In 1981 the corresponding figures were fourteen per cent and less than one per cent. These persons have been excluded from Figure 5.3 wherein the answers are summarized in the form of the mean family size for each (destination) sub-group.

The picture in Figure 5.3 seems unequivocal. In 1971 men tended to want smaller families than women, and degree students tended to want smaller families than non-degree students or those in employment. By 1981, the convergence of all groups suggests that in 1981 there is little more than random variation around what appears to be a norm of 2.4 children. However, the significance of this convergence is problematic. It may be, for example, that in 1981 shared considerations (eg of economic climate) led to common conclusions about family-building. Such an explanation would leave the pattern in 1971 as a puzzle. Alternatively,

Figure 5.3   **'What size family do you think you would like to have?': arithmetic means**

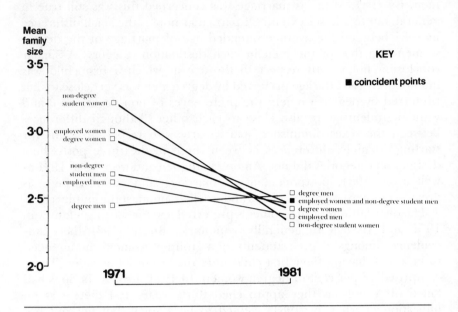

the convergence in 1981 towards a mean of 2.4 may simply indicate that questions about completed family size had come to lie so far in an individual's future (especially given the greater tendency to postpone both marriage and the age of starting a family) that the responses no longer reflected the 'logic' of any set of considerations, shared or otherwise. If so, respondents may have simply inclined towards a notional norm in their attempt to supply a meaningful answer about a remote contingency.

Careers Inside and Outside the Home: Beliefs and Intentions

The two previous sections have indicated, first, that the world of occupations was more salient in the thinking and plans of women in 1981 than it had been in 1971; and, second, that both men and women nevertheless planned to marry and to raise families (albeit smaller families, started later). We now turn to evidence on beliefs and intentions with respect to combining an occupational career with other activities. Part (a) of Figure 5.4 shows the extent of agreement with four items (each measured according to the scale described in the Addendum). In the figure the shaded area indicates the percentages ringing the mid-point that was indicated by a question mark. (It follows, therefore,

Figure 5.4   (a) Beliefs about women and careers and (b) amount of thought about combining an occupational career with a family: percentages

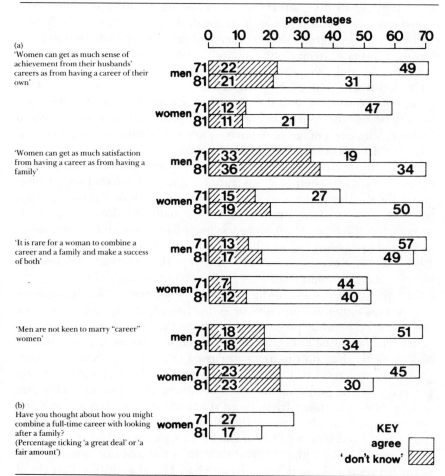

Note The question ran: 'How much do you agree or disagree with the following statements about women and careers? By "career" we mean putting continuous energy over a long period into achieving some success in an occupation – simply taking short-term occasional jobs'

that in each case the residual percentage, which we do not show, is the percentage expressing disagreement with each item.) Except where we say otherwise, the picture within each sub-group did not markedly differ from that over the sample as a whole. Similarities and differences between the sexes are fairly apparent, as also are the changes between 1971 and 1981. Our comments are therefore selective.

The first item indicates that in 1981 both men and women were less likely to affirm that a husband's career may act as a proxy for that of the wife. By 1981, only 31 per cent of men and 21 per cent of women were prepared to agree that 'women can get as much sense of achievement from their husband's careers as from having a career of their own'. Conversely, the decade saw an increase in the percentages of both men and women who agreed that 'women can get as much satisfaction from having a career as from having a family', though it should be noted that, both in 1971 and 1981, more men were uncertain about this, ticking the scale mid-point, than were prepared to express agreement. (Another item, not shown here, asked women how essential it was that their job should be one in which they could 'compete with men on an equal footing'. The percentage of women wanting this attribute rose between 1971 and 1981 from 62 per cent to 75 per cent.)

Despite these changes, men were about equally divided, both in 1971 and in 1981, over whether it was 'rare for a woman to combine a career and a family and make a success of both'. About half the men agreed with this statement in 1981; a little over half had done so in 1971. Women, on the other hand, were less likely to agree with this statement, in 1971 (44 per cent) and in 1981 (40 per cent). Both men and women in 1981 were, however, less inclined to accept that 'men are not keen to marry "career" women' than were their counterparts in 1971.

Interpretation of these findings must be circumspect. Clearly the items may be read either as normative or as descriptive, or both, and we cannot say which or in what proportion. Perhaps the phrasing of these four items articulates the concerns of the feminist movement more directly and explicitly than do the items discussed in the two previous sections. Moreover, the items in Figure 5.4 are general belief statements and do not refer to the respondents' own situations or intentions. This also distinguishes the items from those discussed earlier. When we asked female respondents how much they themselves had 'thought about how (they) might combine a full-time career with looking after a family', the percentages ticking either 'a great deal' or 'a fair amount' actually went down between 1971 and 1981, from 27 to 17 per cent (see Part (b) of Figure 5.4). This is surprising, for one might have expected the increased assent to feminist propositions indicated by responses in Part (a) of the figure to have been accompanied by an increase in the reported consideration given to such matters in the making of life-plans. The slight decrease in the thought reportedly given to them is, however, consistent with the diminished preoccupation, 1971-1981, with when to marry and when to start a family (discussed above). As with occupational choice, it seems that thought tended to be given to choices concerning marriage and family, and the combination of an occupational career with these, for the most part only as the eventualities approached. Young women in 1981 were more inclined to postpone these eventualities than were their counterparts in 1971, and they were therefore, perhaps, more

Table 5.5 Labour market participation: (a) respondents' own intentions and (b) respondents' reports of mothers' participation: percentages

| | Women | | | | | | | |
| | All | | Degree students | | Non-degree students | | Employed | |
	1971	1981	1971	1981	1971	1981	1971	1981
(a) 'What do you think will be the likely pattern of your working life?'								
Will work full-time for most of my married life	15	40	15	44	15	49	14	33
Will work full-time from time to time	34	28	36	33	38	21	28	26
Will work part-time for most of my married life	18	16	20	13	18	12	15	22
Will work part-time from time to time	20	11	19	7	19	11	23	15
Do not intend to work for more than a few years at the most	13	5	11	4	10	7	20	5
PERCENTAGE TOTALS	100	100	101	101	100	100	100	101
(b) 'As far as you can tell, which of the following statements best describes your mother's paid working life?'								
Has worked full-time for most of her married life	11	20	9	23	10	22	13	15
Has had full-time work from time to time	15	18	15	21	16	18	14	12
Has worked part-time for most of her married life	10	22	9	15	12	21	9	30
Has had part-time work from time to time	28	23	30	21	26	22	29	28
Has not worked since marriage	37	17	38	20	37	18	35	15
PERCENTAGE TOTALS	101	100	101	100	101	101	100	100

inclined also to postpone consideration of the problems of combining occupational and familial careers.

Part (a) of Table 5.5 records respondents' expectations as to the 'likely pattern of (their) working life'. Figure 5.5 is a visual representation of the responses in the sample overall. The changes in expectations are striking. Among women only 15 per cent in 1971 expected that they would 'work full-time for most of (their) married life'. By 1981 this had risen to 40 per cent, and 68 per cent of women expected to work full-time either for most of their married life or 'from time to time'. The change was slightly more marked among the students, both degree and non-degree, although differences between the sub-groups were not great. We may also mention here that, compared with 1971, higher proportions of women in each sub-group in 1981 expected to return to full-time work by the time their youngest child was aged seven years (no table shown).

Part (b) of Table 5.5 records respondents' perceptions of their mother's paid working life. The table shows changes that parallel those

Figure 5.5   Occupational and familial plans (from Table 5.5a: all women): percentages

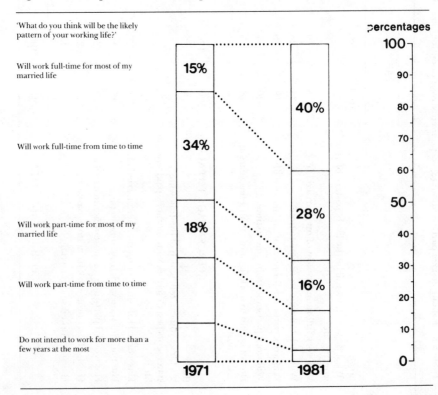

in the respondents' expectations for their own future. The percentage of mothers who were reported to be working full-time rose, as did the percentages working part-time 'for most of (their) married life'. The percentage of mothers reported as not having worked since marriage fell from 37 per cent to 17 per cent. The employed women's reports of their mothers' working lives differed interestingly from those of the students, both degree and non-degree. Among the two student groups, there was a more marked increase, 1971 to 1981, in the percentage of mothers working full-time; whereas, among the employed women, this percentage remained stable at 27 per cent over the decade. More of the employed women's mothers were seen to be working in 1981 as compared to 1971; but the increase was entirely in the category 'has worked part-time for most of her married life'.

The parallel between the trends in daughters' expectations for their own working lives, and in daughters' reports of their mothers' working lives has intriguing implications for the differential transmission of values and of opportunities both in the family and through education, implications which we have not followed through here.

Summary and Discussion

Our analyses relate to the experiences, beliefs and intentions of the academically best-qualified quarter of Scots just under a year after they had left school. This group includes first-year students in further and higher education along with other school-leavers, also relatively well-qualified, who entered the labour market. One of our samples was drawn at the start of the 1970s at a time when postwar expansion was beginning to falter, but before the youth culture of the 1960s had lost much of its new-found exuberance. The other sample, for the 1981 survey, was drawn at the end of the 1970s, by which time economic difficulties had hardened into decline, the growth in higher education had halted, youth unemployment was commonplace, and graduate unemployment and underemployment were growing. By 1981, post-1968 feminism had gained in confidence and effect, giving wide currency to propositions about equal opportunities for women. During the 1970s, both in Scotland and in England and Wales, women had come to participate in higher education on a more equal basis; though, even in 1981, there was still sexual inequality in access to degree-level education, and women's relatively favourable representation in non-degree, full-time, post-school education had been made uncertain by the cuts in non-graduate teacher training. There is also evidence that women degree students in Scotland were less likely to settle for the second best of the Scottish Ordinary degree in 1981 than were their counterparts a decade earlier.

We have used the two surveys to show how beliefs and intentions with respect to occupational and familial careers, and the interrelations between such careers, have changed in ways that parallel the growing participation of women in higher education. Compared with 1971, more women first-year degree students in 1981 had already decided on a career, and more had applied to higher education for reasons connected with the occupational advantages of degree certification. Along with other well-qualified women school-leavers, women degree students had become more certain about the satisfactions they wanted from an occupation; and they also wanted more from an occupation. Compared with 1971, women in 1981 more closely resembled men in the clarity, quantity and quality of their occupational ambitions. For example, women in 1981 placed more emphasis than had women a decade earlier on having a job that was secure, that offered opportunities for promotion and for moving up in the world, and that gave the power to make important decisions. Marriage and child-rearing were less salient in women's plans than they had been a decade earlier, not because fewer in 1981 planned to marry or to have families, but because, compared with 1971, women in 1981 intended to marry later, to continue working for longer before having their first child, to have smaller families, and to return to work earlier after the completion of the family. Somewhat paradoxically perhaps, these changes have meant that today these 19-year-old women are less preoccupied with thinking about marriage and child-rearing than were their counterparts a decade earlier; but many more today plan full-time occupational careers for most of their married life. This is especially true of women on degree courses.

Given the major changes in intention that the decade has seen, it is not surprising that well educated women today are less likely than in 1971 to believe that a husband's career may serve as a proxy for their own; less likely to believe that a woman's occupational career may not be as satisfying as raising a family; or to believe that men are disinclined to marry 'career women'. Nevertheless, educationally able young women in general are just as uncertain today about the difficulties and successes women may have in combining a familial with an occupational career, as were their counterparts a decade earlier.

In considering whether these changes are permanent, or whether their direction will be maintained, it is as well to remember that the two surveys are snap-shots, in two senses. First, they are snap-shots of each young person's life; they offer cross-sectional and not longitudinal information. Second, they are snap-shots of social history: we have not monitored a trend; we have merely compared two points in time. The 1971 observations may have been 'disturbed' by '1968 and all that'. The 1981 observations may have been 'disturbed' both by the level of school-leaver unemployment and also by the recent cuts in teacher-training. This does not mean that the data are atypical, for the question of typicality does not arise. Rather, it means that one is less confident today in extrapolating the future from the present than one was (wrongly, in fact) say ten years ago. More fundamentally, observations for two time-points are insufficient to indicate a trend, especially when no attempt has been made to model on the data causal processes that might underlie such a trend. We emphasize that the present findings are mainly descriptive and the analysis largely univariate.

Nevertheless, the changes we have recorded are, statistically, highly significant and may, we think, have major substantive significance. We have several reasons for saying this. We have not simply measured changes in belief (Figure 5.5); we have also measured changes in intention; and both types of change run parallel to well-established changes in the demographic behaviour of women in post-compulsory and higher education. Many of our measures relate only obliquely to propositions about gender (our measuring of the decline in 'can't say' responses, for example, is very oblique), but all our observations point in the same direction. Taken together they indicate strongly that major change has occurred both in the configuration of men's and women's expectations about women, and also in the expectations that each woman is likely to have for herself. Qualified women have become more ambitious, educationally and occupationally, and more men and women are now prepared to accept such ambitions as legitimate. Finally, similar changes are reported among analogous populations in the USA (Herzog 1982; Regula and Roland 1982).

We think it significant that many of the changes on which we have commented have occurred not just among degree-student women but among all well-qualified women, though not always to the same extent; and not just among all such women but among their male counterparts also. We suggest that the changed economic situation has had a major influence. As to feminism, it is likely that, at the very least, it has helped women to interpret such change and articulate a response; and it may have done more by stimulating and directing both new demands among women and new attitudes to such demands among men. Our evidence is that men's intentions and expectations have changed in the same direction as those of women, and that more men than previously acknowledged the existence and legitimacy of the new futures that the young women of 1981 were planning for themselves. This is not to say that the changes in women's intentions will necessarily translate themselves into practice in the years to come. Much will depend upon the opportunity structure and also upon the resolution of any conflict there may be between occupational and familial careers in this context. We are not unaware of the irony that the occupational emancipation of women appears to be occurring at a time when the world of occupational careers may itself be collapsing.

Nevertheless, it may be that the changes we have remarked will endure. The previous period of expanding women's participation in degree-level education occurred in the 1920s and was rudely terminated by the world economic collapse of 1929. By contrast, women increased their participation in degree-level courses in the 1970s whilst economic stagnation was hardening into contraction. However it may be, the last ten years have seen a substantial change in the meaning of gender in so far as it relates to expectations for occupational and familial careers. But our evidence cannot indicate how this change will affect future occupational and familial experience.

Appendix

Appendix Table 5.1   Uncertainty about qualities sought in 'ideal job': percentages

	Men		Women	
'My "ideal job" would . . .'	1971	1981	1971	1981
Enable me to look forward to a stable secure future	4	2	7	3
Enable me to move up in the world	11	8	15	9
Give me the opportunity to hold a senior position by the age of 30	13	11	24	18
Give me the power to make important decisions	15	10	14	11
Absorb my energy and interests both inside and outside working hours	10	10	9	10
Require me to produce original and creative work	17	20	18	15
Allow me to work full-time with ideas and theories	17	14	17	14
Provide me with excitement or adventure	16	12	15	12
Give me an opportunity to help young people	32	32	17	24
Give me an opportunity to work with young children	21	16	13	13
Give me an opportunity to work with people rather than things	17	18	7	11

Note The set of items was preceded by the following instruction:

'Please read each one carefully, and mark how strongly you feel by ringing the appropriate number. As before, the middle position means ' "can't say" or "neutral" '.

The percentages of respondents ringing each mid-point are shown.

Appendix Table 5.2 'Irrespective of whether you have decided what you want to do, we should like to know your ideas about your "ideal job". How important is it for you that it should fulfil the following conditions?': percentages

'My "ideal job" would . . .'	All				Degree students				Non-degree students				Employed			
	Men		Women		Men		Women		Men		Women		Men		Women	
	1971	1981	1971	1981	1971	1981	1971	1981	1971	1981	1971	1981	1971	1981	1971	1981
Enable me to look forward to a stable secure future	88	90	82	93	85	91	81	90	86	94	84	97	93	87	81	96
Enable me to move up in the world	80	83	65	83	73	81	57	78	77	87	62	87	89	82	75	85
Give me the opportunity to hold a senior position by the age of 30	75	73	44	60	68	72	37	57	69	78	41	66	86	68	55	59
Give me the power to make important decisions	69	72	46	66	66	73	42	72	65	72	46	73	74	64	49	59
Absorb my energy and interests both inside and outside working hours	52	61	51	59	50	58	48	60	60	52	59	73	48	68	44	54
Require me to produce original and creative work	63	62	53	54	67	63	49	66	66	72	59	52	58	55	45	44
Allow me to work full-time with ideas and theories	55	57	42	51	56	53	40	54	61	65	44	54	52	59	41	46
Provide me with excitement or adventure	65	76	63	71	65	76	61	77	68	78	66	76	63	74	61	62
Give me an opportunity to help young people	43	32	64	51	40	31	59	50	49	25	75	57	41	35	52	51
Give me an opportunity to work with young children	15	13	56	38	14	12	44	35	24	14	70	31	11	11	49	41
Give me an opportunity to work with people rather than things	68	60	86	82	64	62	83	81	69	55	90	81	72	59	82	84

Note: The table shows the percentages of respondents who ringed values 6-9 on the scale, thereby indicating that the attribute was 'essential'.

Appendix Table 5.3   'How much do you agree or disagree with the following statements about women and careers?
By "career" we mean putting continuous energy over a long period into achieving some success in an occupation – not simply taking short-term occasional jobs': percentages

(a)

| | All | | | | Degree students | | | | Non-degree students | | | | Employed | | | |
| | Men | | Women | | Men | | Women | | Men | | Women | | Men | | Women | |
	1971	1981	1971	1981	1971	1981	1971	1981	1971	1981	1971	1981	1971	1981	1971	1981
Women can get as much sense of achievement from their husbands' careers as from having a career of their own	49	31	47	21	42	31	42	17	45	25	48	24	58	33	52	24
Women can get as much satisfaction from having a career as from having a family	19	34	27	50	20	30	26	50	18	42	26	47	18	36	27	52
It is rare for a woman to combine a career and a family and make a success of both	57	49	44	40	55	47	43	35	56	57	41	35	59	50	51	44
Men are not keen to marry 'career' women	51	34	45	30	50	33	45	30	46	44	42	24	56	32	49	29

(b)

| | All | | | | Degree students | | | | Non-degree students | | | | Employed | | | |
| | Men | | Women | | Men | | Women | | Men | | Women | | Men | | Women | |
	1971	1981	1971	1981	1971	1981	1971	1981	1971	1981	1971	1981	1971	1981	1971	1981
"Have you thought about how you might combine a full-time career with looking after a family?"																
'A great deal' or 'a fair amount' (* asked of women only)	*	*	27	17	*	*	26	22	*	*	25	20	*	*	29	11

Note Table (a) shows the percentage of respondents who ringed values 6–9 on the scale, thereby indicating agreement with the item.

Methodological Addendum

Our analysis has had two principal and complementary objectives. We wished to ascertain whether the expectations of young women in 1981 had changed from those of young women in 1971; and we also wished to contrast the expectations of women with those of men. That is, we wanted to make comparisons across time, and to make between-group comparisons. We were also interested in the changes that had occurred in the between-group contrasts between 1971 and 1981. In this Addendum we describe the methods used to generate the data and we highlight the threats to our inferences about change that result from changes in the nature of the target population and from differences in the two achieved samples. We also describe the procedures used for assessing the reliability of our conclusions.

Data and Methods

The data come from two separate but equivalent sample surveys and correspond to two separate but comparable target populations. The target population in both instances was young people who had left Scottish schools in the previous school session (ie 1969/70 and 1979/80) and who had passed at least one subject at the Higher grade of the Scottish Certificate of Education. (The SCE 'H' grade is equivalent functionally, though not in all its details, to the GCE 'A' level.) Leavers from independent and grant-aided schools were included but those from special schools were excluded. As Table 5.1 has indicated, the target population comprised 25 per cent of all leavers from Scottish schools in 1969/70 and 27 per cent in 1979/80. The sampling fraction for the 1971 survey was approximately 20 per cent. Sampling was conducted in all secondary schools using the quasi-random procedure of selecting individuals having one of six pre-determined birth dates in each month. The sampling was a joint exercise with the Scottish Education Department (SED) and involved three phases. The SED itself surveyed members of the target sample in order to collect information on post-school destinations. The SED survey achieved an 83 per cent response rate. Members of the SED's achieved sample were able to contract out of the 1971 Centre for Educational Sociology (CES) survey before the sample for that survey was constructed. Fifteen per cent of the 83 per cent did contract out. Further details of the 1971 procedures are available in Jones and McPherson (1972b).

The sample for the 1981 survey was also drawn from leavers from all Scottish secondary schools. A nominal sampling fraction of 4.5 per cent was applied. The sample was drawn using systematic sampling within a stratified design. In 1981 the SED did not conduct a voluntary survey of its own but continued to provide the target sample, again having first offered individuals the opportunity to contract out. Seven per cent did so. Further details of the 1981 survey are available in Burnhill, Lamb and Weston (1982).

The '1971' and '1981' Surveys

The data for both surveys were collected by an identical postal survey procedure whereby the respondent received a printed questionnaire in the Spring following the session in which he or she left school, followed, where necessary, by two reminder postcards and a re-administering of the questionnaire. Based on despatches, the response rates were 92 per cent and 85 per cent in 1971 and 1981 respectively. In relation to the target samples (that is, the target sample first identified by the SED and including non-respondents to the SED's own survey (1971) and also persons declining to co-operate in the construction of the samples for the CES surveys (1971, 1981)), the coverage rates were 65 per cent and 79 per cent respectively. The sample sizes used in this analysis were 2366 for the 1971 survey data and 917 for the 1981 survey data.

Two-thirds of the 1981 questionnaire were reproduced directly from the 'master pages' of that for 1971. Most of the questions offered fixed alternatives for response, some being of the 'yes/no' type and others using multiple-answer categories. In addition, there were many items that offered numerically scaled response categories using a nine-point, bi-polar scale, scored 1-9 with a mid-point (in most instances identified to the respondent as ' "can't say" or "neutral" '). This scale was used to measure variations between the extreme points of 'absolutely essential (9)/definitely not wanted (1)' and 'strongly agree (9)/strongly disagree (1)'. (We deliberately chose a nine-point scale since pilot work had shown that the distributions on many of the items to which this scaling applied were positively or negatively skewed.) We have chosen to regard this discretely scored scale as of an ordinal, rather than an interval, level of measurement.

Analysis

We wanted to produce sets of summary statistics that showed the contrast between the responses of young women in 1971 and those of young women in 1981, and that would also allow the reader to examine differentials in response between women and men. Statistics are therefore presented for each of the four sub-groups defined by sex and year. We further disaggregated the statistics by three categories of post-school destination: those who at the time of the survey were full-time degree students, whether at university or elsewhere; those who were students on other full-time courses in further or higher education, irrespective of the level or institutional location of the course (whom we call 'non-degree students'); and the remainder who were counted as being in the labour market, whether or not they were employed and whether or not they were available for work. With some misgivings we call the labour-market group 'the employed', even though about one-in-five were unemployed at the time of the 1981 survey. This convention sacrifices an important aspect of the data to considerations of fluency. Further description of the destinations of sample members may be found for 1971 in Jones and McPherson (1972b) and for 1981 in Burnhill (1983).

We do not present secondary statistics to indicate the statistical significance of our findings, nor do we attempt to construct causal multivariate models to represent processes whereby individual beliefs, intentions and behaviour come to vary. However, we have taken steps to account for the degree of uncertainty inherent in our analyses and these are described in the section that follows. There we explain how we have satisfied ourselves that the differences we highlight in the text are not merely artefacts of chance.

Target Population

Nominally, the target populations for the two surveys were identical. The 1971 survey of school-leavers was limited to those with passes in one or more subjects at the Higher grade of the Scottish Certificate of Education and the questions in the 'After Highers' questionnaire were devised with this sub-population in mind. In 1981, although the CES did also conduct a sample survey of all school-leavers, the administration of the questions from the 1971 'After Highers' questionnaire was limited to the Highers population. Although this target population has substantive meaning in Scottish education it is a sub-population and, as such, it is subject to a non-random selection mechanism. We are therefore conscious that the changes we detect may be due to a change in the composition of this sub-population brought about by the selection mechanism; a mechanism which is closely allied to that governing the decision whether or not to stay on beyond the minimum school-leaving age. It is reassuring, however, that this sub-population has remained at approximately the same size relative to all school-leavers (about one quarter).

The contraction in the provision of initial teacher-training places, the increase in the provision of higher education outside the university sector, and the onset of youth unemployment might be expected to confound comparisons across time. Partly to avoid this we analysed the data cross-classified into three destination categories. The choice of three categories was inevitably a compromise between the explication of these 'structural' changes and considerations of simplicity and sub-group sample size. Some confounding inevitably remains. As we have stated in the main text, the category of labour market entrants includes both the employed and the unemployed. In 1971 unemployment was not a significant phenomenon among Highers leavers. In 1981 about one in four of the young men with Highers who had entered the labour market were unemployed. Among the young women the figure was one in six. The degree course students on the other hand are members of a relatively stable category, although the mechanism of selection into this particular sub-population (especially with the expansion of CNAA degrees) may have altered the composition even here.

Achieved Sample Data

Although the content and procedures for the 1971 and 1981 surveys were very similar, there were some differences with respect to sample design and with respect to the level of non-response. There were also differences in the essential survey conditions which could have contributed to varying degrees of measurement error.

In the section above on data and methods (pp.104-108) we remarked how in the two surveys the achieved samples fell short of the target samples. This was owing partly to the fact that members of the target sample were offered an opportunity to contract out of the survey before the CES questionnaires were despatched and partly, in the 1971 survey, to the prior attrition brought about by the SED's own survey. The achieved samples for the 1971 and the 1981 surveys represented 65 per cent and 79 per cent of the respective target samples. Moreover, the probability of a response was positively associated with the number of passes in subjects at the SCE 'H' grade, and direct use of the achieved sample data would have introduced bias into the results. One of the advantages of having sampled from a nationally defined population is the ease with which one can obtain population figures, relating to the distribution of passes at the 'H' grade, in order to alleviate this threat of bias. These figures were kindly supplied to us by the SED for the respective surveys, and were used to derive a set of weights which compensated for the differential non-coverage across the qualification groups, thereby reducing the bias in statistics of those variates which were correlated with educational attainment.

In 1971, the selection of the six birth dates in each month meant a large sample size, obtained by quasi-random sampling, and a significant sampling fraction (of 20 per cent). In 1981, the sampling was better than simple random sampling, being double-phase systematic sampling within a stratified design, but with a sampling fraction of less than five per cent.

As mentioned, the 1971 survey design employed birth-date sampling. The six birth dates defined six randomly equivalent sub-samples which could be regarded as (nearly independent) replicates. In 1981 the sampling scheme was also part of a replicated design. Four replicates were defined for this survey, each having the same sample design. In order to assess the net error arising from sampling and from the measurements themselves, without recourse to complex formulae or to elaborate modelling, we made direct use of the replicate structure internal to each survey data-set.

Addendum Table 1   A comparison across time using the replicate structure: comparing the intention to 'work full-time for most of married life' among young men in 1971 with the intentions of young women in 1981: percentages

	Replicate identifier	Percentage intending full-time work	Mean value	(Standard error)
1971	a	12.1		
	b	13.0		
	c	14.1	15.3%	(1.17%)
	d	15.1		
	e	17.4		
	f	19.7		
1981	α	34.2		
	β	37.8	39.9%	(2.42%)
	γ	42.8		
	δ	44.9		
	difference in intention (39.9% − 15.3%)		24.6%	(2.69%)

Comments

In Table 5.5 (p.99) the percentage of women who thought that the likely pattern of their working life would be full-time work was given as 15 per cent in 1971 and 40 per cent in 1981. This substantial change was also illustrated in Figure 5.5 (p.100). The statistical significance of this change is readily appreciated by considering the variation in the value of these percentages across the replicate structure internal to each survey. The change is clearly of statistical significance being many times greater than the corresponding standard error.

Addendum Table 2   A comparison between groups, using the replicate structure: comparing men and women in the percentages wanting an 'ideal job' in which they can 'move up in the world': percentages

(a) 1971

	Replicates						Mean value	(Standard error)
	a	b	c	d	e	f		
Men	77.2	77.2	80.0	85.0	81.3	80.0	80.2%	(1.16%)
Women	59.9	67.4	65.6	67.1	63.3	63.4	64.6%	(1.19%)
Ratio of women to men	0.78	0.87	0.82	0.79	0.78	0.79	0.81	(0.01)*

(b) 1981

	Replicates				Mean value	(Standard error)
	α	β	γ	δ		
Men	80.8	82.0	83.0	86.2	83.0%	(1.16%)
Women	83.9	82.8	81.1	83.1	82.7%	(0.58%)
Ratio of women to men	1.04	1.01	0.98	0.96	1.00	(0.02)

* The finite population correction factor was used in the estimation of this parameter

Comments

Addendum Table 5.2(a) shows the greater tendency in 1971 for men rather than women to want of their 'ideal job' the opportunity to move up in the world. The ratio of women to men wanting this is 0.81, and the standard error about this estimate indicates that this ratio is significantly less than 1. Addendum Table 5.2(b) shows that this differential had completely disappeared in 1981.

It is also worth noting that the small increase from 80.2 per cent to 83.0 per cent among the men has a low level of statistical significance. The difference of 2.8 per cent is less than twice the size of the standard error of this difference. (The variance of the difference between two percentages is the sum of the two error variances, the error variance being the square of the standard error: ie $(1.16)^2 + (1.16)^2 = 2.70 = (1.64)^2$).

Approximate estimates of the error variance may be obtained from a replicated sampling design, for any statistic of interest based on data from any sample design, by measuring the variability in the statistic's value across each replicate (Burnhill and Fisk 1981). The theory of the simple replicate and the jacknife methods is set out in Kish (1965) and in Mosteller and Tukey (1979), respectively. These methods allow one to estimate a standard error which implicitly includes both the sampling error and also the measurement error. This standard error may be used to form confidence intervals and for tests of statistical significance. Addendum Tables 5.1 and 5.2 contain a commentary on the use of the simple replicate method of assessing statistical significance. In this assessment the sampling fraction is allowed to have an effect upon the magnitude of the error variance when the contrast is between men and women in a particular year, inference being made to a finite population. For inter-year comparisons, which invoke an appeal to a common hyper-population, the finite population correction factor is ignored.

The replicate structure also provided an opportunity to conduct analyses in two modes. By first selecting data pertaining to two of the six replicates from the 1971 survey and to two of the four replicates from the 1981 survey, we were able to use the data for exploratory purposes. We were then in a position 'independently' to test propositions derived from the exploration upon the remaining part of the data.

Acknowledgements

Peter Burnhill is an SED-funded Research Fellow in the CES. Our research has drawn on surveys funded by the SED, the Social Science Research Council and the Manpower Services Commission. We are grateful to these bodies, and must also thank Alison Kelly, Lynn Jamieson and colleagues in the CES for their helpful comments on an earlier draft.

References

Acker,Sandra (1983) Women and teaching: a semi-detached sociology of a semi-profession. In Barton,L. and Walker,S. (Editors) *Gender, Class and Education* Lewes: Falmer

Burnhill,P.M. (1983) Destinations of young people leaving school *Statistical Bulletin* 2/E1 Edinburgh: Scottish Education Department (SED)

Burnhill,P.M. and Fisk,P.R. (1981) *Standard Errors, Sampling Design, and Analysis with Standard Statistical Packages: An Overview* Edinburgh: Edinburgh Survey Methodology Group, unpublished

Burnhill,P.M., Lamb,Joanne and Weston,Penelope (1982) *The National School Leavers Survey (NSLS) 1981: A Preliminary Account* Edinburgh: Centre for Educational Sociology, unpublished.

Burnhill,P.M. and McPherson,A.F. (1983) The Scottish university and undergraduate expectations, 1971-1981 *Universities Quarterly* 37 (3) 257-270

Corr,H. (1983) The sexual division of labour in the Scottish teaching profession. In Humes,W. and Paterson,H. (Editors) *Scottish Culture and Scottish Education 1800 − 1980* Edinburgh: John Donald

Coxon,A.P. and Jones,C.L. (1977) Applications of multidimensional scaling in the analysis of survey data. In O'Muircheartaigh,C.A. and Payne,C. (Editors) *The Analysis of Survey Data* London: Wiley

Cruickshank,Marjorie (1970) *A History of the Training of Teachers in Scotland* London: University of London Press

Department of Education and Science (DES) (1982) *Statistics of Education (Vol.6) Universities* London: HMSO

Flett,Una, Jones,C.L. and McPherson,A.F. (1971) *Women Entrants to University and College of Education* Edinburgh: Centre for Educational Sociology, unpublished

Flett,Una, Jones,C.L. and McPherson,A.F. (1972) Women entrants to university and college of education *Scottish Educational Studies* 4,1

Herzog,Regula (1982) High school senior's occupational plans and values: trends in sex differences 1976 through 1980 *Sociology of Education* 55,1

Hutchison,D.A. (1972) Discouraged women *Higher Education Review* 4,3

Jones,C.L. (1972) *Paths to Honours: Some Recursive Models of Academic Achievement* Edinburgh: Centre for Educational Sociology, unpublished

Jones,C.L. and McPherson,A.F. (1972a) College has been second-best *Times Educational Supplement (Scotland)* 16.6.72

Jones,C.L. and McPherson,A.F. (1972b) Implications of non-response to postal surveys for the development of nationally-based data on flows out of educational systems *Scottish Educational Studies* 4,1

Kelly,Alison (1981) Choosing or channelling? In Kelly,Alison *The Missing Half* Manchester: Manchester University Press

Kish,L. (1965) *Survey Sampling* New York: Wiley

McPherson,A.F. (1972) The generally educated Scot: an old ideal in a changing university structure. In Bernstein,O., McPherson,A.F. and Swift,D.F. *Eighteen Plus — The Final Selection*, E282, Unit 15 Bletchley: The Open University

McPherson,A.F. and Atherton,G.F. (1972) Graduate teachers in Scotland — a sociological analysis of recruitment to teaching amongst recent graduates of the four ancient Scottish universities *Scottish Educational Studies* 2,1

Mosteller,F. and Tukey,J.W. *Data Analysis and Regression* Massachusetts: Addison-Wesley

Regan,Mary and Roland,Helen (1982) University students: a change in expectations and aspirations over the decade *Sociology of Education* 55,4

Robbins Committee (1963) *Higher Education* Cmnd 2154 London: HMSO

Rosenberg,N. (1957) *Occupations and Values* Glencoe, Illinois: The Free Press

Scottish Education Department (SED) (1971) *Scottish Educational Statistics 1970* London: HMSO

6 The values and aspirations of English women undergraduate

Helen Weinreich-Haste

This chapter discusses the present position of women undergraduates in Britain, using statistical information and making some historical comparisons, and reports some of the findings of a study of 385 women undergraduates in seven English universities. In this study[1], we explored the career intentions, family plans, political orientation and social and political values of undergraduates of both sexes. I shall present a profile of the British women undergraduate which makes comparisons with male undergraduates and looks at the differences between students reading different subjects.

What Kind of Higher Education for Women?

The entry of women into higher education has always evoked discussion on sex differences, sex roles and the purpose of educating women at all. Are there basic sex differences which, at worst, affect women's capacity to benefit from higher education at all, and, at least, determine their pattern of interests? Secondly, what should the education of women be for? Once there was at least acceptance that women would benefit from higher education, there still remained the question whether there should be total equality of provision for the sexes, or whether there should be special or separate provision for women. The four women whose pioneering work in the middle of the nineteenth century laid the foundation for advanced education for women were divided on this point, and the arguments are still reflected in the debates of feminists today. Emily Davies and Frances Mary Buss, the founders, respectively, of Girton College and North London Collegiate, argued for total equality: Anne Clough and Dorothea Beale, the founders of Newnham and Cheltenham Ladies College, supported a model of girls' education

[1] In collaboration with S.F.Cotgrove and A.Duff, supported by SSRC grant 1980-82

which took into account differences – partly. Anne Clough's position was based in part on her belief that the quality of male education was not particularly good, and she wanted to make women students the vanguard of some educational reforms (Sanderson 1975; Turner 1974). Others argued that special provision for girls would make it possible to compensate for the deficits of opportunity in their earlier education, and also that it would make more salient and publicly visible the particular 'feminine' dimensions which are submerged in the masculine culture of higher education and socialization into professional roles.

The debate continues today. When we try to explain the present differences in representation of women and men in university education, do we seek to explain the differences in terms of different pressures on girls and boys, a form of discrimination in schools and in careers advice; or do we conclude that boys and girls have different expectations of their future lives, and of the relationship between career and family commitments, which undermine the aspirations of girls more than boys? Do we explain the different distribution of the sexes across disciplines by arguing that there is something particularly attractive about the content of arts courses to girls, and science courses to boys, because of some basic sex differences in abilities arising from either nature or early socialization? Cross-cultural studies do not support such generalizations about sex differences; also recent work on science teaching in schools suggests that it is geared to masculine interests and cognitive style, and so tends to alienate many girls (Kelly 1981).

Women first began to enter universities as full undergraduates in the 1870s. London University first awarded women degrees in 1878. In the last two decades, at least in theory, the opportunity for women to enter higher education has increased; the expansion of university education, the development of polytechnics and CNAA degrees, the founding of the Open University and finally, the admission of both sexes to Oxbridge colleges, have all created more opportunities for women.

How far has the situation changed?[1] At first, the proportion of women undergraduates rose steadily, reaching a peak of 31% in the late 1920s; subsequently there was a drop. In 1958-59 women represented 25.03% of undergraduates: in 1968-69, the proportion had risen to 29.01% – not even as high as in 1925. In the last few years, there has been more rapid increase. In 1979-80 there were over 91,000 women undergraduates in UK universities, and over 120,000 women in other forms of higher education at undergraduate level, including Open University students. That means that women make up 39.8% of university undergraduates, but 44% of undergraduates in the local authority sector. The recent expansion in universities has had differing effects on

[1] The statistics which follow are drawn from *Educational Statistics for the United Kingdom* (1982); Open University (1982); *Social Trends* (1982); University Grants Committee (1982a).

male and female students: between 1975 and 1980, male intake into universities increased by 11%, female intake by 30%.

The Open University provides some interesting insights into sex differences in educational opportunity. Part-time, distance learning would appear to be particularly suitable for women wishing to acquire better qualifications while completing their families. Yet the proportion of women studying for Open University degrees has not differed very markedly from the national average. In 1972, the Open University had about 1% more women undergraduates than other universities. Ten years later, the gap had risen to 4%. The qualifications of Open University students also mirror the general pattern of women's participation in higher education. Women Open University students tend to have more school qualifications than men, but there are differences in post-school qualifications — more men students have post-school qualifications. The high proportion of Open University undergraduates who are non-graduate teachers acquiring a graduate qualification also reflects the tendency of girls, a decade ago, to go into non-graduate teacher training rather than to university (McIntosh 1979).

This example reminds us that the problem is not only at the point of university entry; although equal numbers of boys and girls acquire five General Certificate of Education (GCE) Ordinary level passes, fewer girls go on to take the number of 'A' levels usually necessary for university entrance. The relative proportions of school-leavers 'qualifying' (in a nominal sense) for higher education have been changing over the past decade, the proportion with two or more 'A' levels having been 11.5% for girls in 1976, rising to 12.1% in 1980 and to 13.3% in 1982. Comparable figures for boys are 14.1% in 1976, 13.2% in 1980 and 14.4% in 1982. The proportions with three or more 'A' levels have also risen from 1976 to 1982, from 7.0% to 8.8% for girls, and from 10.0% to 10.5% for boys (Burnhill, forthcoming). Thus in England and Wales a differential remains in favour of boys, but the gap between the sexes has narrowed.[1]

Where are Women Undergraduates?

Another difference between the sexes is in their representation in science, arts and social science. As several people have pointed out, if the university cuts are more severe in the arts and social sciences, this will have a deleterious effect upon the representation of women at university, unless there is a massive shift in subject choice. The

[1] In Scotland the proportion of girls with three or more passes at the Scottish Certificate of Education (SCE) higher grade has risen from 16.5% (1976) to 18.5%, 20.8% and 22.1% (1980, 1981 and 1982). The rise for boys from 16.6% (1976) over the same years has also been dramatic (17.7%, 18.6% and 19.4%) but a new differential has emerged in favour of the girls (Burnhill, forthcoming. See Burnhill and McPherson in this volume and Raffle 1984.

arts-science sex polarization begins to take effect at fourteen, when the Ordinary level and Certificate of School Education (CSE) subject choices are made. The Ordinary level pattern shows a clear sex difference, which increases at Advanced level in many subjects. Figure 6.1 reflects the same pattern, with the additional factor that social sciences have their own sex distribution.

Figure 6.1   GCE Ordinary and Advanced level passes: girls and boys

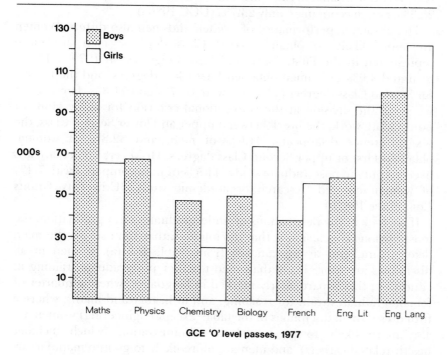

GCE 'O' level passes, 1977

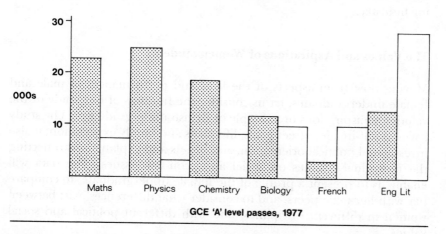

GCE 'A' level passes, 1977

Women are heavily represented in education (68.9%), sociology (64.2%), psychology (66.7%) and languages (67.9%). The only science in which girls are strongly represented is pharmacy (60.4%). In biology they are slightly over-represented relative to the ratio of women to men as a whole (46.4%). In other sciences, men are over-represented; only 15.5% of physics students are women; in engineering, the figure is 6.8% (which represents a considerable increase on 1.4% in 1972). There are relatively few women in some arts and social sciences; in philosophy only 28.3%, and in economics, only 23.7% (UGC 1980a).

The academic performance of women and men also differs. Women are more likely to obtain Second Class degrees; men are more represented in the First, Third and Pass categories; in 1979, 7.1% of men and 4.0% of women obtained First Class degrees, and the figures for Second Class degrees (all types) were 62.7% and 71.8%. However, if we make the division at the conventional criterion for many kinds of postgradate work, the break between upper and lower Second Class, the sex difference disappears; 31.6% of men, and 32.8% of women, obtained First or upper Second Class degrees. However, women are less likely to pursue postgraduate study; 11.5% of men compared with 7.4% of women entered 'research or academic study' (University Grants Committee 1982b).

If we look at the destinations of undergraduates after graduation, the most obvious conclusion is that discipline, rather than sex, is the main determinant. But as we can see from Table 6.1 (a), women in all disciplines are more likely than men to enter postgraduate training in education; this is particularly marked in languages, where a quarter of female graduates train for teaching, and in history and maths, where a fifth do so. In all disciplines in the table (except engineering) women are also more likely to go into local administration (which includes health-related careers), and men are more likely to go into manufacturing industry.

The Values and Aspirations of Women Students

Moving now from aspects of the lives and performances of male and female undergraduates, let us consider the findings of our study of the values and aspirations of a sample of British undergraduates. The study covered self-image, career goals, life plans and family expectation; it also investigated political orientation, and beliefs and explanations reflecting the individual's values on social and economic issues. The data will enable us to present a profile of the female undergraduate, to compare her with her male peers, and to consider what differences exist between women in different disciplines, and with different political and social values.

Table 6.1

a   Destinations of graduates in various disciplines 1980: percentages

MALE STUDENTS

	Biological Sciences	Economics	Engineering	History	Mathematics	Modern Languages	Physics	Sociology
Education Training[1]	6.8	2.8	0.8	12.0	7.6	16.9	6.7	5.2
Education[2]	13.3	2.9	1.5	3.3	4.4	10.34	5.7	5.8
Civil Service[2]	5.2	3.3	3.6	9.6	4.2	7.5	6.6	9.3
Manufacturing Industry[2]	25.5	20.9	83.5	15.2	42.0	19.3	66.8	16.8
Local Authority (inc. Health)	20.2	4.5	2.6	10.7	3.3	4.8	3.0	30.8
Commerce	22.0	62.9	6.0	49.2	43.9	47.6	13.1	25.0

FEMALE STUDENTS

	Biological Sciences	Economics	Engineering	History	Mathematics	Modern Languages	Physics	Sociology
Education Training[1]	12.5	11.1	4.4	21.5	18.7	25.1	14.2	9.0
Education[2]	16.8	2.7	3.7	5.4	3.7	8.1	7.0	4.1
Civil Service[2]	8.1	5.2	2.7	9.0	3.7	9.5	7.0	4.9
Manufacturing Industry[2]	19.9	15.4	73.4	9.5	37.9	20.6	45.0	6.7
Local Authority (inc. Health)	33.2	11.9	2.0	22.1	5.5	12.1	16.0	48.9
Commerce	16.9	61.7	16.2	45.9	45.6	42.6	22.0	17.9

[1] % of all graduates   [2] % of all graduates in employment

Source UGC 1982b

b   Sectors which would be ideal or expected destinations for student samples

MALE STUDENTS

	Biological Sciences	Economics	Engineering	History	Mathematics	Modern Languages	Physics	Sociology
Education	29	10	14	31	38	63	36	75
Civil Service	35	46	28	83	44	46	41	45
Manufacturing Industry	46	59	90	50	54	39	65	31
Health and Social Services	39	11	10	13	15	21	27	80
Commerce	37	92	40	67	67	67	43	53

FEMALE STUDENTS

	Biological Sciences	Economics	Engineering	History	Mathematics	Modern Languages	Physics	Sociology
Education	51	26	19	57	53	54	58	69
Civil Service	47	56	16	66	61	54	49	45
Manufacturing Industry	40	44	81	13	60	16	76	26
Health and Social Services	69	44	36	45	33	34	33	89
Commerce	39	97	50	49	72	84	52	42

Note Figures exceed 100% because respondents could give multiple responses

Source Cotgrove and Weinreich-Haste 1982

The sample was made up of 385 women and just over 400 men from seven English universities. They were drawn from a range of arts, social science, and science disciplines, with an attempt to sample disciplines where women are over-represented (sociology, languages), where they were under-represented (physics, engineering, mathematics, economics), and where there is moderate equality (history, biological sciences).

Self-Image

First, how do undergraduates see themselves, and what qualities do they admire and aspire to? If we first make a sex comparison, we find that in general, the usual sex differences emerge; female undergraduates perceive themselves as more people-oriented, sociable, intuitive, hard-working and responsible, and less technical, scientific, skilled, competitive and risk-taking. The differences are significant, but not large. But when we look at the 'ideal self' measure — 'me as I would like to be' — we find that sex-typed characteristics converge. Both sexes want to be more scientific, technical, skilled and practical, and more people-oriented, sociable, intuitive, accepting and service-oriented. At the same time, each sex wishes to be more feminine or masculine. These findings suggest that the supposed stereotypes of what constitutes 'masculinity' and 'femininity' may be somewhat less important than a general perception of what constitutes the 'good' or 'nice' person.

If we look at differences between disciplines, however, we find that on several traits it is discipline rather than sex which is more important in how one perceives oneself. This is particularly true of technical, scientific, practical, skilled, analytical and realistic. On these dimensions, being a student of a science discipline is more predictive of one's score than is one's sex. Sex, however, remains the main variable in determining sociability, risk-taking, hard work, responsibility, radicalism, people-centredness, and being accepting rather than critical.

Career Satisfactions

What kinds of rewards and satisfactions do women seek from their careers? Again, we find sex differences. Women were less interested in good pay, status, being their own boss and being involved in new developments. They were more interested in helping and working with people, in variety, and in making full use of their abilities. So the expected stereotypical sex differences emerge, but, as with self-image, discipline differences considerably moderated the effects of sex. Making full use of one's ability was important to everyone, but most particularly to historians and physicists. Helping people and working with people was important to sociologists; helping the economy important to economists, engineers and physicists. Travel, not surprisingly, was important to linguists. Physicists and engineers wanted to be involved in new developments.

The figures quoted earlier from national statistics indicate the sex and discipline variation in the career fields which graduates enter. Our sample produced a similar variation, with the predictable expectation that women were more likely to wish to enter education and health, and (on the whole) less likely to enter manufacturing industry. The exceptions were mathematicians and physicists. We asked respondents 1) what fields of work they <u>expected</u> to enter, and 2) what field of work would be <u>ideal</u> for them. The figures in Table 6.1 (b) reflect the combination of these two positive responses.

Family Plans and Career Conflicts

Women's long-term career plans necessarily take into account family plans and expectations − if only to make the decision not to have a family. Despite some changes in climate of opinion about sex roles, and the increase in 'dual-career families', only a tiny minority of people − in selected middle-class enclaves, or sometimes where the male partner is unemployed − have made any substantial change in the pattern of child care responsibility (Beail and McGuire 1982). Parenting is still much more likely to interfere with the career pattern of women than men. Over the last two decades there has been an increased number of working mothers and of married women in general. It is now less likely that young women will regard their careers as an interlude between education and motherhood: full-time childcaring is a relatively brief period after which they will take up their careers again. The problems which arise from such interruption vary from one career to another; economic recession increases the uncertainty of job prospects for everyone, of course, but in jobs where there is rapid change in techniques, the need for retraining is a significant issue. Some young women engineers on one of the country's élite engineering training courses believed that taking time off to have a family would certainly bring their industrial career to an end; they saw their long-term futures in management, or in consultancy, rather than in technological innovation. In contrast, young women entering teaching can reasonably expect to find that a return to the profession after a break will not be ruled out on the grounds of technological advances. Also school teaching is a career which fits in reasonably well with holidays and daily family routine.

These are practical considerations. Any changes in the situation do not depend upon the attitudes of the working woman, but on employers and institutions. But a variety of individual factors affect women's long-term plans and their expectations of resolving conflicts between family and career: How important is work, relative to family and other life considerations? How much time does she wish to spend full-time with young children before returning to work? How does she envisage reconciling possible conflicts between her own career and that of her partner?

It is only of limited <u>predictive</u> value to ask women undergraduates such questions; but such predictions and long-term plans reflect underlying attitudes, and assumptions about appropriate or desirable rôle behaviours and relations between male and female partners, which are central factors in an individual's career motivation. Family life was seen as most important by the women in our sample and work was second. But the gap between the importance of the two – the relative importance, in other words, of family life and work – differed according to discipline. For engineers and sociologists the gap was small: .26 and .37 respectively. Family and work therefore have almost equal importance. For economists and linguists the gap was greatest: .81 and .74. There were also discipline differences in how soon women intended to return to work after their children were born: sociologists expected to return earliest, economists latest. However, almost all women expected to return at some point; the differences between the groups largely depended on whether people expected to return to work (part-time or full-time) while children were under five years of age.

The career conflict situation we presented to the students was a realistic, if oversimplified one. 'Suppose you and your partner are offered equally attractive jobs in different places, what would you do?' The options were: follow their partner ('surrender'), expect their partner to follow them ('my way'), live equidistant and commute ('compromise') and end the relationship ('call it quits'). There were some predictable sex differences: males were more likely to choose the 'my way' option (45%) or the 'compromise' option (39%). 40% of women chose 'surrender', and 49% chose 'compromise'. 13% of men and 10% of women expected the relationship to end.

We also asked about factors which might influence their decision: relative earning power, promotion opportunities, attractiveness of the area, intention to have children, partner's commitment to own career, and the opportunity for alternative employment. For students of both sexes, in all disciplines, partner's commitment to career was rated highest, with opportunities for alternative employment second.

There were discipline differences amongst women students both in option choice and in the importance of the factors affecting the decision.

Biologists, sociologists and engineers were more likely to choose the 'compromise' option and economists, mathematicians and linguists the 'surrender' option — which reflects the same pattern as that found on the measure of relative importance of family and work (Table 6.2). There was a strong relationship between childcare plans and resolution of the 'dual-career' conflict; the women who would 'surrender' expected to spend much longer at home than those who 'compromised'; the ones who thought the relationship would end expected to spend least time. So it is not surprising that the 'surrender' respondents were similar to the longer-term childcare respondents, and the 'compromise' respondents were similar to those who would return early.

Table 6.2   Family plans and conflict with partner

	Would expect partner to follow	Would expect to follow partner	Would live equi-distant and commute	The relationship would end	Mean score on return-to-work scale (low = return earlier)
JOB CONFLICT RESOLUTION	%	%	%	%	
Sample:462 males					
372 females					
Males	45	4	39	13	
Females	2	40	49	10	
JOB CONFLICT RESOLUTION AND RETURN-TO-WORK SCALE					
Women only; sample as above					
Economics N=35	0	49	41	11	13.68
Engineering N=25	3	28	62	7	13.66
Biology N=51	5	37	53	5	13.66
Languages N=80	0	46	42	12	13.97
History N=31	3	40	49	9	13.74
Maths N=40	0	50	43	8	13.72
Physics N=27	0	44	47	9	13.66
Sociology N=49	2	25	58	16	12.75
Mean score on return-to-work scale	13.16	14.72	13.56	13.64	
Number	5	143	153	28	

There were discipline differences on two factors — the importance of relative earning power, and the intention to have children. Biologists were most concerned about earning power; economists least. Economists and linguists gave greater weight than others to the intention to have children. From this evidence there is emerging a pattern of values and expectations concerning the family and the feminine role in the broadest sense, which appears to relate to discipline. The traditionally 'feminine' style in terms of both self-description and family role expectations and values – is found among economists and linguists. Less traditional are sociologists and, depending on the issues, biologists and engineers.

We also found that a conservative or traditional view of family roles was related to more general conservatism in social and political attitudes. Women who were likely to take longer off work with their children tended to support more conservative and controlling policies and to be less egalitarian. In contrast, those who were likely to return to work sooner endorsed the social provision of welfare, believed in the importance of the individual's autonomy, and were more egalitarian – especially on sex-role issues.

Social and Political Values

In the study of social and political values we used various measures; goals for an 'ideal society' which differentiated between 'materialist' and 'post-materialist' values;[1] and two scales which measured attributions about the origins of social order and about the causes of unemployment, the first devised by ourselves, the second by Furnham (1982). These two measures differentiate individualistic and institutional explanations of social issues, that is, locating causes within individual traits or behaviours versus locating causes within the institutions of society or the policy of government. We also asked about the respondents' desired goals for the government, which political party they thought most likely to endorse those goals, and where they saw themselves on a left-right dimension.

The most striking preliminary finding was the relative conservatism of the student body as a whole. Overall, 38% of the sample (both sexes) would vote Conservative, 40% Liberal or SDP and only 15.5% would vote Labour. The study was undertaken at the height of the Alliance popularity in the winter of 1981-82; these figures would suggest that, amongst students, the SDP had taken more from Labour than from Conservative; however, the sample was relatively conservative on other issues; only history and sociology students saw themselves as left of the centre point of the left-right scale. A global description of the sample might be 'centre right'. Sex differences did not follow the usual pattern; amongst this sample, women were less conservative both in terms of party support and on the left-right scale (Table 6.3).

The discipline differences in voting intentions amongst the women students are marked: only 6% of economists, 4% of engineers and 3% of physicists would vote Labour, compared with 37% of sociologists. Alliance support was generally stronger amongst women students (in line with national trends), and the Conservative party appealed to engineers and linguists. Engineers also saw themselves as most right wing (Table 6.4).

[1] This scale was developed by Cotgrove and Duff (Cotgrove 1982).

Table 6.3 Political affiliation by discipline: percentages

MALE STUDENTS

	Conservative	Labour	Alliance		Ecology	Other
			Liberal	SDP		
Biological Sciences	35	21	6	35	3	0
Economics	42	19	22	14	3	0
Engineering	55	10	12	19	2	4
History	28	22	6	33	4	6
Mathematics	36	16	18	28	0	2
Modern Languages	39	23	4	31	0	0
Physics	38	15	19	17	11	2
Sociology	10	24	5	43	0	19

FEMALE STUDENTS

	Conservative	Labour	Alliance		Ecology	Other
			Liberal	SDP		
Biological Sciences	35	15	15	29	4	4
Economics	38	6	27	27	3	0
Engineering	56	4	19	19	0	4
History	28	13	19	28	6	6
Mathematics	35	13	11	28	8	0
Modern Languages	46	11	30	29	1	1
Physics	36	3	5	27	3	0
Sociology	12	37	5	32	4	11

What policy aims do these women endorse? There were eleven aims which represented a broadly conservative-socialist dimension. Overall, both sexes tended to conservatism on restricting the unions, staying in the Common Market, restricting immigration, and retaining the House of Lords, but to liberalism on social services spending, police power, taxation of the rich, and increasing opportunities for women. Women students were significantly less conservative on social services spending, increasing opportunities for women, and unilateral nuclear disarmament. Comparing women students of different disciplines, on six of the dimensions engineers were the most conservative, on seven, sociologists were the most radical. The disciplines were differentiated most sharply on social services spending (engineers $\bar{x} = 2.96$; sociologists $\bar{x} = 1.62$), nuclear disarmament (engineers $\bar{x} = 3.32$, sociologists $\bar{x} = 1.98$), taxation of the rich (engineers $\bar{x} = 3.41$; sociologists $\bar{x} = 2.10$), and abolition of the House of Lords (economists $\bar{x} = 4.08$; sociologists $\bar{x}$ 2.84).

There were interesting sex differences on the measures of goals for an ideal society and on attributions of the causes of social order and unemployment. Female students were generally in favour of greater participation by the ordinary citizen in government decision-making, more egalitarian, and more in favour of public interest rather than market forces. Female students were more likely to attribute social order to proper upbringing, clear rules and guidelines, people having a sense of individual worth, and community concern. They attributed unemployment more to sickness, automation and weak trade unions. Males in contrast were more likely than females to cite government policy, overmanning, incompetent management or the fussiness and unadaptability of the unemployed.

These sex differences suggest that women are more people-oriented, and place more emphasis on community and interpersonal values, less on institutions and less on hierarchical organization. There were, however, marked discipline differences amongst women students, and also differences according to political affiliation, which tended to swamp sex differences. In particular, there was a tendency for sociologists and either economists or engineers to be highest and lowest on the majority of social and economic values scales. Sociologists contrasted with economists on 'economic' issues — market forces versus public interest, economic growth, the importance of community needs, responsiveness of policy makers to the ordinary citizen. Economists were least likely to attribute unemployment to inefficient industry or incompetent management. They were most likely to want to leave management to the experts.

Sociologists contrasted with engineers on egalitarianism versus élitism, and the role of the expert in decision-making. Engineers were in favour of the individual looking after herself, rather than relying on social provision, were inclined to explain unemployment more in terms of individual deficiencies amongst the unemployed, industrial overmanning and Trade Union power. However, party affiliation was an even stronger factor in explaining these differences; part of the difference between engineers, economists and sociologists can be attributed to their voting preferences — though these are, of course, not separable from their social values. Another finding was that linguists tended to be politically conservative, and to be most in favour of law and order on all the scales which tapped this parameter.

Conclusions

From the material I have presented, it seems that there are two kinds of 'conservatism' emerging which to a degree are discipline-linked. Sociologists are relatively radical on family, social control, economic and political issues, but the political conservatives tend to be engineers, and the family and social control conservatives are the economists and linguists. There is consistency across a range of social, personal, political and family aims and goals amongst these young women. Expectations of family and career do relate to what people believe about the wider world. Women who expect to remain at home longer with their children tend to be politically more right wing, endorse a less egalitarian ethic, support law enforcement and advocate clear rules and firm upbringing. They are more likely to give individualistic explanations of unemployment, and support expertise rather than participation, and central planning rather than community involvement. Women who intend to return to work earlier and to have more equal marriage relationships are more supportive of individual autonomy and of participation by the ordinary person in policy-making, and expect social provision and sensible planning of resources. They blame the government or social institutions rather than the individual for social ills.

This difference is partly a left-right dimension, but it also involves a dimension of control versus individual autonomy. It is not reducible to saying that there is a contrast between traditionalists and feminists, and that the former are politically and socially conservative, and the latter are more liberal. While there is clearly a body of feminist socialists, many of whom are sociologists, there are at least two types of 'conservative'. One is traditional in her family and work expectations, in her self-definition and in her political and social values. She is likely to be an economist or a linguist. The other is more work-oriented; although relatively traditional about childcare, she is not so likely to abandon her career for her husband or family; she is élitist, individualistic and conservative politically and economically, but this does not seem to be simply an acceptance of the dominant social paradigm. She is more likely to be a biologist, physicist or engineer.

Throughout this chapter, the evidence I have presented affirms the relationship between discipline and values in the broadest sense. It is an interesting question as to why this relationship should be. Does it precede the experience of university, in some way determining choice? Or is it a consequence of socialization within university − in which case, is it the result of membership of social groups, the anticipation of professional roles, or the outcome of learning to think about social issues in ways particularly associated with the content of different disciplines? At this stage, no clear answer can be given. However, other data which we obtained amongst sixth formers suggest that there is already, by seventeen years of age, a clear pattern of general intellectual orientation to science, arts, technology or social sciences which does relate to politics and to social and personal values.

Finally, how far do the data presented in this chapter forecast a continuing increase in women undergraduates, and a future narrowing of the gap between the qualifications and career opportunities of men and women? While this depends a great deal on government policies regarding higher education, in particular the selective cutbacks of disciplines in which women have been well represented, the evidence would seem to be that a high proportion of the population of undergraduate women are motivated to pursue careers and to organize their lives overall in a way which will put them at least potentially on an equal footing with male graduates. But the question remains open as to whether this is simply opting into the male definition of higher education and subsequent career patterns and values, and we have not explored the forms of discrimination, overt and covert, which may hamper the fulfilment of these aspirations.

References

Beail,N. and McGuire,J (Eds) (1982) *Fathers; Psychological Perspectives* London: Junction Books

Burnhill.P. (forthcoming) *Key Issues in Higher Education Projections* Centre for Educational Psychology, University of Edinburgh. Mimeo

Central Statistical Office (1982) *Social Trends* 12 London: HMSO

Educational Statistics for the United Kingdom: 1979 (1982) London: HMSO

Cotgrove,S.F. (1982) *Catastrophe or Cornucopia?* Chichester: Wiley

Cotgrove,S.F. and Weinreich-Haste,H.E. (1982) *Career-Choice: With Special Reference to Engineering* Report of a project funded by SSRC, 1980-82. SSRC

Furnham,A. (1982) Explanations for unemployment in Britain *European Journal of Social Psychology* 12, 335-353

Kelly,A. (Ed.) (1981) *The Missing Half* Manchester: Manchester University Press

McIntosh,N. (1979) Women in distance education; the Open University experience *Educational Broadcasting International* 12, 178-183

Open University (1982) *Digest of Statistics 1971-1981 Vol.1: Students and Courses* Open University

Raffe,D. (Ed.) (1984) *Fourteen to Eighteen: the Changing Patterns of Schooling in Scotland* Aberdeen University Press

Sanderson,M. (1975) *The Universities in the Nineteenth Century* London: Routledge and Kegan Paul

Turner,B. (1974) *Equality for Some* London: Ward Lock

University Grants Committee (1982a) *University Statistics Vol.1: Students and Staff 1980* Cheltenham: Universities Statistical Record

University Grants Committee (1982b) *University Statistics Vol.2: First Destination of University Graduates 1980* Cheltenham: Universities Statistical Record

7 Sexism in teacher education

Dale Spender

The evidence for the existence of sex discrimination in many areas of higher education has often rested on revealing the under-representation of females in a particular student community, and the consequent virtual exclusion of women from the area of expertise. This is not the pattern which has predominated in teacher-training where, in part because teaching has been perceived as 'a good job for a girl' (see Lou Buchan 1980), women have often comprised the majority of the students. Little research has been undertaken in relation to the provision of equal educational opportunity within teacher-training and perhaps this is because the presence of women has been taken as an indication that there are no pressing problems.

Yet teacher-training would seem to demand research attention because the provision of equal educational opportunity within it is distinctively different from that in any other area of higher education: the education that trainee teachers receive has implications not only for the students' own growth and development but for the consequences of their future behaviour within their own classrooms. It is difficult to explain why it is that when so much emphasis has been given to eradicating inequality between the sexes through the medium of education, so little attention has been given to the preparation of the teachers who are to bear the burden of promoting such change. This cannot be because there is widespread confidence in the belief that teachers are free from sexist assumptions or above and beyond the practice of discriminating against females in the classroom, for the evidence that many teachers construct sexual inequality within their own classrooms is quite clear, convincing — and condemnatory (see Katherine Clarricoates 1978; Sara Delamont 1980; Dale Spender 1982 a and b; Michelle Stanworth 1981). If there is a rational basis for the failure of

This chapter has arisen from a research project funded by The Equal Opportunities Commission, *An Investigation of the Implications of Courses on Sex Discrimination in Teacher Education*, undertaken in 1980 — 1981 by Elizabeth Sarah and Dale Spender.

teacher-training institutions to prepare their students for the promotion of equality of educational opportunity, it cannot be because they are currently confident of their student's competence in this area.

It was partly because so little was known about the issue of sex discrimination in relation to teacher-training that in 1981 the Equal Opportunities Commission funded a research project in this area with the aim of ascertaining what attitudes and values future teachers brought with them to their training, and what form of training would equip them to combat sexual inequality within the classroom (see Dale Spender and Elizabeth Sarah 1982). The project produced some startling findings and led to some unanticipated areas of further research.

First of all it became abundantly clear that among a representative group of students entering a teacher-training college, attitudes and values were displayed which, at best, would be likely to reproduce the practices of unequal treatment towards the sexes in the teachers' future classrooms, and, at worst, to be responsible for the structuring of gross inequality between the sexes within education. But what also emerged as a 'side effect' of the study was that if the 'official' response to the issue of sex discrimination is any guide to the action that will be taken to preclude or pre-empt discriminatory behaviour among future teachers, then the future looks very bleak indeed.

What is presented here is by no means an attempt to provide a comprehensive picture of sex discrimination within teacher-training: it is not even an attempt to summarize the basic findings of the research project (and readers are referred to the report itself for fuller details (Dale Spender and Elizabeth Sarah 1982)). No one research project and no one paper can even begin to map the diversity and the complexity of the issue. Rather, this is an attempt to provide two 'examples' − one related to the students themselves and one related to the educational policy of the institutions in which they are being educated − which will help to illustrate the dimensions of the problem of sex discrimination within teacher-training.[1]

Both 'examples' are ones that were not initially planned for. The first arose from student response to a classroom exercise designed to alert them to the presence of sexually discriminatory attitudes and its implications for the classroom. The second emerged as a result of the criticism of some students of teacher-training institutions: an attempt was consequently made to examine a sample of recent educational documents as a basis for evaluating student criticism of the attitude of the educational community in general toward the issue of sex discrimination.

[1] Both examples are drawn from the two appendices of the EOC Report (Dale Spender and Elizabeth Sarah 1982).

Example One: Student Response

There is a widespread belief among well-intentioned individuals that the practice of sex discrimination is to be deplored and is confined to a dastardly minority. It is common to find that while teachers, for example, claim to be committed to the principle of fair treatment, their behaviour nonetheless reveals that they regularly provide boys with preferential treatment and are often, at times without conscious intent, responsible for constructing the very sexual inequality of which they are critical (see Dale Spender 1982 a and b).

It is not easy to change the perception of individuals on this matter – partly because the recognition that one is displaying qualities not held in high esteem can leave one feeling threatened. As a result, among those who are concerned with teaching students about the dynamics and dimensions of discrimination, much energy has gone into finding non-confrontational ways of raising the issue that sexist societies generally produce sexist members, and that one of the primary steps in the quest for the elimination of sexual inequality is the questioning of sexist practices in relation to the self.

It was with the aim of facilitating self-analysis that a class of Post Graduate Certificate of Education (PGCE) students was provided with a *Report Card* (see Table 7.1). The students were members of one class within the college and along with one other class were being given a course which related to sex discrimination in education: in total there were twelve members of the class but only ten were in attendance when the *Report Card* exercise was undertaken as part of the course. The students were not aware that half the class had been issued with a card which had the name 'Jane Smith' at the top, while the other half had received a card with the name 'John Smith' on it. The *Report Cards* were identical in all other respects.

While no rigorous planning had gone into the *Report Card* it was designed to be intentionally ambiguous in relation to sex stereotyping and school performance. The students, however, who made their recommendations and gave their advice, did so on the basis of sex stereotyping – according to whether the *Report Card* they had been issued displayed the name 'Jane Smith' or 'John Smith'. The responses of the ten students who undertook the exercise (from a range of discipline backgrounds and of both sexes) are contained in Tables 7.2 and 7.3.

The students' responses indicated stereotyped views about the sexes – and their abilities – and that they believed that boys had more ability than girls. The implications of their responses (and the underlying assumptions which informed them) for the provision of equal education-al opportunity within their own future classrooms are serious – and sobering. Yet these were students who (a) claimed that they were against

Table 7.1

Minerva Comprehensive

REPORT CARD

Name ....

English	Shows aptitude. Obviously reads texts and benefits from it. Comes to terms with basic issues. Could pay more attention to detail – instead of broad sweeps.
Mathematics	Understands fundamentals, but too careless. Needs to be more diligent. Could be a more able student.
Social Studies	Has covered the course quickly and is aware of the significance of much of the material. Adopts a questioning approach, does not take things on trust. A very thoughtful student.
Science	Too concerned with complicated questions and not sufficiently concerned with finishing experiments. Needs to be better organized if going to continue with science.
French	Can answer questions on French literature but makes many mistakes with grammar. Pronunciation good and conversation quite fluent, but needs more thorough grounding in rules.
General Comments	General agreement that insufficient attention to detail. A well balanced and cheerful student with many friends. Well adjusted and good natured.

IF YOU WERE TEACHING THIS STUDENT, WHAT EXPECTATIONS WOULD YOU HOLD? WHAT ADVICE AND RECOMMENDATIONS WOULD YOU OFFER IN TERMS OF SUBJECTS THAT SHOULD BE CHOSEN AND CAREER PATHS FOLLOWED?

Table 7.2

Jane Smith

1   Seems there is a need to be organized especially in maths and science. The more literary subjects seem to be a strength.

2   It seems that she fits in and does what is expected of her, but avoids the complicated issues in maths and science.

3   Obviously gets on well with all the other students – should work in some public relations type job. Would be a good secretary or receptionist.

4   Looks as though she does not concentrate enough, doesn't take enough time and care with her work. More interested in social things. Wants to talk French without learning the rules. Probably won't want to stay on at school.

5   Doesn't seem to be very well organized. Needs a job where routine is laid down, one where she can talk to her friends.

Table 7.3

John Smith

1   Should persevere with mathematics. Is probably able enough but needs extra help.

2   Discuss with student the need to master the ground rules of the subject otherwise he will find he is unable to progress to his desired aims. Imagination may be vital but it is not enough. Could have an arts/social science bias but hasn't given mathematics or science a fair try. Needs to do some solid work on these subjects.

3   Seems to have ability but should give much more attention to details. Would have to ask him why so careless on some of these important issues. Probably just needs some personal attention and discussion about need for detail.

4   Would probably do very well in the Civil Service – gets on well with people, could manage them and fluent at French literature and conversation. Sounds as though just a bit immature in mathematics and science and this could be overcome. Thoughtful and questioning and interested in complex issues. Suspect his teachers don't understand him.

5   I think this boy could do anything if he wanted. Seems to be good at everything and gets on well with all the other students. What teachers call 'careless' and 'not enough attention to detail' could be impatient with the subject as taught in school. Could be very bright.

---

sex discrimination, and (b) were probably more aware than some, being engaged in a course on sex discrimination and education.

First of all it must be noted that when the trainee teachers believed they were dealing with a male they treated the student as more significant, as worthy of greater and more perceptive attention: their comments were longer and they were concerned with finding the reasons behind his performance. 'Jane Smith's' performance however was taken for granted and no one suggested that she or her teachers be consulted in the interest of improved performance.

This is probably because of the expectation that boys are intellectually competent and should do well, whereas girls are not perceived to have the same intellectual ability and academic excellence is not considered so important for them (see Katherine Clarricoates 1978; Matina Horner 1976; Dale Spender 1983). Although the information on 'Jane Smith' was exactly the same as it was for 'John Smith', 'Jane's' intellectual competence was assumed to be of little or no significance with no mention made of it, while in 'John's' case it became a matter for some concern, with references made to possible ways in which it could be fostered and encouraged. Whereas 'diagnosis' and strategies based on 'individual programming' were the response when trainee teachers thought the student to be male, critical comments on poor organizational ability were offered when the student was thought to be female. The image of the male student in the mind of the trainee teachers appears to be one of a serious student, capable of considerable achievement and needing only the appropriate facilitation for his 'true ability' to emerge, while the image of the female student is one of a flighty 'miss', neither suited for nor interested in academic things, and in need of castigation.

Through the filter of debilitating and damaging stereotypes, 'John Smith' is seen as bright, as capable of doing mathematics and science, and as embarking on a career path – with very good prospects! The same information, however, is used to classify 'Jane Smith' as not very bright, not very self-disciplined, not able to do mathematics and science, not about to follow a career path, and not the stuff from which 'successful' students are made.

It is interesting to note that when 'John Smith' did not conform to the stereotyped and successful image the trainee teachers did not question the accuracy of the stereotype or take advantage of the deliberate ambiguity contained within the *Report Card*: the stereotype held firm and 'explanations' for the 'failure' were sought. If 'John' was not living up to the traditional image of good performance in mathematics and science then it was suggested that there was something wrong with the education he was receiving – that his teacher was not doing the job properly or he was not receiving the right attention! The assumption of the competence of the male student overrides the assumption of the competence of the teacher! No such faith – or concern – was shown in relation to 'Jane': massaged into meeting the stereotypical image of girls and mathematics and science, her 'weaknesses' in the area were not assumed to be problematic, appear to have been expected, and were therefore passed over without comment.

(Anyone wishing to find an explanation for the enhanced perform-ance of boys and the hindered performance of girls in mathematics and science may need to look no further than to the attitudes and expectations of trainee teachers to locate a major part of the problem. Yet trying to promote change is not easy: like most other well-intentioned teachers few of these trainees would have taken kindly to the suggestion that they were culpable.)

The contrast in the evaluation of 'Jane' and 'John' is really quite extraordinary: lack of attention to detail on 'John's' part was interpreted as evidence of his ability and an impatience with inconsequential matters, whereas on 'Jane's' part it was viewed as carelessness and a disqualifica-tion for responsible future education and employment. That 'John Smith' was judged to get along well with his peers made him a management candidate and a suitable appointment for the Civil Service whereas the same qualities when seen to reside in a female suggested that she should be managed – she was suitable for an appointment as receptionist or secretary. While the future was seen to be open to the responsible 'John', it was even suggested that the irresponsible 'Jane' would probably soon leave school!

This is no extensive analysis of the student population but it does help to convey how deeply entrenched – and pernicious – are the sexually differentiated educational expectations that are held for girls and boys among one group of teacher trainees who were considered representative within the college. It would seem that no matter what these particular students do, their behaviour is filtered through a belief system which is likely to favour boys and penalize girls. Under the circumstances the chances of implementing equality of educational opportunity are remote – and unrealistic.

Example Two: The 'Official' Picture

Given that trainee teachers reveal a range of attitudes and behaviours which, unless challenged, are more likely to perpetuate rather than modify existing practices of inequality in education, the question arises of what remedial steps are being taken. It seems to be perfectly sensible to ask whether policy and decision makers within education are aware of the nature and extent of this problem, treat it as a serious issue, and are disposed if not committed to bringing about change – particularly in teacher-training institutions. It would, however, entail a mammoth project to ascertain the individual stance of influential members of the educational community, and such a study – for many reasons – is not feasible. But policy and decision makers in education do make public decisions and formulate policies, and these can be used as a guide to the status which they accord to the problem of sex discrimination and as an indication of their commitment to promoting equality.

An analysis of official educational publications is salutary and saddening. Sex differences in educational achievement receive brief analysis in some of these publications (for example, Assessment of Performance Unit surveys on mathematical development). And there appears to be an increasing concern about girls' 'under-achievement' in mathematics and science, as shown by the Cockcroft Report (Committee of Inquiry...1982, Appendix 2) and the HMI pamphlet *Girls and Science* (DES 1980c). However only one educational publication since the mid-1970s has focused in detail on sexual inequality across the school curriculum: *Curricular Differences for Boys and Girls*, also known as Education Survey 21 (DES 1975), certainly revealed that there was a problem and that change was considered desirable, but one could be forgiven for suggesting that, in so far as the official response was concerned, it is as if this survey were never undertaken. The Department of Education and Science has shown few if any signs of acting on its own findings.[1]

[1] Anna Coote is currently engaged on a research project on the politics of male resistance, in which she is analysing the way in which male controlled institutions do not act upon information about sexual inequality: the response of the DES is in her estimation typical.

Even the concern for girls' under-achievement in science surfaces only sometimes. Survey 21 specifically concentrated on the sex-discriminatory practices which characterized the teaching of science as well as student performance in science, and suggested that many changes were in order. *Girls and Science* investigates schools where girls did comparatively well in science and nevertheless finds that many changes are required. On the other hand the Science Progress Report (APU 1979) for which the terms of reference explicitly state that the aims were 'to identify the evidence of under-achievement' makes no reference to sex differences and sexual inequality!

Other areas where concern about sexual inequality would seem to be needed − higher and further education, teacher training, schemes like YOP and YTS − receive almost no attention to the matter in official documents. Perhaps most distressing are the proposals for the future: *Higher Education in the 1990s* (DES 1978) does not address the issue of sex inequality and it could be assumed that there are no plans for combating sexual discrimination in teacher education in the years to come.

The 1979 *Annual Report* of the DES (1980) fails to mention sex discrimination in its section on 'Educational disadvantage' and there are no entries for 'equality of educational opportunity' for females under the headings 'The school curriculum', 'Co-operation with the training and manpower services' or 'Education and industry'. There are a number of appendices to the report and in none of them is sexual inequality referred to as an issue, despite the fact that the appendix 'Research and Development' reveals that out of the twenty-nine funded research projects in 1979 only one was related to sex discrimination, that none of the fifteen projects completed during 1979 was concerned with sex discrimination, and that none of the 108 publications listed for 1979 addressed the issue.

Even the HMI pamphlet *A View of the Curriculum* (DES 1980d) which in a just and rational society could be expected to build on the earlier findings of sexual inequality in Survey 21 (DES 1975), contains no discussion of sex discrimination. While Appendix 2 of this report deals with mathematics, no acknowledgement is made of sex differences and the issues they raise.

One of the more positive features that can be salvaged from official publications since the mid-1970s is in *A Framework for the School Curriculum* (DES 1980b), which states that schools should avoid sex discrimination. The trainee teachers who filled in the *Report Card* were of the same opinion − that sex discrimination should be avoided − but this did not immunize them against the practice − nor did it provide them with any strategies for overcoming its existence.

Of course, one should not be surprised that both trainee teachers and the occasional official educational publication should state the desirabil-

ity of avoiding sex-discriminatory practices. It is unlikely that anyone –
whether they be in prestigious or lowly positions within the educational
community – is going to take a stand for sex discrimination. There has
been a change in rhetoric perhaps, in the last decade, but it seems that
little else has changed. Christabel Pankhurst's slogan seems appropriate
under the circumstances – Deeds not Words!

Policy and decision makers in education (and Eileen Byrne (1978) has
disclosed that 97 per cent of them are male) have not treated the issue of
sex discrimination seriously, yet this cannot be because they are oblivious
to its existence. They are influential, informed and professional people
who are required to keep abreast of current literature and research –
and more research has been undertaken and more literature produced
in this area than in any other educational area in the last decade! So why
this reluctance to address and tackle the issue? Why has sex discrimination not become a priority problem in teacher-training?

In the face of convincing evidence that there are gross sexual
inequalities within education (among the convincing evidence one would
include the DES's own Survey 21), why is it that the predominantly male
influential circles in education persist in providing an education which
affords preferential treatment for males?

Conclusion

In a society based on sexual inequality most members of the society
develop attitudes and values which are consistent with that sexual
inequality, and neither trainee teachers or teachers, neither educational
policy or decision makers constitute an exception. The sexual inequality
of the society is reflected in the sexual inequality within education and
the pattern will persist until deliberate and concerted efforts are made to
change it. The realm of teacher education would appear to be the logical
place to start if a programme for promoting equal educational
opportunity for both sexes were to be embarked upon – but apart from
the dedicated efforts of a few individual tutors it seems that there is little
or no such activity within teacher training (see Dale Spender and
Elizabeth Sarah (1982) for fuller details).

And there is no easy solution to the problem, for like the trainee
teachers who unwittingly revealed the pervasive and pernicious nature
of their sexism, the policy and decision makers in education – who could
institute a programme for change – are just as likely to hold similar
values and attitudes to the trainee teachers.

Yet even this is not the full picture: much more is needed to explain
the reluctance of educational officials to act upon their own research
findings and to reduce the likelihood of boys being provided with

preferential treatment. What are the alternatives when in educational circles rational arguments are not enough to hold sway?

References

Assessment of Performance Unit (1979) *Science Progress Report 1977-78* London: HMSO

Byrne,Eileen (1978) *Women and Education* London: Tavistock

Buchan,Lou (1980) 'It's a good job for a girl (but an awful career for a woman)'. In Spender,Dale and Sarah,Elizabeth (Eds) *Learning to Lose; Sexism and Education* London: The Women's Press, pp. 81-9

Clarricoates,Katherine (1978) 'Dinosaurs in the classroom': a re-examination of some aspects of the 'hidden' curriculum in primary schools *Women's Studies International Quarterly* 1 (4) 353-364

Committee of Inquiry into the Teaching of Mathematics in Schools (The Cockcroft Report) (1982) *Mathematics Counts* London: HMSO

Delamont,Sara (1980) *Sex Roles and the School* London: Methuen

Department of Education and Science (1975) *Curricular Differences for Boys and Girls* Education Survey 21. London: HMSO

Department of Education and Science (1978) *Higher Education in the 1990s: A Discussion Document* London: HMSO

Department of Education and Science (1980a) *Annual Report 1979* London: HMSO

Department of Education and Science (1980b) *A Framework for the School Curriculum* London: HMSO

Department of Education and Science (1980c) *Girls and Science* HMI Series: Matters for Discussion 13. London: HMSO

Department of Education and Science (1980d) *A View of the Curriculum* HMI Series: Matters for Discussion 11. London: HMSO

Horner,Matina (1976) Toward an understanding of achievement-related conflict in women. In Stacey,Judith et al. (Eds) *And Jill came Tumbling After* New York: Dell Publishing, pp. 43-63

Spender,Dale (1982a) *Invisible Women: The Schooling Scandal* London: Writers and Readers

Spender,Dale (1982b) The role of teachers: what choices do they have? In The Secretariat of the Council of Europe *Sex Stereotyping in Schools* Lisse: Swets and Zeitlinger, pp. 50-62

Spender,Dale (1983) Introduction. In Spender,Dale (Ed.) *Feminist Theorists: Three Centuries of Women's Intellectual Traditions* London: The Women's Press

Spender,Dale and Sarah,Elizabeth (1982) *An Investigation of the Implications of Courses on Sex Discrimination in Teacher Education* Equal Opportunities Commission Report. Manchester: EOC

Stanworth,Michelle (1981) *Gender and Schooling: A Study of Sexual Divisions in the Classroom* London: Women's Research and Resources Centre

8 The professional socialization, integration and identity of women PhD candidates

Daphne Taylorson

Very few women in Britain, compared with men of similar ability, continue their education to the level of a PhD. Whilst there has been considerable interest in gender differentiation in the last decade, much of this has been focused on schooling; the researcher on women in higher education in Britain is faced with a remarkable paucity of information. Although there has been research on British postgraduates and research students (Glennerster 1966; Rudd and Hatch 1968; Rudd 1975), little of this information is divided by sex, so that the data available on women as postgraduates are limited and those on women PhD candidates are negligible. The participation of women in academic life in America has not been much higher than in Britain in this century (Bernard 1964; Rossi 1973) but they have attracted more research interest, particularly in recent years. In consequence there are studies of women PhD recipients in America (Simon et al. 1967; Astin 1969; Holmstrom and Holmstrom 1973, 1974) and studies of doctoral recipients which divide their data by sex (Centra 1974; Cartter 1976). This chapter reports some of the findings of a study of women PhD candidates at a large British university in the 1970s which explored antecedent and current factors of their experience that might account for their high academic achievement, continuing studies and career motivation (Taylorson 1980). In the following discussion the focus will be on aspects of women PhD candidates' integration into academic life and related aspects of their identity.

We need to begin with a profile of the respondents, who were women PhD candidates at a large Northern university.[1] Women comprised only a tiny minority (9%) of the PhD candidates registered there in 1972, and 25% were the only woman PhD candidate in their department. The majority (82%) were full-time candidates. Over two-thirds (69%) were scientists, just under a fifth (18%) were social scientists and only 13% were registered in the arts faculties. Just over half had a grant and a further quarter a salary, the remainder relying on a variety of other sources to finance their studies. Just over a fifth were employed as staff at the university and half of these were lecturers. A quarter of the respondents had a First Class Honours degree, although three-fifths had 'good' Honours. The scientists were the most and the social scientists the least likely to have 'good' degrees. Two-thirds had obtained a Masters degree, or completed a Masters course, before registering for a PhD, and nearly a fifth had been awarded a distinction. Almost two-thirds had studied for their undergraduate degree, and over a third had had postgraduate experience, at other universities. Four-fifths of the respondents were British. The respondents were older than might be expected, as a quarter were over thirty. However four-fifths had proceeded straight from school to university for their undergraduate degrees but some then had employment experience before continuing their studies. Almost three-fifths were currently married but only a quarter of the respondents were mothers. It was notable that, apart from their very different numerical representation, the demographic data on all the PhD candidates at this university[2] indicated only slight differences between the women and men. These slight differences included women being more likely than men to study arts but less likely to study science, less likely to have a grant, more likely to be part-time, to be married, to be older and to be British.

Study and Career Orientations and Experiences

The literature on the current experiences of highly educated women and men in Britain has indicated considerable gender differentiation in continuity of education and career prospects and progress (Kelsall et al. 1972; Chisholm 1978; Chisholm and Woodward 1980; Fogarty et al. 1971a, 1971b). The employment histories and study and career aspirations of these women PhD candidates were therefore analysed in the light of data on male research students.

First, a much higher proportion of these women PhD candidates had an employment history than would have been expected from previous research on postgraduates in Britain (Rudd 1975; Kelsall et al. 1970).[3] That work mainly concerned men postgraduates. Of the present sample of women candidates two-thirds had had some employment experience. One-fifth of all respondents had been employed prior to going to university (although mainly for short periods), 44% had been employed between graduation and registering for their PhD, and 38% had been employed during their PhD studies.

For a few respondents this employment experience had been rich in variety and interlinked with periods of further study. One respondent had started as an 'itinerant waitress', then had a year as a student, left to have a baby, returned to work as a laboratory assistant, left again to be a full-time housewife for a couple of years, before returning to complete full-time studies which were followed by a variety of research posts and eventually a lectureship. Another, a single woman, had had twenty-three years of varied employment before obtaining a university lectureship. She had started with three years of various unskilled jobs before studying for 'O' and 'A' levels. She then spent six years as an apprentice engineer, followed by several years in designing and research, before returning to postgraduate studies, followed by research posts and eventually a lectureship. However, the majority who had some employment experience had worked for less than five years. Most, as is usual among highly educated women (Astin 1969; Kelsall et al. 1972; Chisholm 1978; Williamson 1979; Chisholm and Woodward 1980) had been employed mainly in the education sector. A fifth were already established as lecturers or researchers in higher education and half of these were university lecturers, although a few had had manual or clerical jobs before they went to university. Few of those now established as staff in higher education had had a straightforward path to their present status. Hardly any had been creamed off to join the 'closed loop' of the apprenticeship for an academic career that Rudd and Hatch (1968) depict as usual for brighter students.

Surprisingly, marital status did not distinguish between respondents employed at different stages of their educational career. Although single women were less likely to have been employed, this was because they tended to be younger and still to be continuous students. However, those with 'poorer' degrees were much more likely to have some employment experience than those with good Honours. Thus to some respondents a PhD was a necessary qualification to step onto the first or next rung of the ladder to an academic career, but for others it was simply consolidating yet another stage in a varied career.

A higher proportion of these women PhD candidates had had discontinuous educational careers when compared with the national sample of research students (85% male) at British universities (Rudd 1975)[4], but not in comparison with American women doctoral recipients (Astin 1969). Nevertheless, three-fifths of the respondents had no time off during their higher education. Those who did have gaps said this was for employment. The discontinuous candidates were more likely to be arts or social science candidates and, surprisingly, to be slightly more likely to have a 'good' degree. They were also twice as likely to be married, but nevertheless the traditional association between 'returners' and married women (Myrdal and Klein 1968) was not applicable to these women PhD candidates: time out was for employment not child care. Several married respondents, some of whom were also mothers, had no gaps in their educational careers. Time out for child care or the three-phase model (ibid.) of training, family and work does not appear to apply to women who continue to this more advanced level, as Williams et al. (1974) note for academic women and Astin (1969) found among American doctoral recipients, although it does appear to be common among women graduates who do not continue their studies further (Kelsall et al. 1972). Moreover, prominent among the 'returners' were the women, whether married or single, with continuous careers, who 'returned' to a PhD because it was a normal, if not necessary, step in the development of their career, women who, after periods elsewhere, had moved into universities, where they wished, or were expected, to obtain qualifications similar to more conventional members of the academic staff. Nevertheless it is difficult to assess whether some of the discontinuity in the respondents' higher education was attributable to their gender. Women seem to suffer more than men from lack of both self-confidence (Bardwick 1971; Maccoby and Jacklin 1975; Feldman 1973; 1974) and sponsorship (Williams et al. 1974). More research is needed on the reasons for the more discontinuous educational careers of women.

This picture of gender differentiation changes when we turn to study and career motivation. Firstly, there was remarkably little indication of any significant gender differentiation in motivation to study for a PhD when the reasons the respondents gave were compared with those in Rudd's (1975) national sample. The largest group of women PhD candidates were 'dedicated scholars' (Rudd 1968, 1975). There were, however, slight differences between these women PhD candidates and Rudd's (1975) sample. These respondents were slightly more likely to be 'dedicated scholars' and less likely to be 'vocationally oriented' or 'drifters'. They were also less likely, firstly, to be concerned with the promotion or salary prospects which might accrue from obtaining the qualification and, secondly, to consider registering for a PhD was a normal step for anyone with a good degree.

Secondly, these women PhD candidates show considerable career motivation. The majority were clear about their occupational aspirations before they went to university and in contrast to the 1960 women graduates (Woodward 1974) their occupational motivation increased or was reinforced during their higher education. Most of the respondents were breaking away from traditional female occupational stereotypes (such as school teaching), and instead aspired to male-dominated, high status careers, especially academic careers, which three-quarters were considering. Certainly from the literature (Williams et al. 1974, p.98; Rudd and Hatch 1968, p.182) one would expect PhD candidates to be oriented to academic careers. Some of the respondents were undeterred by any handicap of low social origins or even of a poor academic record.

However a few were still undecided about their future careers, but not because they lacked ambition. Rather they were realistic and often pessimistic about the limited employment opportunities for PhD recipients in general and women in particular. The scientists were the most undecided about their future careers. So also were the married rather than the single women, although those married respondents who had made up their minds did not restrict their occupational choice any more than those who were single.

Thus it is suggested that women who continue their studies as far as a PhD differ in career commitment and occupational aspirations from other graduate women (Kelsall et al. 1972), being more ambitious and oriented towards a wider range of the traditionally male dominated high status careers. In this they resemble male graduates and PhD students (Kelsall et al. 1970, 1972; Rudd 1975) more than other educated women in Britain, although of course they resemble in ambition and occupational orientation the American women doctoral recipients (Astin 1969; Simon et al. 1967; Centra 1974). Thus whilst these women PhD candidates differ from other research students in Britain in terms of their greater employment experience and more discontinuous educational careers, they approximate 'men's models' (Ardener 1978) in terms of their study and career orientations. This suggests that whilst the ambitions of women PhD candidates may be the same as men of similar status, their experiences may not. In the following sections further aspects of the respondent's experiences of studying for a PhD will be explored in greater depth, concentrating firstly on professional socialization and integration into university life and secondly on the development of academic rather than gender identity.

Professional Socialization and Integration?

Two important ingredients of a successful graduate career mentioned in the American literature on graduate education (Husbands 1972; Feldman 1974; Solmon 1976) are a close relationship with an academic sponsor and integration with a student reference group. These provide the essential professional socialization and foster the development of the appropriate self-image. However, it has been suggested by several authors (Solmon 1976; Schwartz and Lever 1973; Epstein 1970; Williams et al. 1974; Carnegie Commission 1973) that the gender of the graduate student will affect the likelihood of their receiving sponsorship from academic staff, so that male students have a better chance of being sponsored than females. Gender will also be one of the factors influencing membership of student peer groups. Women may be less likely than male peers to be included in those informal learning situations that arise from the social activities of students outside the research situation or the formal university seminar (Whitehead 1976; Deem 1978; Smith 1978). The woman student is therefore in a particularly difficult situation in trying to accomplish a successful graduate career. Moreover it is suggested that in order to minimize the comparative disadvantages associated with female socialization and status, which may include *inter alia* a lack of prior socialization to an occupational role orientation, conflicts over the perceived deviance of graduate studies from the socially expected 'wife-mother' female role, plus a more general lack of confidence, women have a greater <u>need</u> for sponsorship and supportive relationships with peers (Sommerkorn 1967). It has been notable that a lack of occupational role orientation was not a problem experienced by the majority of these women PhD candidates. Only a third had not made up their mind about a future career at university entrance and only one respondent was not considering any future career by the onset of her studies for a PhD. The question remaining is whether these women PhD candidates also received these supportive relationships. Did they have an attachment to some form of academic reference group, and did this consist predominantly of staff or students?

The problem for research, however, is what is meant by sponsorship by staff or membership of a peer group (of precisely what would these relationships consist?). Such complex and possibly sensitive relationships are not readily measurable. It would involve an assessment of the intensity and form of various relationships which was beyond the scope of this research. Particularly, the concentration here was on individual women PhD candidates and their interpretation of the significance and meaning of various events and relationships, rather than their interaction patterns with significant others. The latter would have required some questioning of staff and relevant students which was not attempted. The concern was more to see if the respondents felt they had the basis of an academic reference group in the sense of meeting regularly a group of people with whom they could discuss their research, or their subject in general as well as other intellectual matters, career opportunities and the other day-to-day concerns of academics. That is, the reference group could be expected to assist in the process of professional socialization of the respondents so that they 'learned the requirements of continuing' in their graduate career 'and of success in it' (Becker and Strauss 1970, p.279). To try to tap the relationship of the respondents with academic reference groups of staff and other students they were asked who they mixed with in their work and leisure time, and what was the status and gender of their companions and the bases for their selection. Moreover, were there any barriers to their interaction in the university?

It was found that during work time at the university the majority (three-fifths) of the respondents did have the basis of an academic reference group. However this did not apply outside the formal work situation. The respondents' reference groups during work time predominantly comprised other PhD candidates rather than staff. Most of the minority (18%) who mainly mixed with staff were themselves employed in their department and thus already had collegial relationships. There was thus little overt evidence of the sponsorship of these women PhD candidates by staff, but since other research (Rudd 1975; Acker 1978) suggests high levels of interaction with staff are unusual, there is no evidence that these respondents are particularly disadvantaged. The social scientists were the most likely to have a predominantly staff reference group and the scientists a predominantly student reference group. Those who mixed regularly with staff tended to have better degrees, an indication perhaps of sponsorship or encouragement of the 'more able' (Rudd and Hatch 1968). Marital status did not appear to limit integration into university life.

The reference groups comprised, of course, mostly men (only 7% of the respondents mostly mixed with other women during work time in the university), so that cross-sex relationships with all their attendant problems were the norm (Solmon 1976; Schwarz and Lever 1973). As so many of these women respondents were the only women registered for a PhD in their department, they could be considered 'tokens' (Kanter 1977). If these cross-sex relationships were to provide the respondents with the support and informal socialization necessary for a successful graduate career, they needed to be able to adapt to the male 'models' (Ardener 1978). It was clear that a majority were able to do this, as so few (11%) felt that 'being a woman' was a barrier to social mixing in the university or would prefer to mix with more women.

It was concluded that overall the respondents appeared integrated into the formal academic and social life of their departments centring on research and seminars. However this did not continue into the more informal interaction during leisure time in the university, coffee breaks, lunch or an evening drink. Then half the respondents were isolated, they belonged to no social grouping in the university. Without more intensive research on interaction patterns in departments, and a comparison with a control group of male PhD candidates, it is impossible to assess the effect of gender on isolation outside the formal work situation. We do not know whether these women have 'formal equality' but not the 'informal signs of belonging', or 'acceptance' into the 'club', as Simon et al. (1967) found in the professional lives of American women doctorates. This question merits further research.

Academic or Gender Identity?

The next question to be explored is whether the respondents had an academic or gender identity. It has been suggested that the experience of being in a minority in academic life might have a negative effect on women's self-images and performance (Feldman 1974) and additionally that women may experience conflicts between educational or occupational role orientations and a domestic role orientation. Thus 'being a woman' might not readily combine with 'being academic'. How far then did these women PhD candidates feel 'being a woman' affected their PhD experience? Initially the respondents were asked whether they thought there were any particular advantages or disadvantages in being a woman studying for a PhD compared to a man. Three-fifths of the respondents felt there were no advantages whereas two-fifths felt there were no disadvantages.

Among the advantages of being a woman mentioned by these respondents was the differential treatment associated with being in a minority. Nearly a tenth of the respondents felt that as women it was 'easier' to get some things done. Another popular response was that 'women can be less competitive'. Thus one advantage of the more limited career opportunities for women is that less is expected from them, so that the pressures to be successful may not be so strong or burdensome nor failure so publicly condemned. The minority status of women was also perceived by a few to be an advantage in that 'women are scarcer — and a novelty'. This has both intellectual and social potential. There is also little competition for the attentions of the opposite sex and it is quite likely that as women they will be treated by male staff and peers 'with courtesy', at least. A small number also felt there were advantages in being a married woman. Particularly it was possible 'to study without finance', assuming a co-operative and supportive spouse, and also to be socially 'less tied to the university'. Again, marriage enables the woman PhD to escape from some of the problems and pressures of postgraduate life. Thus most of the advantages of being a woman studying for a PhD are those that arise primarily as compensations for the secondary status that women hold in academic and professional life.

The disadvantages the respondents felt were equally connected with having a secondary status; they were the other, less pleasant, side of the coin. A fifth commented specifically on the various ways they felt women as a whole met with social disapproval or were not accepted or not taken seriously. 'People tend not to take one seriously — this also tends to influence one's own assessment of oneself.' Some were philosophical about this; as one scientist said: 'It's difficult to be accepted by an almost 100% male research group — you just have to learn to live with this.' Others were more exasperated by male academics' ambivalence to their women students. 'One tends to be patronized on the one hand, or set apart on a pedestal to be admired as a freak, on the other.' Whilst others spoke of more bitter experiences: 'Some lecturers consider that women are inferior.'

A further fifth of the respondents felt the disadvantage of being a woman PhD candidate arose either from the actual problems of combining a domestic role of marriage and possibly motherhood with a graduate career or because the female domestic role, either existing or as a normal expectation for the future, affected staff and peers' perceptions of their potential. The actual disadvantages which the respondents associated with being married women, and which they felt affected men less, were three-fold. First, domestic responsibilities left less time for study and participation in the 'loose-knit life of university'. Motherhood intensified the domestic labour. Secondly, marriage and motherhood tended to isolate women from activities in the university as domestic concerns could not be integrated with those of academic life. 'My colleagues are all men and have different problems.' Moreover, following the traditional pattern (Holmstrom 1972; Edgell 1980), the woman's career is normally considered secondary to her husband's so that her studies 'must be organized so as to interfere minimally with his.' The limitations this places on the woman's ability to be successful in her graduate career were also felt to restrict her future choices. Thirdly, the domestic role of women impinges on the lives of the women who have not chosen it. Some of the single women felt that women's aspirations as postgraduates or for their future careers were not taken seriously because 'you were expected to marry at any time.' Thus although a woman PhD candidate may well have developed an occupational role orientation, the perceptions of staff and peers that this may be incompatible with what they expect to be her domestic role, may affect both her ability to successfully pursue her goals and the support she will obtain.

A smaller group of respondents felt that the disadvantages of being a woman studying for a PhD arose from what they perceived to be the differential mental and physical attributes of women or from female programming or conditioning. Thus women, they felt, have a 'lack of mental aggressiveness both in approach to experiment and in discussion with colleagues,' are 'more emotional in approach' and lack physical strength and stamina. These respondents were predominantly scientists and it is conceivable that the nature of achievement or originality in the natural sciences, the 'cognitive style' (Webb 1977), emphasizes gender differentiation more than in the humanities and social sciences. A final disadvantage which concerned a few respondents was a lack of female colleagues with whom to share their experiences.

To explore further how far these women PhD candidates felt their experiences as postgraduates were affected by the minority status of women in academic life they were asked to speculate what changes in their experiences could be expected if women, instead of being a small minority, constituted a half or more of the PhD candidates, so that, using Bernard's (1975) term, a 'social tipping point' had occurred. Just under a third of the respondents (31%) felt that it would have affected their experience. Most of these felt that women's status would automatically improve if they were not in a minority and this would 'more accurately reflect the ability distribution'. This change would, firstly, bring emotional benefits to the respondents. 'I would feel it was easier mainly because it would be normal, less freaky.' There was the possibility of more supportive relationships. Thus, as Darley (1976) suggests, they would not have to search for supportive reference groups to convince themselves they are not just deviant, and would consequently have more time available for the pursuit of their careers. Secondly, an increase in the proportion of women students would bring changes in the working situation. 'Work would change because of women's abilities and also disabilities.' It might also improve career chances as 'employers' condescending attitudes towards female applicants might change.' Thus the effect that a better balance in the distribution of the sexes would have on the respondents' experiences as PhD candidates would be one of improvement in the direction of equality. They would be considered normal, would be able to have more supportive relationships and the working environment would change to fit their needs.

However, almost twice as many of the respondents (58%) did not feel that reaching a 'social tipping point' in the distribution of the sexes in universities would affect their experience as PhD candidates. Increasing the proportion of women would not necessarily change the way those women were treated. Equality was not just changing numbers in universities. As one respondent said: 'Several undergraduate courses already have mostly women and there they are not taken more seriously.' Further, a small number of respondents, notably in medical departments, pointed out that they already had an equal proportion of PhD candidates from both sexes. Rather the problem was the general lower status ascribed to women in most areas of society. It was also the greater domestic obligations of women either actual or potential that affected their experiences and opportunites. As one said: 'It wouldn't have any effect because the majority of these women would still marry and I feel it is being married which has the strongest influence on my personal career.' Moreover, a change in the distribution of the sexes would not necessarily affect the way in which individual women, particularly the reserved or shy, were able to manage social relationships. Indeed a third of the respondents felt that increasing the proportion of women PhD candidates would not have an effect on their experience as they did not see their gender to be such an important determining factor. More important for some of them were various aspects of the university organization, particularly what they felt were inadequate inter-departmental contacts and the limitations this imposed on postgraduates with inter-disciplinary interests. For others, increasing the proportion of women PhD candidates would not affect their experience as they did not mix with other research students.

It is important therefore not to over-emphasize the respondents' consciousness of the effects of female status. Only a third felt that equalizing the proportions of men and women would affect their experience in studying for a PhD, and in contrast an equal number felt that gender was not an important determining factor in their PhD experience. How far then did their experience as PhD candidates override that of being women? That is, could their identity be considered more academic-salient than gender-salient? It has been argued earlier that there were many similarities in the undergraduate and postgraduate careers of these respondents and research students in general (Rudd 1975). On the whole these women PhD candidates are more similar to men who are research students (Rudd 1975) than to women educated to graduate level (Kelsall et al. 1970, 1972). In terms of self-ambition and qualifications the majority of the respondents seemed so similar to male research candidates that it is suggested that their salient identity (Kando 1977) had become 'a PhD candidate' rather than 'a woman'[5]; that is they were developing an 'academic' rather than a 'gender' identity. However the transformation of identity has to be negotiated and legitimated by others (Strauss 1962). Acquiring the identity of a PhD candidate may be a more complicated process for women than men, firstly because gender identity is so fundamental, and therefore more difficult to transform, and secondly because women comprise such a minority in academic life that there are fewer institutionalized means of negotiating the trans-formation. Although a respondent's self-concept may well emphasize that at the university being a PhD candidate is more salient than being a woman, for this to become a new identity it must be legitimated by others. But the rituals involved in the respondent's interpersonal relations may affirm gender identity rather than academic identity. Those respondents who felt 'being a woman' did affect their experience as PhD candidates may be expressing precisely this situation. So however determinedly a respondent may try to transform her identity (Strauss 1962) she can only succeed if this process is acceptable to others.

It is argued therefore that the woman PhD candidate is in a crisis stage, in that she is no longer similar to other educated women but has not yet been accepted as similar to her male peers; she operates between the woman's and man's models (Ardener 1978). She is rejecting a traditional feminine identity in pursuing high status qualifications and a career. But to be fully assimilated to the current definition of an academic identity she is confronted with the impossible task of denying her gender identity and adopting the man's model. Thus the differential experience of women PhD candidates, for example their greater experience of employment, lack of grant aid and more discontinuous educational careers, compared with research students in general, could be explained first in terms of their own lack of confidence to continue their studies and apply for grants because they are still unsure or insecure about their academic identity and secondly, closely connected with this, by the fact that male staff and peers may be less supportive because they are continuing to emphasize these women's gender identity and have not yet legitimated their academic identity. Women will only be able successfully to pursue graduate careers if, first, there is a change in the definition of an academic identity which allows for female experiences as well as male, and if, secondly, staff and male peers in universities accept that the gender identity of women allows for considerable variation. The traditional feminine wife and mother is only one of the available women's models, a committed career woman is another, and between these exist many patterns for women to develop for themselves. What is required is for universities to legitimate a woman's adoption of an academic-gender identity of 'woman PhD candidate', which neither questions her commitment to a graduate career nor negates her identity as a woman.

Academic or Subject Identity?

It has been argued that for the majority of the respondents their academic identity seemed more salient than their gender identity, although some were experiencing problems as they were still negotiating the legitimation of this transformation. In this context 'academic' is being used very generally to refer to a commitment to their PhD studies. However, it is recognized that there are differences between disciplines, even if these are not so strong as to entail 'two cultures' (Snow 1951) so that being a PhD candidate in a science department may involve a different experience to being a PhD candidate in the humanities. This may, however, be mediated by gender. Indeed it remains common currency that gender is an important determinant of work orientation and ambition. At the undergraduate level the available evidence suggests this association remains valid. For example Williams et al. (1974) quote the research on the academic aspirations of second-year university students at Manchester and Edinburgh (Jones et al. 1971), and in particular the decisions to study for a PhD where the effect of gender was large: notably larger than the effect of subject. By the graduate level it would appear the effect of gender declines; women students become less distinguishable from men in commitments to their studies, career orientation and ambition. In conjunction with this shift the effect of subject as a distinguishing characteristic increases. Feldman (1973, p.74) argues from his research on American graduates that 'in general, the data suggest that, although attitudes vary by sex, women and men within a given academic discipline are quite similar. Women in chemistry resemble their male colleagues more than they resemble women in French.' It was beyond the scope of this study to compare these women PhD candidates with their male peers. On the other hand considerable differences between the respondents from the various faculties were noted in terms of their graduate experiences and aspirations. These would suggest that although, as argued, an academic identity was more salient among most of the respondents than gender, academic identity might be further differentiated by subject.

The experience of being a woman PhD candidate in a science department differed in several ways from the same experience in arts or social science. Part of this arises from the differences in the type of departments in the various faculties. Particularly the larger departments with big graduate schools were more likely to be found in the science faculties. But the experience the scientists had acquired before they started their studies for the PhD differed from that of their peers in humanities. Fewer scientists had registered for a Masters degree so that the PhD was their first postgraduate experience. They were less likely to have any employment experience or to be employed whilst studying for the PhD. Only a minority had had any time off from their education, being instead continuous students. The scientists were less likely to be employed in their department as lecturers, teaching assistants and research staff or to mix socially with staff either in work or leisure time in the university. Instead they were most likely to have a student reference group, mixing predominantly with male students from their own department. Their experience of studying for a PhD was therefore most likely to be as a full-time student. Few were doing a PhD for vocational reasons but instead had either a scholarly orientation or had drifted on to a PhD. More were undecided about their future careers and tended to consider a wider range of possibilities than their peers in humanities. Many scientists were very conscious that women were at a disadvantage in academic life and felt they encountered social disapproval. They were especially positive that increasing the proportion of PhD candidates who were women would improve their experience in the university.

The arts candidates in contrast were the least likely to be having a 'student experience' during their studies. They were more likely to be studying part time for the PhD. All were employed during their period of registration for the PhD and most had some previous employment experience. Indeed over two-fifths were members of the teaching staff of their department. Three-quarters of the women registered for a PhD in the arts faculty were the only women PhD candidates in their department so these respondents had the experience of being a novelty and were particularly conscious of the significance of gender, feeling that 'being a woman' was a barrier to social interaction in the university. Nevertheless, they were more likely to have women as regular work-time contacts. But outside work time they seemed the least socially integrated into academic life. Although they all had a scholarly orientation to their studies they had moved away from an interest in an academic career during their PhD registration. Whilst undergraduates they had also been interested in the more traditionally female careers but in contrast some were now more interested in careers such as industrial management. At the same time they felt that the domestic responsibilities of women placed them at a disadvantage, compared with men, in participating fully in university life. The arts respondents thus appeared to find their experience in studying for a PhD difficult and despite their scholarly interests and greater experience of university teaching did not see their future in academic life.

The social scientists were similar to the arts PhDs in terms of their prior experience; equally having had periods of time off, and most of them also having had some employment experience both before and during PhD registration. But their experiences whilst registered for a PhD seemed much easier than those of the arts respondents. Particularly they seemed the most integrated into academic life. They had a staff reference group and spent both their work and leisure time in the university with male staff. Although they were the least likely to be the only woman registered for a PhD in their department, none had women as regular contacts either during or outside work time. Their interest in an academic career had increased during the time they had spent studying at university. On the whole they seemed the best assimilated as PhD candidates. Either female status was less problematic in the social science faculties or these respondents were particularly adept at coping with it.

Overall, it appeared that the transformation from a gender identity to an academic identity had been successfully accomplished for the social scientists. The scientists were still experiencing conflict in negotiating the process. Their self-concepts were academic but their gender remained sufficiently salient to significant others that the transformation to an academic identity had not yet been successfully accomplished. The arts candidates seemed to have had particularly negative experiences so that, although at the onset of their studies their self-concepts were academic, their gender identity still appeared more salient both to themselves and to significant others.

In conclusion, becoming a PhD candidate and negotiating an academic identity was an easier process for these women respondents to accomplish in some disciplines than in others. Gender status was differentially experienced, making a shift from gender identity to academic identity a more complicated process in certain subjects. However, the information available is insufficient to suggest that subject identity was more salient than academic identity. But subject is a differentiating characteristic. More research is necessary to assess whether this arises because of the nature of the discipline, or of the social patterns and relationships peculiar to particular faculties or departments. Or, on the other hand, whether it was more a reflection of differences in the type of women candidate recruited to particular disciplines and the ability they have to adapt and be accepted or assimilated.

Conclusion

It has been argued that women PhD candidates approximate to 'men's models' (Ardener 1978) in terms of qualifications and study and career orientations, but differ from them in terms of their greater employment experience, more discontinuous educational careers and less grant aid. Thus their ambitions are more similar to those of men of similar status (Rudd 1975) than to those of women educated to a graduate level (Kelsall et al. 1970, 1972). The respondents appeared to be integrated into the formal academic and social life of their department centring on work in the sense of having regular contacts, but this did not extend into the more informal interaction of leisure time in the university, when half became isolated. It is suggested that the differences found in the careers of these women PhD candidates, when compared with the data on men, may arise because of a continued emphasis on their gender identity rather than a legitimation of their academic identity. Further, gender status is differentially experienced, making the transformation of a gender identity to an academic identity a more complicated process in certain subjects. Approximating 'men's models' and thus eventually 'belonging to the club' is easier for women to achieve in some academic situations than in others.

Future research on the experience of women in higher education needs to continue to focus on aspects of sponsorship, peer-group membership and professional socialization, on formal and informal 'belonging' in comparison with the experiences of men. But this is a particularly difficult area to research for two reasons. First, these experiential factors are perhaps best explored interactionally and it is difficult for one person to undertake participant observation in a large number of departments spread over a wide range of disciplines. For example, the attempt at participant observation in this study was particularly unsuccessful among the scientists. Secondly, making comparisons between men and women is difficult when there are so few women; there is very often only one woman PhD candidate in a department, but several men. The situation is similar among academic staff. There are more women students at earlier stages of higher education and an alternative would be to concentrate research here. One possibility is an action research programme to support and encourage women to continue their studies. This could concentrate on the final undergraduate year or an early stage of the postgraduate career. Cartter (1976) has argued that affirmative action in America has now brought American women PhDs equality at the point of entry to a profession. Further research on the differential experience of being a graduate student in different disciplines is also required. It was found in this study that the experience of being a woman PhD candidate in a science faculty differed in various ways from the experience of women studying in the arts or social science faculties. Why is this so? In particular, are such patterns replicated for the male PhD candidate? Much more research on the interaction patterns in universities is needed before we can begin to answer these questions.

Notes

1   The data were collected by questionnaire sent to all women registered for a PhD at the university in 1972, and by a small number of interviews and some participant observation to check responses and clarify and explore further issues. The response rate was 67%. The 55 respondents were comparable with all the women registered for a PhD at the university with the exceptions that they were rather more likely to be married and were overall rather younger.

2   Although the focus of the research was on women PhD candidates it was obviously important to make some comparisons with men, and male comparison groups were used. First, the university Registrar's records contained data (eg age, faculty, marital status, full-time or part-time, finance, nationality) on all men and women PhD candidates then registered. Some aspects of their university experience could thus be compared by analysing the data. Secondly, questions used by Rudd and Hatch (1968) and Kelsall (1970, 1972) in their studies of postgraduates were included in the questionnaire in this present study of women PhD candidates so that results could be compared with their findings.

3   Rudd's (1975) sample comprised 85% men. He does not divide his data by sex when discussing employment. He found only 17% of research students had been in employment (p.40) between first degree and graduate study compared with 44% of these women PhD candidates. Moreover, 64% of these women PhD candidates had been employed at some time whether prior to going to university or during some interval in their postgraduate career. As far as can be ascertained from Rudd's data (1975, Table 3.9, p.36) the difference between the faculty distribution of his sample and these women PhD candidates (Taylorson 1980, Table 4.3, p.123) was sufficiently small for it to be unlikely that the differential employment histories result from faculty affiliation and not from sex. Further, the proportions of these women PhD candidates in each faculty with some employment experience were much higher in each case than in Rudd's sample (1975, p.40), eg 86% of social scientists compared with Rudd's 26%, and 50% of scientists and technologists compared with Rudd's 8% of scientists and 25% of applied scientists. For further details and discussion of the sample see Taylorson 1980, Ch.4.

4   42% of these women PhD candidates had had discontinuities in their university education compared with 26% of Rudd's (1975, p.40) sample of research students.

5   This is not to suggest that they ceased to be women but rather that they were moving away from traditional conceptions of woman-hood or femininity.

References

Acker,S.S. (1978) *Sex Differences in Graduate Student Ambition* Summary of unpublished PhD thesis, University of Chicago. Available from School of Education, University of Bristol

Ardener,S. (Ed.) Introduction: the nature of women in society. In *Defining Females: The Nature of Women in Society* London: Croom Helm, in association with the Oxford University Women's Studies Committee, pp.9-48

Astin,H.S. (1969) *The Woman Doctorate in America* New York: Russell Sage Foundation

Bardwick,J.M. (1971) *Psychology of Women* New York: Harper and Row

Becker,H.S. and Strauss,A. (1970) Career, personality and adult socialisation. In Becker,H.S. (Ed.) (1970) *Sociological Work* Chicago: Aldine. Reprinted from *AJS* 62 (Nov) 253-63 (1956)

Bernard,J. (1964) *Academic Women* University Park, Pennsylvania: Pennsylvania State University Press

Bernard,J. (1975) Adolescence and socialisation for motherhood. In Dragastin,S.E. and Elder,G.H. (Eds) (1975) *Adolescence in the Life Cycle* New York: Wiley

Carnegie Commission on Higher Education (1973) *Opportunities for Women in Higher Education* New York: McGraw-Hill

Cartter,A.M. (1976) *PhD's and the Academic Labour Market* New York: McGraw-Hill

Centra,J.A. (1974) *Women, Men and the Doctorate* Princeton: Educational Testing Service

Chisholm,L. (1978) The comparative career development of graduate women and men *Women's Studies International Quarterly* 1 (4) 327-340

Chisholm,L. and Woodward,D. (1980) The experiences of women graduates in the labour market. In Deem,R. (Ed.) (1980) *Schooling For Women's Work* London: Routledge and Kegan Paul, pp. 162-176

Darley,S.A. (1976) Big time careers for the little woman: A dual role dilemma *Journal of Social Issues* 32, 85-98

Deem,R. (1978) *Women and Schooling* London: Routledge and Kegan Paul

Edgell,S. (1980) *Middle Class Couples: A Study of Segregation, Domination and Inequality in Marriage* London: George Allen and Unwin

Epstein,C.F. (1970) *Women's Place: Options and Limits in Professional Careers* Berkeley: University of California Press

Feldman,S.D. (1973) Impediment or stimulant? Marital status and graduate education. In Huber,J. (Ed.) (1973) *Changing Women in a Changing Society* Chicago: University of Chicago Press

Feldman,S.D. (1974) *Escape from the Doll's House: Women in Graduate and Professional School Education* New York: McGraw-Hill

Fogarty,M., Rapoport,R. and Rapoport,R. (1971a) *Sex, Career and Family* PEP. London: George Allen and Unwin Ltd.

Fogarty,M., Allen,A.J., Allen,I.A., and Walters,P. (1971b) *Women in Top Jobs* PEP. Oxford: George Allen and Unwin Ltd.

Glennerster,H. (1966) *Graduate School* London: Oliver and Boyd

Holmstrom,E.I. and Holmstrom,R.W. (1973) *The Plight of the Woman Doctoral Student* Washington DC: American Council on Education

Holmstrom,E.I. and Holmstrom,R.W. (1974) Plight of the woman doctoral student *American Educational Research Journal* 11 (Winter) 1-17

Holmstrom L.L. (1972) *The Two-Career Family* Cambridge, Massachusetts: Schenkman Publishing Co

Husbands,S.A. (1972) Women's place in higher education *School Review* 80, 261-274

Jones,C.L., McDonald,K.M. and McPherson,A.F. (1971) *Aspirations to Post-graduate Training at Edinburgh and Manchester Universities* Working Paper No 10 from the Student Surveys Section of the Edinburgh-

Manchester Universities Project, Mimeo. Edinburgh: University of Edinburgh

Kando,T.M. (1977) *Social Interaction* St Louis: C.V. Mosby Co.

Kanter,R.M. (1977) *Men and Women of the Corporation* New York: Basic Books

Kelsall,R.K., Poole,A. and Kuhn,A. (1970) *Six Years After: First Report on a National Follow-up of Ten Thousand Graduates of British Universities in 1960* Dept. of Sociological Studies, Sheffield University: Higher Education Research Unit

Kelsall,R.K., Poole,A. and Kuhn,A. (1972) *Graduates: The Sociology of an Elite* London: Methuen and Co.

Myrdal,A. and Klein,V. (1968) *Women's Two Roles: Home and Work* 2nd Edition. London: Routledge and Kegan Paul

Maccoby,E.E. and Jacklin,C.N. (1975) *The Psychology of Sex Differences* London: Oxford University Press. Previously published by Stanford University Press, California (1974)

Rossi,A.S. (1973) Summary and prospects. In Rossi,A.S. and Calderwood, A. (Eds) (1973) *Academic Women on the Move* New York: Russell-Sage Foundation, pp.505-529

Rudd,E. in association with Simpson,R. (1975) *The Highest Education: A Study of Graduate Education in Britain* London: Routledge and Kegan Paul

Rudd,E. and Hatch,S. (1968) *Graduate Study and After* London: Weidenfeld and Nicholson

Schwartz,P. and Lever,J. (1973) Women in the male world of higher education. In Rossi,A. and Calderwood,A. (Eds) (1973) *Academic Women on the Move* New York: Russell-Sage Foundation

Simon,R.J., Clark,S.M. and Galway,K. (1967) The woman PhD – a recent profile *Social Problems* 15 (2) 221-36

Smith,D. (1978) A peculiar eclipsing: women's exclusion from man's culture *Women's Studies International Quarterly* 1, 281-295

Snow,C.P. (1951) *The Two Cultures and the Scientific Revolution* Cambridge: Cambridge University Press

Sommerkorn,I. (1967) *The Position of Women in the University Teaching Profession in England* Unpublished PhD thesis, University of London

Solmon,L.C. (1976) *Male and Female Graduate Students: The Question of Equal Opportunity* New York: Praeger Publishers

Strauss,A. (1962) Transformation of identity. In Rose,A.M. (Ed.) (1962) *Human Behaviour and Social Processes* London: Routledge and Kegan Paul

Taylorson,D.E. (1980) *Highly Educated Women: A Sociological Study of Women PhD Candidates* Unpublished PhD thesis, University of Manchester

Webb,D. (1977) *Women in Sociology* Paper read to British Sociological

Association, Sexual Divisions Study Group, University of Sheffield (April)

Whitehead,A. (1976) Sexual antagonism in Hertfordshire. In Barker,D. and Allen,S. (1976) (Eds) *Dependence and Exploitation in Work and Marriage* London: Longman, pp.169-203

Williams,G., Blackstone,T. and Metcalfe,D. (1974) *The Academic Labour Market: Economic and Social Aspects of a Profession* London: Elsevier

Williamson,P. (1979) Moving around in the room at the top *Dept. of Employment Gazette* 187 (2) 1220-8

Woodward,D. (1974) *The Implications of Sex for the Life Styles of Graduates* Paper presented to the British Sociological Association Annual Conference (April)

9 Women academics in the seventies

Margherita Rendel

At a time of cuts and threatened redundancies, why should the promotion prospects of academic women in universities matter? Academic women, it is said, are an élite. There are many reasons why this simplistic view is inadequate. First of all, among academics, women are not an élite; many of them are doing the most work for the lowest pay with the least security under the worst conditions and subject to close scrutiny. Women are, in disproportionate numbers, the proles of the academic profession. Secondly, it must always be a matter of concern that groups should be fairly and justly treated. Furthermore, universities and their academic staff directly and indirectly perform licensing and gate-keeping functions throughout the educational system, and greatly influence what constitutes knowledge and the ideological machinery of the state and the society.[1]

What opportunity have women had to share in these activities? At what levels and in what subjects have women been located in universities? In 'How many women academics?' (1980), I found that the proportion of academics who were women had risen to about 10% by 1921 while the proportion of women holding senior posts had risen to about 5% by 1930, after which dates neither proportion appeared to increase. I also found, not surprisingly, that women were concentrated in relatively few subjects: education, French, English, botany, chemistry, history and, by 1951, mathematics. Between 1912 and 1951 the proportional distribution of women changed and women appear to have entered a wider range of subject-departments suggesting strongly that their representation in any one subject decreased. Here I am exploring what happened to women in the 1970s.

The number of both men and women academics employed full-time in universities increased between 1972 and 1979[2], as did the proportion of women academics, but there are big differences between the sexes in the grades and subjects in which the increases occurred, that is to say there is vertical and horizontal segregation. Hakim (1979, p.19) defined these terms as follows:

'Horizontal segregation exists when men and women are most commonly working in different types of occupation. Vertical occupational segregation exists when men are most commonly working in higher grade occupations and women are most commonly working in lower grade occupations, or vice versa.'

Writers on women's employment have commented on the extent of both vertical and horizontal occupational segregation in this country and abroad (eg Routh 1965; Barron and Norris 1976; Blaxall and Reagan 1976; Hakim 1979; Willms 1982). American writers (eg Bernard 1964; Carnegie 1973; Feldman 1974; Sandler 1973) have shown its prevalence in American higher education. In what ways does such segregation show itself in British universities? A few studies have demonstrated its existence (Blackstone and Fulton 1974, 1975, 1976; British Sociological Association 1975; Lovenduski 1981). My earlier work suggested that horizontal segregation was diminishing as women obtained posts in a wider range of subjects, but that vertical segregation (between grades) was untouched. My examination of the Universities Statistical Record (USR) data for the years 1972-1979[3] suggests that both vertical and horizontal segregation are increasing.

The Grades of Women and Men

I look first at the grades of women and men, beginning with the representation of women in different grades and the distribution of women between grades. Representation means how many women are in a grade and what proportion they form of it. Distribution means how many of the women are in a grade and what proportion of the women hold that grade. It will be seen from Table 9.1 that between 1972 and 1979 the representation of women among the professoriat increased very substantially from 61 to 105 women (1.8% to 2.7%) but the distribution of women between the professoriat and other grades scarcely increased, from 1.6% to 1.9%. In contrast the distribution of women in the reader, senior lecturer and lecturer grades declined, with the result that the proportion of women holding senior posts has declined from 11.9% to 10.4%. The proportion of 'others and not known' comprising 5.8% of all staff in 1972 and only 8.6% in 1979 accounts for 38% of the proportionate increase in the number of posts held by women.

Table 9.1   Number and percentage representation and distribution of women in each grade 1972-1979

	1972			1979		
	No.	%	%	No.	%	%
PROFESSORS						
Representation	61		1.8	105		2.7
Distribution		1.6			1.9	
READERS, SENIOR LECTURERS						
Representation	382		6.3	468		5.8
Distribution		10.3			8.5	
LECTURERS						
Representation	2729		12.1	3698		15.0
Distribution		73.8			67.4	
OTHERS[3], NOT KNOWN						
Representation	528		26.8	1216		35.3
Distribution		14.3			22.2	
ALL GRADES	3700		10.9	5487		13.7
		100.0			100.0	

Source Derived from data from the Universities Statistical Record, Cheltenham.

The developments can be summarized as follows: whereas by 1979 there were forty-four more women professors than in 1972, there were proportionately fewer women readers, senior lecturers or lecturers and far more women paid on scales the minima of which are below that of the lecturer scale.

Table 9.2 is directly concerned with comparisons between men and women[4] and in particular with vertical segregation. It shows the number of men and women observed in each grade in each year, the number of women who would have been expected in each grade in each year had they been distributed between the grades in the same proportions as the men were, and the ratio of the number observed to the number expected. The closer the ratio is to 1.0, the closer women are to being distributed between grades in the same proportion as men. Table 9.2 shows more clearly than Table 9.1 the segregation of women in the lowest ranks of the profession. Only in the lecturer grade is the ratio near 1.0. There are nearly three and a half times as many women in the lowest grade, 'other', which is below the basic grade of the profession. For readers and senior lecturers, the ratio worsens quite sizeably. The increase in the number of women professors from 61 to 105 looks

Table 9.2 Ratio of vertical segregation; number and proportion of men, and observed expected number of women, in each grade

	1972			1979		
	No.	%	Ratio	No.	%	Ratio
ALL GRADES						
Total men	30168			34500		
Total women	3700			5487		
PROFESSORS						
No. of men	3297			3745		
% of all men		10.9			10.9	
Women observed	61			105		
Women expected	403			598		
Women observed/ women expected			0.15			0.18
READERS, SNR						
No. of men	5638			7621		
% of all men		18.7			22.1	
Women observed	382			468		
Women expected	692			1213		
Women observed/ women expected			0.55			0.39
LECTURERS						
No. of men	19788			20904		
% of all men		65.6			60.6	
Women observed	2729			3698		
Women expected	2427			3325		
Women observed/ women expected			1.12			1.11
OTHERS, NOT KNOWN						
No. of men	1445			2230		
% of all men		4.8			6.5	
Women observed	528			1216		
Women expected	178			357		
Women observed/ women expected			2.97			3.41

Note 'Women expected' = no. of women who would hold the rank if women held it in the same proportion as men. No increase is involved in the total number or proportion of women.

Source Derived from data from the Universities Statistical Record, Cheltenham.

gratifying until it is set against the 598 there would be if the small number of women in academic jobs held professorships in the same proportion as the men. There would be nearly 600 women professors if 10.9% of women, like 10.9% of men, held chairs.

The decline in the proportion of women readers and senior lecturers is especially serious as it casts doubt on whether the increase in the number and proportion of women professors will be maintained. No doubt a number of individuals move from lectureships directly to chairs, but the vast majority do not. Table 9.2 also makes clear that the decline in the proportion of women readers and senior lecturers cannot be accounted for by a shortage of posts as the proportion of men readers and senior lecturers has increased markedly, and this increase accounts for more than half the decline in the proportion of men lecturers.

It is sometimes suggested that the decline from 1972 to 1979 in the proportion of senior lectureships and readerships held by women can be accounted for by women dropping out of the academic profession for marriage or childbearing in the 1950s and 1960s. When the ages of men and women in the lecturer grade in 1972 are examined, it is clear that drop-out for marriage is an insufficient explanation. This conclusion can be reached in the following way. First, what is the 'pool' for promotion? In 1972 only 5.2% of all readers and senior lecturers were under 35; by 1979 only 2.2% were. Most people over 54 in 1972 would probably have left the profession by 1979. In 1972, 37.8% of the men and 37.3% of the women fell within the age-range 35-54. This suggests that equal proportions of men and women were available for promotion. Why then were women less likely to be promoted? Salary data in 1972 show that proportionately more men (49.6%) than women (35.3%) were on the upper half of the lecturer salary scale.[5] If position on the salary scale can be taken as a rough indicator of seniority and experience[6], the argument can be made that in 1972 fewer women were in the ideal position to be considered for promotion, ie near the top of the scale, and 'marriage' need not enter into the discussion. However, some might question why women in 1972 were more likely to be in the bottom half of the scale. While this situation could have resulted from some women having been out of academic employment for child-rearing, it might equally and perhaps more plausibly result from women having had greater difficulty than men in obtaining academic employment and then having been placed at a lower starting point on the salary scale than their experience and qualifications might have warranted.

The Subjects of Women and Men

The data I compiled for 'How many women academics?' showed that the subject groups (eg education, medicine, science)[7] used by the UGC masked important differences within as well as between groups. In the present study I have examined the data for the seventy-four individual subjects used by the UGC. I divided them into five groups, according to the total number of academic staff and the number and proportion of women in the subject.

The seventy-four subjects ranged in size from mathematics, with about 2500 staff altogether, to surveying, which in 1972 had only five staff. Some subjects decreased sharply during the period, for example physiology from 299 to 80, while others increased, for example clinical medicine from 1210 to 2082. The decline in physiology may reflect a change in classification. As the distribution of women and men in subjects differed and the changes in them usually affected the sexes differently, I did not attempt to combine subjects to eliminate the small ones. Nor have I attempted to examine the definitions of the subjects themselves.

I divided the subjects into five groups:

i   Subjects with 'very large' numbers of women: ie twice the average number of women per subject in both 1972 and 1979 (11 subjects).
ii   Subjects with large numbers of women: ie above the average in both 1972 and 1979 (10 subjects).
iii Medium subjects: ie subjects which had less than the average number of women, but which had at least half the average number of women either in 1972 or 1979 or in both years (19 subjects).
iv   Small subjects: ie those with fewer than half the average number of women in both 1972 and 1979 (21 subjects).
v   Very small subjects: ie those which never had as many as 101 total staff (men and women) at any time and which had ten or fewer women in both 1972 and 1979; to which subjects I added aeronautical engineering which never had more than 117 staff or more than two women (13 subjects).

To arrive at this classification and to analyse the data, I compiled time series for each grade and for all staff while also ranking the subjects by size for women and for all staff for 1972 and 1979. The Appendix lists the subjects in each of the five groups (pp.177–78).

Women were present in all except one subject in 1979 as opposed to all except three in 1972. The median number of women in the very small subjects was two in 1972 and five in 1979. In half the small subjects women increased their representation considerably, sometimes more than doubling or trebling their numbers, but the median number was only nine in 1972 and rose to eighteen in 1979. This group of subjects includes nearly all the engineering subjects, a number of vocational subjects and a few of the smaller arts subjects.

In the nineteen medium-sized subjects, the median number of women rose from thirty-five to forty-one, but there were more than seventy women in three of these subjects. The proportionate increase was largest in some of the subjects which were smallest in 1972; examples are town and country planning, and other professional and vocational. In five subjects (Russian, Hispanic, social anthropology, other social studies, and physiology) the number and proportion of women declined, although the number of men increased marginally in four of them. As none of the five was particularly small, the decrease in the proportion of women cannot be adequately explained by the departure of individuals. The number of women increased most in government and public administration, adult education and veterinary science, which are relatively large members of this group.

In the ten large subjects the average number of women increased from 73 to 106 and fell in only one subject. But the number of women in law increased one and a half times and in biochemistry nearly doubled. Whereas the increases in other subjects lay between 8.2% (German) and 45.3% (chemistry). All these subjects, with the exception of other medical and health, have large numbers of staff.

All the very large subjects are among the eighteen largest subjects both for women and for all staff, with the exception of French, which decreased slightly between 1972 and 1979. Where the men are, the women are also, even if in only small proportions. In mathematics and chemistry, two of the largest subjects for both men and women, the proportions of women were only 6.3% and 5.9% respectively in 1979.

In these very large subjects, the average number of women increased from 185 to 281, but the median number dropped from 196 to 193. This is because the number of women in clinical medicine more than doubled, from 319 to 744. Whereas in no other subject was the increase anything like as large: in biology the number of women increased from 101 to 176, in pre-clinical medicine from 214 to 363, in education from 205 to 316 and in sociology from 279 to 404. In French and in mathematics the number and proportion of women remained virtually unchanged.

The examination of the data so far confirms an increase in vertical segregation and suggests an increase in horizontal segregation. The changes in the distribution of women between subjects are, however, quite complex. Women are becoming more numerous, especially in professional and vocational subjects, some, but not all, of which are increasing in size, but they are tending to become relatively less numerous in languages, traditionally a subject-group with relatively large numbers of women.

The Grades of Women in Ten Selected Subjects

Before seeking explanations of the changes in the numbers of women in particular subjects, it is necessary to discover in which grades in which subjects these changes are occurring. That information will help to show whether or not women are obtaining access to a wider range of academic posts.

A disproportionate increase in the number of women below the lecturer grade, that is of research assistants, junior research officers and demonstrators, has implications very different from an increase in the number of women in senior grades or even in the lecturer grade. Even quite a small increase in the number of women professors can greatly influence the shape of a subject and the contribution that women can make to it; but it is extraordinarily difficult, if not impossible, for individuals in purely token numbers to exercise any influence at all.[8] Senior staff are able to exercise an influence not only on the shape of the subject, but also on research, publications and appointments[9] not only in their own institutions but also through the professional associations, and in other institutions through their work as external examiners, referees and assessors. For all these reasons it is important to analyse the grades of women in particular subjects.

Ten subjects have been selected for detailed examination: education, clinical medicine, biology, biochemistry, mathematics, chemistry, law, sociology, French and history (Table 9.3). In these subjects the fortunes of women and men have varied. The subjects selected include both those that have increased in size, and those that have not, and a range of vocational, science, social science and arts subjects.

In the sciences and law, women have made virtually no gains in chairs. In contrast, they held eighteen chairs in sociology (which includes social administration and social history) in 1979 compared with seven in 1972. In the other subjects the gains have been much smaller, ranging between three and five. The extent to which women are disadvantaged is evidenced by the fact that a gain of between three and five can be described as a gain at all. Even in sociology, only 4.5% of the women hold chairs compared with 10.8% of the men.

Only in chemistry did both the representation and distribution of women among readers and senior lecturers increase between 1972 and 1979 – and this is the only one of the ten subjects with no woman professor in 1979. As regards all senior staff, it is the only subject in which the ratio of vertical segregation for senior staff improved between 1972 and 1979 and then only from 0.21 to 0.24; the number of women readers and senior lecturers rose only from five to twelve forming 2.0% of all readers and senior lecturers in 1979. In law, however, the representation of women improved at every level although the ratio did not. The ratio declined most in biochemistry, sociology, history and education. Table 9.3 shows the details.

In the lecturer grade, the representation of women has increased in nine subjects (mathematics being the exception), usually by about 2% to

Table 9.3 Ratio of vertical segregation: selected subjects: 1972 and 1979

	Education		Clinical medicine		Biology		Bio-chemistry		Mathematics	
	1972	1979	1972	1979	1972	1979	1972	1979	1972	1979
No. of men senior staff	294	419	247	360	190	261	158	171	664	782
% of men senior staff	28.9%	31.2%	25.2%	24.0%	26.8%	27.8%	26.1%	32.6%	28.6%	31.9%
No. of women professors	1	5	–	5	–	2	–	1	1	2
No. of women readers & senior lecturers	26	31	23	34	8	11	8	5	19	18
No. of women senior staff expected	59	99	80	179	27	49	17	42	47	51
Ratio of women senior staff observed/expected	0.46	0.36	0.29	0.22	0.30	0.27	0.47	0.14	0.43	0.39

	Chemistry		Law		Sociology		French		History	
	1972	1979	1972	1979	1972	1979	1972	1979	1972	1979
No. of men senior staff	641	816	186	260	223	367	173	204	352	448
% of men senior staff	29.2%	36.4%	32.2%	33.3%	23.2%	30.4	28.6%	35.0%	34.4%	41.1%
No. of women professors	1	–	1	3	7	18	3	6	3	7
No. of women readers & senior lecturers	5	12	6	13	33	40	29	29	23	28
No. of women senior staff expected	28	50	20	54	65	123	56	68	42	68
Ratio of women senior staff observed/expected	0.21	0.24	0.35	0.34	0.62	0.47	0.57	0.51	0.62	0.51

Source Derived from data from the Universities Statistical Record, Cheltenham.

4%, but by about 10% in biochemistry and law. The proportion of women holding lectureships increased slightly in education and French, and remained virtually the same in mathematics and law. In all other subjects, but especially in clinical medicine, biology and biochemistry, the increase in the number and proportion of women in the lowest grades is reflected in a decrease in the lecturer grade.

Clinical medicine, biochemistry and biology have a high proportion of staff (both men and women) in the lowest grade (26.0%, 21.7% and 18.4% respectively in 1979).[10] In clinical medicine and in biochemistry the proportion of women in this grade increased and stood at 57.6% and 40.6% respectively in 1979. More than half of the total increase in the number of women in clinical medicine occurred in this lowest grade. The number of women in the other grades increased also, by about one half in biology and biochemistry, and by about 26% in clinical medicine.

Women's Promotion Chances

In general, the proportion of senior posts and the proportion of men and women holding them were remarkably stable over the eight-year period. However, the likelihood of a woman holding a senior post varies a great deal according to subject and the variation is far greater than for men. The number of women in senior posts as a proportion of all teaching posts (here defined as lecturer and above) ranged from 22.7% in history to 8.2% in biochemistry in 1979. In 1972, the proportions had been 22.2% and 16.3% respectively; in that year, women were worst off in chemistry (8.1%). For men, the range is between 39.0% (history) and 23.4% (clinical medicine) in 1979 and 33.5% (history) and 22.0% (sociology) in 1972. Nor can an absolute shortage of women explain the discrepancies. Women did much better in biochemistry in 1972 when there were fewer women lecturers, forty-one instead of sixty-seven as in 1979, and more men lecturers, 417 instead of 327. It is clear from the data that in subjects of the size of these ten subjects, promotion chances cannot be explained in terms of the number and proportion of women. It would also seem to be the case that many universities could rectify the under-promotion of women and increase the number of senior posts within the permitted 40:60 senior:junior ratio.[11] The present cuts and the contraction of universities will make it more difficult to improve the position of women.

The Equal Pay and Sex Discrimination Act

Attempts have been made to use the Equal Pay Act and Sex Discrimina-

tion Act to remedy individual grievances. There have been some half
dozen cases. Nearly every woman academic who has brought a case
against a university has lost.[12] It would be quite wrong to conclude from
this record of apparent failure, which parallels the experience of the US,
that women have made no gains as a result of this litigation. Anecdotal
evidence suggests that several women in institutions which have been
sued, as well as the women who themselves brought cases, were better off
in the end. Promotions and pay rises for women in both categories have
followed fairly quickly (within one or two years) upon the litigation and
after the consequences of it had been settled. At the very least
consciousness was raised. Some of the improvements almost certainly
could not have taken place without the crisis created by the litigation. For
the individual, the crisis is the culmination of a process of attempting to
get a grievance about pay or promotion[13] righted or even seriously
attended to. In some of the cases, litigation was perceived as the only
means of getting a grievance even listened to. While the litigation is
traumatic for the university as well as the woman, the crisis compels the
institution to examine and re-consider policies and actions which have
been taken for granted and to take actions and establish procedures
which are fairer both to women and to all staff. Such developments can
vindicate staff who had been seeking open criteria and fairer procedures
for deciding pay and promotion.

It is quite impossible to assess the effect of such cases on other
universities. Although many senior staff probably think that such things
cannot happen to them, joint decision-making and participation by
committees provides opportunities for the expression of less complacent
views, so that rather more care would be taken now than in the past. The
problem, especially now, is to maintain even this slightly higher
standard, to make things stay changed. Old habits tend to re-assert
themselves.

Equal opportunity legislation and the campaign for it in this country,
as in the United States (Carnegie 1973), has legitimized and supported
women's academic pressure groups and their activities on behalf of
women's careers and the development of their disciplines.[14]

Conclusions

We should, until the contrary is proved, assume that universities recruit
able, promotable women in the same proportion as they recruit able,
promotable men; that is, that they do not seek out worthy, hardworking,
ordinarily competent women whose function it will be to do all the work
no one else wants to do and who, because of their own limitations, will
not be suitable for promotion.

In the 1970s the increases have been in the lecturer and lower grades apart from the few cases where individuals have obtained chairs. During this period, there have been demands for greater equality for women, and the Sex Discrimination Act has been passed. It seems possible that university appointments and promotions committees have responded to these pressures by appointing more women in the lower grades where, as I have shown, they make the most impact on proportions and the least on power and policy, and a very few to chairs, where they are prominent but will as a result of their small numbers have difficulty in being as effective as many would wish them to be in securing equality for women and the conditions that make equal opportunity meaningful.

It is possible to discuss only briefly the trends in the distribution of women between subjects. Patterson (1973) and Blackstone and Fulton (1974) suggest that women are more likely to be found in the less prestigious subjects. The data I have examined does not entirely bear this out. There are in any case problems of definition. One is the difference between the representation of women and the distribution of women. As I showed in 'How many women academics?' despite the very small representation of women in sciences there was also a quite substantial distribution of women in sciences. Secondly, we have no data for the distribution of women within branches of subjects.[15] Nor do we know which are most generally thought to be the prestigious subjects and for what reasons.[16]

Blackstone and Fulton (1974, p.137) thought that the subjects in which women were better represented might be those with a small proportion of senior posts. The data as shown in Table 9.3 does not support this hypothesis. In both 1972 and 1979, of the ten subjects history had the largest proportion of senior posts and a relatively good proportion of women in senior posts.[17]

Blackstone and Fulton (1974), in speculating on the effect of the Women's Liberation Movement, thought that increases in the numbers of women engineers and business executives were not very likely because of the potential conflict between the radicalism of the Women's Movement and the masculine and conservative image of these subjects. In fact, as we have seen, women's participation in these subjects has grown fast and business and management sciences ranks as a 'large' subject in my classification; it is also one in which women's representation has grown relatively fast. Perhaps women resolve the conflict by choosing research and teaching; alternatively they may find more jobs or a less uncongenial environment in university departments than in professional work.

Willms (1981) suggests that the participation of women is likely to be greatest in those industries which are declining, for example textiles, or those which are growing but which need an unskilled labour force. In the academic labour force, women seem to have been losing ground in declining or static subjects. Perhaps it is thought that jobs should go to men when jobs are scarce; with a large number of good candidates for any post, appointments committees probably feel safe in preferring men, other things being equal. In contrast, women have made progress in fast-growing subjects: some of these are long-established subjects with clear entry qualifications, for example law, and others are subjects new to universities with more diffuse entry requirements, for example business and management sciences and, among medium or smaller subjects, town and country planning, other professional and vocational, and home, hotel and institutional.

These conclusions make clear the need, whenever possible, to look behind aggregated figures. Superficially, women appear to have made progress. A more detailed examination reveals the ambiguous nature of the changes that have occurred both in grading and in subjects. Hence gains need to be defended since the continued advancement of a disadvantaged group can never be assumed. The demand for legislation may result from a feeling that gains are not being consolidated or even that they are slipping away. At the very least the expression of such demands and the organization needed to make them effective can reduce losses.

Notes

1 In 'How many women academics?' (1980, pp. 143-144) I set out the arguments for studying women academics.

2 Data for universities (excluding the Open University, which receives its grant directly from the Department of Education and Science and not via the University Grants Committee) are available from the UGC statistics published by the Universities Statistical Record, Cheltenham (USR), are compiled on a consistent basis and refer to broadly similar work throughout all the institutions concerned. The work of the academic staff in polytechnics and other non-university institutions providing higher education is far more disparate than it is in the universities and includes a considerable body of work not found in the universities at all. Also, polytechnics and other institutions of higher education, unlike universities, are subject to the supervision of the CNAA in formulating the curriculum of the degrees for which they teach. I have throughout used data from the USR for full-time staff. Equal Opportunities Commission (1982) gives some data for part-time staff. The first year for which information is available from the USR showing the numbers of men and

women academics separately is 1972. My previous work was based on a count of the names in the Commonwealth Universities Yearbooks. Those data indicate at least an order of magnitude.

3   I am indebted to the Universities Statistical Record (USR) at Cheltenham for the data which show the numbers of men and women in four grades (professors, readers and senior lecturers, lecturers, and others and unknown) in each of seventy-four subjects. Teaching and research staff not appointed as professor, reader, senior lecturer, lecturer or assistant lecturer, but with salaries matching these grades are included irrespective of the title used to describe the post. Staff classified as 'other' include those on scales where the minimum is below the minimum of the lecturer/assistant lecturer scale, eg demonstrators, research assistants. The record includes all full-time teaching and research staff both permanent and temporary. The staff record maintained in the USR was restructured in 1976 so that some staff previously excluded were afterwards included. These seem to have been chiefly very senior technical staff paid on academic scales. Most subjects show no apparent effect resulting from the change.

4   The distribution of men between grades in this table can be compared with that for women in Table 9.1. The representation of men by grade can be deduced simply from the representation of women in Table 9.1.

5   I have counted the upper half of the scale from steps 10 − 17 inclusive, leaving 9 steps in the lower part of the scale.

6   Academic salaries were restructured following the NPBI Enquiry. This showed that there were no fixed salary scales for reader and senior lecturer; consequently, the level of a lecturer's salary was probably less likely to influence promotion to senior lecturer or reader than may be the case now. It is not possible within the scope of this paper to do a full analysis of salaries or of age in relation to subject and grade.

7   There are nine subject-groups altogether: education, medicine, dentistry and health; engineering and technology; agriculture, forestry and veterinary science; science; social, administrative and business studies; architecture and other professional and vocational subjects; language, literature and area studies; arts other than languages.

8   Kanter (1977, Ch.8) discusses the implications of numbers in working relationships and the effect on women managers of being very few in number.

9   Morlock (1973, p.260) suggests that the presence of women faculty tended to be associated with a higher proportion of women doctoral students. Unfortunately Feldman (1974), in his

analysis of relations between students and professors, did not include the sex of the professors as a variable.

10 None of the other subjects examined has more than 7.7% of all staff in this grade.

11 The Government has fixed a maximum ratio of senior posts (professor, reader, senior lecturer) to all teaching staff of 40:60. The figures given in this paragraph may not coincide with the exact senior/junior ratio, which in any case applies to each university and not to subjects, because some research posts may be included and some teaching posts excluded from this particular USR classification, but the data should be accurate enough to give an order of magnitude.

12 But at least two cases have been successful: *Grundy v Keele University*, and *Dicks v Dundee University*.

13 The cases brought have concerned pay and/or promotion, but the Acts apply also to other aspects of work and conditions of service.

14 There is not space here to discuss this aspect of the contribution of equal opportunity legislation to intellectual developments.

15 Patterson (1973, p.330) has made such an analysis for the US.

16 We have no rating comparable to that presented by Feldman (1974).

17 It is clear that many universities do not make senior appointments up to the maximum permitted senior/junior ratio of 40:60. Since some universities do, the figures in Table 9.3 suggest that some are very substantially under the ratio or that senior posts are distributed very unevenly indeed between subjects. A number of senior posts will now be vacant for financial reasons, but that would hardly have been the case in 1972.

Appendix: Subjects Arranged in Groups According to Size

The groups of subjects analysed on pages 168–69 are set out below. They are kept in the order in which they appear in the USR lists so that comparisons may be made between subjects in the same subject-group and sense made of categories beginning with 'Other'.

Very large subjects: education; pre-clinical medicine; clinical medicine; biology; mathematics; economics; psychology; sociology; English; French; history.

Large subjects: other medical and health; botany; zoology; biochemistry; chemistry; business and management sciences; geography; law; German; Code 67: other languages and literature.

Medium subjects: adult education; pharmacology; Code 18: technologies; agriculture; veterinary; physiology; physics; geology; government and public administration; social anthropology; other social studies; town and country planning; other professional and vocational; Hispanic; Code 61: other European languages and literature; Russian; classical; philosophy; art and design.

Small subjects: institutes of education; clinical dentistry; pharmacy; chemical engineering; civil engineering; electrical engineering; mechanical engineering; production engineering; metallurgy; Code 16: other engineering; agricultural biology; Code 30: other biology; environmental; accountancy; architecture; home, hotel and institutional; Oriental, Asian and African languages; archaeology; theology; drama; music.

Very small subjects: pre-clinical dentistry; mining; surveying; agricultural chemistry; forestry; maths/physics; Code 37: other physical sciences; Welsh and Celtic; French/German; Slavonic; Chinese; arts general; aeronautical engineering.

References

Barron,R.D. and Norris,G.M. (1976) Sexual divisions and the dual labour market. In Barker,Diana Leonard and Allen,Sheila (Eds) *Dependence and Exploitation in Work and Marriage* Longmans

Bernard,Jessie (1974) *Academic Women* University Park, Pa: Pennsylvania State University Press

Blackstone,Tessa and Fulton,Oliver (1974) Men and women academics: an Anglo-American comparison of subject choices and research activity *Higher Education* 3, 119-140

Blackstone,Tessa and Fulton,Oliver (1975) Sex discrimination among university teachers: a British-American comparison *British Journal of Sociology* 26 (3) 261-275

Blackstone,Tessa and Fulton,Oliver (1976) Discrimination is the villain *Times Higher Educational Supplement* 9 July

Blaxall,Martha and Reagan,Barbara (1976) *Women and the Workplace: The Implications of Occupational Segregation* Chicago: University of Chicago Press

British Sociological Association (1975) *Report of the Working Party on the Status of Women in the Professions* (Mimeo)

Carnegie Commission (1973) *Opportunities for Women in Higher Education* New Jersey: McGraw-Hill

Equal Opportunities Commission (1982) *Women in Universities: A Statistical Description* Manchester

Feldman,Saul (1974) *Escape from the Doll's House* New Jersey: McGraw-Hill for Carnegie Commission

Hakim,Catherine (1979) *Occupational Segregation* Department of Employment Research Paper No.9. HMSO

Kanter,Rosabeth Moss (1977) *Men and Women of the Corporation* Basic Books: New York

Lovenduski,Joni (1981) *Women in British Political Studies* Studies in Public Policy No.78. Glasgow: Centre for the Study of Public Policy, University of Strathclyde

Morlock,Laura (1973) Discipline variation in the status of academic women. In Rossi and Calderwood (1973) *op.cit.*, pp.255-312

National Board for Prices and Incomes (1968) *Report No.98, Standing Reference on the Pay of University Teachers in Great Britain, First Report* Cmnd 3866

Patterson,Michelle (1973) Sex and specialization in academe and the professions. In Rossi and Calderwood (1973) *op.cit.*, pp.313-331

Rendel,Margherita (1980) How many women academics? In Deem, Rosemary (Ed.) *Schooling for Women's Work* Routledge and Kegan Paul

Rossi,Alice S. and Calderwood,Ann (Eds) (1973) *Academic Women on the Move* New York; Russell-Sage Foundation

Routh,Guy (1965) *Occupation and Pay in Great Britain 1906-60* Cambridge: NIESR CUP

Sandler,Bernice (1973) A little help from our government: WEAL and contract compliance. In Rossi and Calderwood (1973) *op.cit.*, pp.439-462

Willms,Angelika (1981) The socialization of women's work: The case of Germany 1882 – 1979. In Hvidfeldt,K., Jørgensen,K. and Nielsen,R. (Eds) *Strategies for Integrating Women in the Labour Market* European Women's Studies in Social Science, No. 1, Copenhagen, pp.121-144.

10 The double marginalization of women in research

Sue Scott and Mary Porter

'Despite the contribution made by contract researchers to the University, ... (they) are discriminated against when compared with permanent staff. Contract research workers have appalling job security and no proper career structure. Nearly all have had to sign away their rights...under the Employment Protection Act 1978. Is this really the way to treat a group of people who make such an important contribution to university life?'

The above extract from a study carried out in the University of Bristol by an Association of University Teachers Working Party (AUT 1982) describes an explicit and material two-tier system, within which researchers are marginalized in academia. Similarly material is the systematic marginalization of women in academia, such that women researchers are doubly marginalized. From the same report, we find that:

'For example, women are less likely to be paid on scale 1A or above, irrespective of their age and experience. ... Also, women are far less likely to hold senior research posts than men.'

It would seem apparent then, even using solely objective criteria, that women research workers are disadvantaged.

Rather than leaving it at that, however, we want here to open up the complexity of women's position in research, to attempt to discover if there are ways in which the objective facts of women researchers' marginalization may present less than the 'truth'. We want to suggest that women's experience of marginalization within research can both enhance our understanding of how that marginalization is effected and provide information about the ways in which one can contend with and attempt to subvert it. As a beginning, we want to describe some of our own experiences as researchers.

The following descriptions and analysis are based on experiences during the course of a three-year longitudinal study of the context and process of postgraduate education in the social sciences, which was funded by the Social Science Research Council, and on which we were employed as research associates. Our position as researchers based in a sociology department, doing research on the context of postgraduate research in other academic departments, made us particularly vulnerable to critiques of and assumptions about our role from within sociology, but also made us particularly well-placed to understand and comment upon our own positions within research structures. Our understanding of the marginalization of women in sociology, brought out in the data we collected, was reinforced by consciousness of our own marginal position, both within the department in which our research was centred, and in terms of our entry as women researchers into the departments in which our sample of postgraduates was registered.

From the beginning the research was already meshed into the structural marginalization of women academics. It was initiated and funding was secured by a senior male academic. Two women researchers were appointed, one from postgraduate study within the research director's own department, one from a recently completed undergraduate degree elsewhere. Dingwall (1980) has noted that it is the conventional wisdom that women make more empathetic interviewers than men:

'It is quite clear that certain sorts of data are made more readily available to personable young women.'

While we would not argue that we were appointed for this reason, and we felt that our research director employed two women because he is supportive of feminist critiques of women's numerically disadvantaged position in academia, our appointments did fit into the traditional model of male director/female research workers and secretary; and the way in which our research was often viewed by our male colleagues bore this out.

Whilst we were technically on the staff of a sociology department, we felt and were often made to feel that we were in a marginal position, since we could only contribute marginally to what was seen as the main business of the department, teaching. This would not have been the case, of course, if we had been employed within an organization devoted to research. In this we find no argument for the separation of research from academic departments, but the suggestion that an attempt at re-asserting the value of contract research within an academic setting is necessary.

At the very beginning of our research, one of our male colleagues made the 'lighthearted' comment 'haven't you finished yet, you could write that up in ten minutes.' Now different academics obviously have different views about the relative merits of various kinds of research, but we considered that it would be highly unlikely for a male academic to make such a statement in a public place (the college bar) if he had not been addressing his comments to two young women in (for him) a comfortably marginal position. It is true that this kind of joking aside may be common currency in academic settings, but its use in this situation showed a marked lack of understanding both of power relations in general and of the different meanings which may accrete round such a statement in terms of the relative positions of those it is aimed at. The result of the generalized attitude displayed in such statements was that we tended to go along with them and distance ourselves from the research, downgrading what we were doing as not 'proper' academic activity, and attempting to 'prove' our academic respectability by becoming engaged in the type of work which was defined for us as 'respectable'. We undertook several hours teaching per week (for which we received no additional payment), we became involved in other people's research, and we assumed service roles within the department, in an effort to offset with 'credits' the perceived devaluation of our own research efforts.

We noted a circular process in the devaluation of the work we were involved in. First, since 'research' is more often understood by academics to be the angst-laden process of critique, the desperate, 'privatized' search for something new to say for the next book, the kind of research that we were undertaking placed us as 'interviewers' rather than researchers. Interviewing has been down-valued because it is the time-consuming part of research which other people (most often women) are paid to do. Interviewing is a service job and is therefore seen by many men as 'women's work'; after all, establishing rapport is what women are good at. This (perhaps subconscious) reasoning often leads to a generalized denigration of the kind of research which is dependent on interviewing, the consequent reification of 'academic' research and the completion of the circle.

Our own understanding of doing interviews was coloured by this generalized lack of respect for the task. By and large, we enjoyed the interview process, but this enjoyment was tempered by the anxiety that these 'little chats' were not proper work. The quality of the data we collected, however, reinforced our thinking that interviewing is an extremely important and enjoyable aspect of the research process. The importance of interviewing for the qualitative nature of our work often resulted in the methodology itself being called into question. Qualitative methods are seen as being close to what women do 'naturally' and as such are easier to dismiss and harder to defend. We found ourselves frequently being asked for 'numbers' and for 'actual data'. Since we were 'only interviewers' and not 'proper sociologists' it was often assumed that we simply chose the methodology which most closely fitted our own inclinations and abilities, and that we were largely unaware of the theoretical arguments about research which the sociologist seems most concerned with.

The view that interviewing was a menial task was apparent within many of the interviews which we carried out with male academics, and this was often linked to the interviewee's understanding of our position as women. The interview was often seen by men as an opportunity to 'personalize' and thus control the relationship, and this, we believe, mirrors the relationships which develop between women in academic settings and their male 'superiors', whether supervisors or colleagues. We were often patronized by remarks apparently designed to impose a male/female power relationship over the interviewee/interviewer relationship. One male interviewee, when asked if he objected to the interview being taped, said 'Oh dear, that means I won't be able to chat you up'. On the other hand, we often found the devaluation of the interview useful, in that many interviewees, because they did not feel threatened by feelings of responsibility to an academic method, or by the position of the interviewer, felt able to reveal much more in such a 'chat' than we think they would have had they considered the situation to be more formal. This usefulness, however, was not in itself unproblematic; many proponents of qualitative methods have noted that the interview often produces revealing data precisely because the relationship is personalized rather than formal, and that this is enhanced if women are used as interviewers because they are able to construct this informality more easily:

> 'I do not advise an interviewer to adopt views of which he (sic) does not approve. He will do well to remember that a coquette is in a much better position to learn about men than a nun.' (Wax 1971)

This rationale for using women as interviewers can, however, lend itself to the possibility that it will be women who are labelled devious rather than that the method itself constructs informal and information-laden situations. If men were to extract revealing data it would be because they had assumed the role of 'coquette', if women extracted the same data it would be because they were 'coquettes'.

During our visits to academic departments we were often reminded quite forcibly of our lack of status, sometimes through our position as researchers, and sometimes simply as women in an academic setting. Women's lack of status tends to be somewhat hidden if a woman is a member of staff within a department, and has achieved some success. She often becomes one of the boys, or her academic achievement is seen as warranting an explicit admission of equality. When we entered other departments, however, we were not known and our position was unclear. In this way we were able to see the assumption of lack of status which is hidden when achieved status is known. In one department where we had an appointment with a male academic, we went to the departmental secretary to announce our arrival. She asked us to wait since the person in question had gone to lunch. When we stressed that we had an appointment, she said 'you are first-year students aren't you'. At the time this had its element of humour, but on reflection it raised several interesting points. It showed, first, that we had not developed the assurance of status and the ability unquestioningly to suppose that we ourselves were worthy of deference. Partly this was a result of a laudable desire not to 'pull rank', but partly it seemed to result from our own internalization of our marginal position. It also showed that it is not only men who assume the marginal position of women, and that the male domination of the social sciences and academia in general is not just a matter of a few sexist men in positions of power.

This short description of some of our experiences as researchers brings out, we hope, some of the many contradictions inherent in the position. Although the position of women researchers is problematic, we enjoyed doing the research; although we often felt (with some reinforcement) that fieldwork wasn't 'proper' work, we enjoyed doing it and got a lot out of it; although we often tried, by assuming teaching responsibilities, to be seen as 'real' academics, we were loyal to the research and defended it.

One of the most important understandings that we gained from our experiences was that although women researchers are marginalized they are not powerless, only less powerful. In one sense women researchers' power may simply consist of the turning back of marginalization on the more powerful, the use of marginalized positions to gain knowledge which may be used against the more powerful. More importantly, and perhaps less problematically, we found that our own marginalization was not uniform, it was not the same, in quantity or quality, in every situation, and that we were able to control, to an extent, the effects of that marginalization. The structural disadvantages of women researchers are constraints which women can affect, rather than moulds which simply squeeze them into conformity. Women researchers may not be able to break free completely from those constraints but they can and do, at the same time as they struggle to abolish them, work within them. This situation is not new to women; indeed, it is a central fact of many women's lives. The option of ceasing to work within research is always open. But we prefer to think that there is the possibility for women working in structurally marginal positions to influence that marginalization and that the recognition of the compexity of women's marginal positions in research need not result in a paralysis of effective action.

References and Further Reading

As our chapter is a personal reflection rather than a research report we have used few references. But for the reader who wishes further to explore the issues raised, we have added to the references below some suggestions for further reading.

Acker,S. (1977) Sex differences in graduate student ambition: do men publish while women perish? *Sex Roles* 3 (3)

Acker,S. (1980) Women, the other academics *British Journal of Sociology of Education* 1 (1)

AUT Working Party (1982) Contract research survey *University of Bristol Newsletter* 18 March

Bell,C. and Newby H. (Eds) (1977) *Doing Sociological Research* London: George Allen and Unwin

Bernard,J. (1966) *Academic Women* New York: Meridian

Blackstone,T. and Fulton,O. (1975) Sex discrimination amongst university teachers: a British/American comparison *British Journal of Sociology* 26, 261-275

Delphy,C. (1978) *The Main Enemy* London: WRRC

Dingwall,R. (1980) Ethics and ethnography *Sociological Review* 28 (4) 871-891

Eichler,M. (1980) *The Double Standard* London: Croom Helm

Hanmer,J. and Leonard,D. (1980) Men and culture: the sociological intelligentsia and the maintenance of male domination: or superman meets the invisible woman *Transactions of the British Sociological Association*

Mackinnon,C. (1979) *Sexual Harassment of Working Women* New Haven: Yale University Press

Morgan,D. (1981) Men, masculinity and the process of sociological enquiry. In Roberts,H. (Ed.) *Doing Feminist Research* London: Routledge and Kegan Paul

Oakley,A. (1981) Interviewing women: a contradiction in terms. In Roberts,H. (Ed.) *Doing Feminist Research* London: Routledge and Kegan Paul

Smith,D. (1974) Women's perspective: a radical critique of sociology *Sociological Inquiry* 44, 7-13

Smith,D. (1978) A peculiar eclipsing: women's exclusion from man's culture *Women's Studies International Quarterly* 1, 282-295

Spender,D. (1980) *Man Made Language* London: Routledge and Kegan Paul

Stanley,L. and Wise,S. (1979) Feminist research, feminist consciousness and experiences of sexism *Women's Studies International Quarterly* 2 (3)

Wax,R. (1971) Doing fieldwork. Quoted in Dingwall,R. (1980) Ethics and ethnography *Sociological Review* 28 (4) 871-891

Woodward,D. and Chisholm,L. (1981) The experts' view. In Roberts,H. (Ed.) *Doing Feminist Research* London: Routledge and Kegan Paul

Part 4

Points of view

11 How the social science research process discriminates against women

Liz Stanley

Feminists working in the social sciences have addressed a number of important aspects of their operation. One is the position and treatment of women in the social science professions. A second involves the products of the social sciences – how women's lives are conceptualized and presented in theory and research. Closely related to this is a third concern, which is with the social science research process. Work here has focused on an examination of particular 'methods' and on whether and to what extent these are appropriately used by feminists.

Feminist work concerned with sexism in the products of the social sciences has resulted in a critique which is well-developed and massively documented (Barker and Allen 1976a, 1976b; Oakley 1974; Roberts 1976; Millman and Kanter 1975; Spender 1981a). Its reception has included blanket rejection and scorn; but this has perhaps been outweighed by the grudging admission of feminism as an alternative 'perspective', akin to interactionism, marxism and the like.

Feminist work on the research process, in contrast, is really only just beginning. Until fairly recently the main line of approach has been to identify particular 'methods' as sexist and others as non- or less-sexist (Bernard 1973; Roberts 1981). That is, the concern has been less with what 'feminist research' might be like and more with which of the existing methods are appropriately used by feminists. However, feminist work in this area is presently changing a great deal; in particular an increasing number of academic feminists are starting with the idea of 'feminist research' and trying to derive its essential features from feminist principles and beliefs. As part and parcel of this approach, emphasis is moving away from individual 'methods' and towards a broader concern with 'the research process'.

This changing approach to feminist research, in addition to the possibilities it raises, also reveals some of the grounds on which discrimination against women and against feminism in higher education already takes place, and some of those on which future discrimination might take place. Discrimination against women is found throughout the operations of the social sciences; but of particular concern here is the research process and the influence of professional-ideological under-standings about its nature as they are experienced and related to by feminists and 'newcomers' to research work.

The first section introduces the notions of 'gatekeeping' and 'discrimination', particularly as these are presently experienced by feminists in the social sciences. The second section examines three key themes in feminist social science and outlines feminist ideas about various 'methods'. The third section looks at 'the research process' as it is described in conventional social science. In doing so it considers some of the problems with what are sometimes seen as 'alternatives' to the so-called 'scientific method'. The fourth section discusses some ideas about the nature of 'feminist consciousness' and thus feminist experience of research; and it outlines the grounds for arguing that a clearly identifiable model of 'feminist research' exists. It goes on to discuss various ways in which such a model might bring its users into a more direct confrontation with conventional social science, and so is also concerned with how the nature of 'discrimination' might change.

'Gatekeeping' and 'Discrimination'

The experience of newcomers to social science research work is interesting and useful to examine because it reveals the existence of extremely subtle forms of 'discrimination'. The relationship between the theory and reality of research is experienced by newcomers in a particularly problematic way. Succinctly, the longer we're members of our profession the more we tend to forget or disregard the fact that 'experience' is often treated as somehow inferior to theoretically-derived accounts of social phenomena. Newcomers are less advanced on this path; but both for them and for 'initiates' frameworks exist which legitimate this process of theoretical imperialism. Later on I shall be discussing some of these; however, ideas about the nature of 'the research process', about what are to be seen as 'facts' and what as 'opinion', about what is and isn't 'collectable data', about what constitutes 'knowledge', are all involved here. All are located in the ideologically-constituted practices of the social science professions, all are the outcomes of political processes, and all have changed over time (Outhwaite 1972; Halfpenny 1982).

The gap between professional knowledge-claims about the research process and individual research experience is absolutely crucial for feminists; and the reality of the subtle forms of discrimination embedded in them is potentially acutely felt by feminists. An example may help to explain this. Some kinds of feminism reject the conventional distinction between 'fact' and 'opinion', construct 'knowledge' in different terms, and collect it through different means, and also reject conventional social science distinctions between 'researchers' and 'researched' (Kleiber and Light 1978; Stanley and Wise 1979; Smith 1974). Thus a style of feminist research based on these principles and beliefs would bring its practitioners into a more direct confrontation with the practices of conventional social science and thus with its 'gatekeepers'.

The importance for feminists of 'gatekeeping' in the processes of academic professional control has been noted by Dorothy Smith and Dale Spender. Both suggest that particular kinds of people set standards, decide what counts as knowledge, monitor what is distributed as such, and decree what is to be seen as innovatory (Smith 1978; Spender 1981b). I prefer to write of 'gatekeeping' rather than of 'social control', because the notion of gatekeeping makes it apparent that the people involved in such practices act on the basis of frequently exemplary motives in guarding and protecting what seems to them, to us, to be right, good and correct. The notion of control, in contrast, is much more suggestive of a deliberate power-seeking and maintaining which I think is only rarely found. However, it is important to keep in mind that the underlying practices, whatever we call them, can involve sanctions against women for being feminist and attempting to 'do feminism' in our academic lives. This is because 'doing feminism' can be seen as 'acting unprofessionally'. Another example here might concern academic feminists interested in 'non-subjects' such as the realm of the emotions (Hochschild 1975).

I also prefer to write about 'discrimination' rather than 'bias'. This is because, to me, 'discrimination' makes it much more apparent that involved here are processes actively carried out by some people which 'discriminate against' others; while 'bias' is a much more neutral word. All professional practices are in a way 'discriminatory' in this active sense, for they select-in some behaviours and attitudes for approval and select-out others for negative sanction. It is in this very broad sense that I am using the notion of discrimination in this chapter, rather than in a morally negative sense. This is because I think that examining and analysing 'discrimination' doesn't necessarily require seeing the practices involved as bad or unacceptable. After all, most of us would see at least some of them as professionally and morally justifiable while disagreeing with others; and of course some of these practices are acceptable to feminists and others not (and, indeed, different forms of feminism would find different ones acceptable and unacceptable). I use the term, then, only to point out the existence of 'professional practices' which differentially affect different people within the profession, in particular feminists.

'Discrimination', so-defined, has three aspects, that are in practice indissolvably interlinked — 'overt discrimination', 'covert discrimination' and 'self-discrimination'.

'Overt discrimination' I see as the enforcement of professional practices acknowledged as designed to guard and protect existing standards, beliefs, procedures and productions. These are to be found in the rules and codes of all professional bodies as well as in sets of academic practices presented in research manuals and teaching. 'Covert discrimination' I take to include all the mundane assumptions made about 'right', 'correct' and 'valid' ways of thinking, behaving and writing that are not ordinarily formulated into coherently presentable codes but are nevertheless routinely applied as part of the everyday business of professional work. Major sources of both these forms of discrimination include peers (whether academic colleagues or other students) and referees and examiners, including research supervisors.

'Self-discrimination' cuts across both covert and overt discrimination because one's self is a — often the — major source of gatekeeping activity. Most of us come into our profession not entirely at odds with it, having accepted at least some of its thinking as interesting and pertinent. A result is that we monitor, often extremely stringently, our own activities and outputs against what we see as existing and validated standards, practices and knowledge.

Existing feminist research can incur each of these forms of gatekeeping activity from a multiplicity of sources (as indeed can other forms of research, although this isn't my concern here). Concentrating on women can be, and often is, taken as prima facie evidence of bias or of a concern with the merely trivial aspects of social life by many non-feminists in the social sciences. It has been suggested that to be a feminist is to be tainted with 'values', and/or that feminist research is overtly and therefore unacceptably political research. These kinds of comments I think derive from feminism's implicit, often indeed unwilling, threat to what Kuhn calls 'normal science' (Kuhn 1964), a point I return to later. They can translate into gatekeeping activity and probably do so fairly widely. However, this kind of gatekeeping activity can be demonstrated only indirectly, for this is the quiet talk of senior common rooms and departmental corridors, the anonymous remarks in reader's reports, the chance remarks of examiners and interviewers. It only rarely appears in print or in public and when it does it is even more rarely associated with anyone by name. However, there are ways of demonstrating its existence, and various of the other chapters in this book do so very successfully (see Taylorson, Rendel, and Scott and Porter: chapters 8-10 in this volume).

Having said that this gatekeeping activity derives from the presumed threat of feminism to existing 'normal science' and its power structures, to my mind far too little actual academic feminist work in fact does constitute such a threat (Stanley and Wise 1983). But, as I have said, increasing numbers of feminist researchers are now becoming aware of the multiple contradictions involved in our accommodation to conventional research models and methods (Roberts 1981; Spender 1981b), and in particular how this helps to maintain a conventional social science fundamentally antipathetic to feminist principles and practices. In the past many feminists have coped with this through self-discrimination, often as the only way of lessening the possibility that other forms of discrimination will be applied to our work. Also, in practice and no matter how aware of the contradictions, few academic feminists have felt able to do anything other than accommodate at a time when many people feel that higher education is under attack and jobs are at risk.

Even the present style of feminist research produces discrimination on what seems to be a wide scale. It seems more than likely, then, that a style of feminist research which doesn't accommodate and which is committed to 'doing feminism' within the research process will do so on an even wider scale – but with one important exception. In such a situation I think that self-discrimination will sharply decline.

In relation to academic feminism, the origins of self-discrimination seem to lie in the convergence of two factors. One is the existence of coherent conventional social science research models and of covert and overt discriminatory practices designed to protect them. The other is the absence of any coherent comparable model/s of 'feminist research'. When such a thing exists then a clash between any of its practices and those associated with the conventional social science models will be clearly seen to be (by feminists at least) sexual political in nature. However, in the following section I locate this discussion of research models within the general concerns of feminist social science.

Three Themes in Feminist Social Science

At a very general level, three key themes can be discerned within feminist social science. They are: the existence of a powerful 'feminist critique'; the implication that feminist research ought to be 'research on, by and for women'; and the argument that the processes of research involve 'sexist methods'.

The 'feminist critique' involves the simplest but in many ways the most powerful criticism of the social sciences. One of the best examples of it is to be found in Ann Oakley's demonstration that sexism in the social sciences is located in their almost total concern with the interests and activities of men only (Oakley 1974). This affects not only the focus of research but also the way a discipline is constructed, including the division of labour within it. A consequence is that although women's 'social presence' is high in most areas of social life, nevertheless their 'academic visibility' is low, sometimes almost non-existent.

An extension of this argument is that even where women's social presence isn't ignored it is viewed and presented in sexist ways. Feminist work here has argued that the research that does exist is based on inadequate perceptions of women, men and relationships between the sexes; for these rely heavily on ideas about the supposed biological determination of female personality and behaviour. Associated with this is the consequence that women's lives and experiences are often treated as less than fully human because different from the assumed norm of male experience.

One implication of these criticisms is that the social sciences are 'moral theories' (Friedan 1963). 'Moral theories' describe the world according to sets of moral beliefs rather than in terms of the precepts and understandings of the people who inhabit it. Here 'moral' refers to those beliefs which justify and so legitimate social divisions between, and differential treatment of, various groups of people; and these are, of course, political beliefs.

Another implication is that future feminist research ought to be 'research on, by and for women'. In practice this aspect of feminist social science has been largely 'corrective' in its emphasis, because it has been concerned with filling in gaps in our basic knowledge about women. That these gaps should be filled is obviously desirable; and this point of view has been discussed by a number of feminists (Bernard 1973; Daniels 1975; Erhlich 1976; Smart 1976; Tobias 1978). However, at least some of these women have also expressed concern in case too much emphasis is placed on this at the expense of other needs.

The danger here is that if academic feminism becomes 'ghetto-ized' as 'women's studies', and 'women' thus separated-off as a topic area, then the rest of the social sciences may remain untouched by feminism. In particular, the danger is that conventional social science will continue in its old sexist fashion, while along side of it but unconnected to it a new feminist social science concerned with 'women' comes into existence.

For me, a second danger exists here as well. If academic feminism becomes ghetto-ized then this separating-off of feminism from the rest of the social sciences will cut it off from ideas and debates of crucial importance to it. Isolation from research and thinking in specialist fields and particular disciplines drains the life-blood of academic feminism as much as isolation from feminism itself. Of course in Britain we are perhaps much more discipline-orientated than elsewhere; and for a contrary view of women's studies see Duelli Klein in this book (Ch.13).

A third danger is that feminist research might become research on women only. If 'sexism' is the name of the problem addressed by feminism then men are importantly involved, to say the least, in its practice. Analysis of women's oppression cannot exclude the part played by men, for that oppression is fundamental to the meaning of feminism. However, much academic feminism seems to see this kind of analysis as outside its field of interest.

In marked contrast to the continuing debate about feminist research being research 'on and for women', the emphasis on it also being research 'by women' has lessened. This seems to me a logical development. As long as it is seen as 'research on women' then there's no obvious reason why men shouldn't do it. Indeed, there's every reason in the sexist world why they should. Separating off 'women' as a topic area in fact provides the existing academic community with suitable means of colonizing 'women's oppression' and de-politicizing it − the fate of 'black studies' should act as a warning here. However, I see 'feminist research' as absolutely and centrally 'research by women' because of the way that I understand the relationship between consciousness and research; and I examine this in more detail in the last section. In addition, something of this is also hinted at in feminist ideas about 'sexist methods' and I now turn to examine this third theme in feminist social science.

Centrally involved in feminist ideas about sexism in the social sciences is the contention that methods, along with all other aspects of their operation, are so to be seen. Until comparatively recently the focus in this kind of work has been on the distinction between 'sexist methods' and 'non-sexist methods'. Some academic feminists have argued that particular methods, but not others, contain 'machismo elements' (Bernard 1973). This involves the creation of controlled realities which can be manipulated by researchers, who at the same time remain safely distant from the 'objects' of their research; and many feminists have identified such 'controlled realities' with methods yielding 'hard' or quantified data.

However, there are at least some academic feminists who find this depiction of quantitative or 'hard' data and accompanying methods as sexist quite inadequate (Kelly 1978; Jayaratne 1981). The kernel of their argument is that the use of methods involves the simple application of technical procedures which, unlike other aspects of the research process, can and should remain uninfluenced by values of any kind. Indeed, a large number of academic feminists routinely utilize arguments about value-freedom, objectivity and science, and criticize the social sciences for failing to embody these qualities in the sexist work produced in them; and some go further than this, to argue that through feminism the social sciences can achieve true objectivity.

The simple dichotomizing of methods and equally simple association of women with one kind (non-sexist qualitative 'soft' methods) and men with the other (sexist quantitative 'hard' methods) has been rejected on rather different grounds by other people. Some feminists object to such a use of dichotomies, arguing that the complexities of social (and academic) life are denied in these; and that, moreover, they are themselves part and parcel of sexist ways of seeing the world (Spender 1978). Other people have pointed out that even the so-called 'non-sexist methods' in practice have 'their own brand of machismo' (Morgan 1981). And a central feature of both arguments here has been that behind the dichotomizing of methods lies a vision of research which can be value-free, objective, and truly, really, absolutely scientific. The implication is that there is 'a' way of doing research which avoids values, beliefs and the presence within the research process of the researcher as a person (with all that this entails in the impact of preferences, likes and dislikes, feelings and emotions on the intellectual processes of interpretation and conceptualization).

This essentially nineteenth-century vision of 'science' has of course been rejected by many social scientists and some academic feminists (Robert 1976; Spender 1978; Stanley and Wise 1979; Duelli Klein 1980; Rinehartz 1981). Importantly involved here has been the production of alternative models of the research process derived from experientially-based descriptions of research (Glaser and Strauss 1968; Lofland 1971; Johnson 1977; Kleiber and Light 1978); and I discuss something of this in the next section.

'The Research Process'

Newcomers to the social sciences, including newcomers to the practicalities of research, are confronted with two main models of the research process. The first of these models, the 'positivist' model, is that often referred to as 'the traditional scientific method'. This is frequently contrasted with the second main model of the research process, the 'naturalist' one. These models are of course connected with the distinction between 'hard' and 'soft' methods referred to earlier. Indeed, in much academic work 'positivism' is almost exclusively interpreted as 'hard' methods and data and 'naturalism' as 'soft' ones.

In the 'positivist' model the first stage in research is an involvement with theoretical concerns, which may involve a particular discipline or the particular theoretical interests of a researcher in general problems. This leads to the formulation of an hypothesis, or a series of them, which expresses the nature of the problem or interest to be investigated. The second stage involves the use of a set of technical procedures or 'methods' designed to collect information or 'data' from the chosen research population; and this may involve people or documentary sources of various kinds. The third stage is one in which the products of the data collection are analysed and the results then interpreted and related back to the theoretical concerns which started off the process.

The second model of the research process, the 'naturalist' one, similarly describes a linear movement but this time one in which theory is seen to come out of the research rather than precede it. It suggests that a researcher enters a natural setting of some kind and then 'lives' in it for some time. This 'living within' may be as a member of a community or as someone with a recognized 'research role' in it. Information is thus derived about the day-to-day activities of the people for whom this is 'life'. The researcher then goes away to produce both a description of the natural setting and an interpretation of what has occurred within it.

Presenting the research process in terms of one or other of these two models, and thus as orderly, coherent and logically organized, has consequences. The main one of concern here is the shock which occurs when newcomers to research are faced with discrepancies between the models and their practical experiences of research. Most researchers start off by believing that what is presented to us in such models is a reasonable representation of the reality of research. However, the point at which we begin to realize that the models present something quite unrealistic – 'hygienic research' in which no problems occur, no emotions are involved – is a crucial one. It is the point at which we are required to present our research outcomes to academic colleagues, supervisors, publishers and examiners. In other words, it is also precisely the point at which we are most vulnerable and least able to resist pressures to conform because we may face 'discrimination' in one way or another if we don't. But there are additional consequences of the gap between the theory and the experience of research.

All newcomers to research confront in some form or other the discrepancy between textbook description and research experience. Most end up dealing with the problem in the same way that others have before them – simply presenting the models rather than the experience. Importantly involved in this is the influence of professional ideology and, in particular, ideas about objectivity, detachment and the like. Within the social sciences subjectivity isn't highly valued. To be subjective is seen to be unscientific, irrational, illogical. What I mean here can be summarized in the homily 'not able to see the wood for the trees.' The implication is that involvement brings with it an incapacity to truly, really, understand what is going on.

As we become increasingly assimilated into our profession we learn to discount experience where there are any gaps between it and the products of research and theory – including, that is, our own experience as researchers as well as the experience of those upon whom we do research. Essentially we learn to treat 'experience' as a faulty representation of theory, and to treat theory as 'real reality'.

Asserting that we need to reclaim our experience as researchers and move away from what I earlier called 'theoretical imperialism' is double-edged. On the one hand it can be (and often is) read as a special plea that the researcher's view should be privileged because it is 'scientific' and thus conceptually, analytically and also often factually preferable. On the other hand, I prefer it to be read as an insistence that we recognize that, fundamentally, all research is no more than 'the researcher's experience'. This experience may be, indeed usually is, worked up, analysed, re-formulated and re-written; but it starts off from the experiences of a person in a social situation and remains as such, although in a worked-up form and presented as something very different. I also prefer that it should be read in conjunction with the presentation of 'the researcher's experience' in a specific form.

For the purposes of this chapter I find it useful to distinguish between 'biographical experience' and 'intellectual experience'. The former includes temporal description (first I did this, then I went there, then...), significant events (the agency refused to allow me research access, the people knew straight away I was really a researcher...) and persons (she turned out to be the most useful informant, the community leader spent all his time chatting me up...) and the like. Research which includes this kind of information is usually more accessible, readable and interesting than that which doesn't, but my prime concern is with making a case for the inclusion of the latter form of experience − 'intellectual experience'. More often than not research presents us with outcomes, with products, and very rarely with the intellectual processes involved. We know <u>what</u> the researcher found out, but not <u>why and how</u> it was found out. The result is that we can take research or leave it − believe it or not, in a sense. Even if we don't believe it we usually do so in an intuitive way, for only very rarely indeed are we allowed access to the intellectual processes of interpretation, conceptualization and analysis in relation to the specific settings, persons and events which produced this interpretation, that conceptualization and so on.

Including 'the researcher's experience' in this sense in research has produced some of the most insightful, exciting and intellectually rigorous and stimulating research currently to be found in the social sciences (Garfinkel 1967; Wieder 1974; Cuff 1980; Lury 1982). It has other benefits as well, principally that it makes the researcher less invulnerable, and goes some way to even-up the gross inequalities embedded in conventional research outcomes. In particular it makes it apparent that 'the researcher's view', 'the researcher's experience', is precisely that − and that alternative views and experiences exist which may be equally rational, logical, sensible and sound. This is exactly what the adherents to conventional research models and their outcomes find anathema, for 'science' has recognized only one 'reality' and so only one valid view of it.

The idea that reality is one dimensional and unseamed and permits only one true description of it is 'positivism'. In the sense I'm using this term, 'positivism' is a way of interpreting our experience of social life which insists that 'facts' of various kinds exist and can be separated from 'opinion'. Within it 'opinion' is seen as multi-dimensional and varying between people, time and place, while 'facts' are seen as invariable. An example here might be a road accident in which various people who were witnesses to it, and the professionals who interpret material evidence of various kinds, disagree about 'what happened'. Here, most people would agree, 'the facts' of the accident can be discovered, for something really happened and this is what constitutes 'the facts'.

Described around such an example the positivist view of social reality sounds eminently sensible — after all, we all of us behave like this in our everyday lives. We sift the evidence, look for what really happened, decide what was really meant. But use of a different example can show up some of the problems here, problems which are particularly important for feminists.

In this other example we might imagine a middle-aged woman going to see her general practitioner because she feels depressed and suicidal. The doctor sifts among the collected evidence, examining possible physical ills, possible mental ills, and also social factors such as possible money worries or problems about family relationships. If the result of this is that there are no physical ills, no mental ills, no money worries, a lovely house, charming husband and wonderful children, then the verdict may well be that here is a case of neuroticism or symptoms produced by the menopause.

However, feminism suggests that the diagnosis in this example of 'the problem without a name' should have been 'sexism' and the prescription personal and societal change. In other words, in situations such as this feminism disputes 'the evidence', 'the facts' and 'technical expertise'. And, by doing so, it also denies the positivist insistence that only one 'real reality' exists. One of feminism's main messages is that all of this can and must be seen differently.

The above example is a particularly useful one to use, for doing so also raises an interesting point about the feminist challenge to 'sexist evidence', 'sexist facts' and 'sexist technical expertise'. In effect this challenge has said 'there is an other way of seeing this, the feminist way'. Effectively this is to replace one 'real reality' with another. What I am suggesting here is that feminism has as yet failed to solve (not surprisingly, given both the complexities and the fact that no one else has either) the practical and philosophical conundrum of how we can disagree with other people's constructions of reality without either denying its-validity-for-them or attempting to impose our own on them as the correct one. That is, in situations such as this the temptation is to treat ourselves as right and correct and other people as wrong, rather than different. Here the central difficulty lies in arguing that feminism and feminist versions of 'reality' are preferable without also falling into the same trap that anti-feminists and other misogynists fall into, and asserting the 'one reality — my reality' line. And of course, it must be said, some kinds of feminism are quite happy with the 'one reality — feminist reality' line and that in holding it they thereby deny the ontological validity of other kinds of feminism.

It is because of factors such as these that there could have been a constant tension in this chapter between what could be said on behalf of 'feminism' generally and what I could say only on behalf of 'my feminism'. Like most other feminists who write, I have rejected this on practical and stylistic grounds — the result would have been unwieldy and unnecessarily convoluted. I have instead written of 'my feminism'. With some of this most other feminists will agree; with some of it only a few. And I think that as long as readers know this and that feminism is as internally diverse as any other ontological framework, this is sufficient in an essay such as this.

The approach to feminism and feminist research I favour is one centrally concerned with the kinds of issues, possibilities and problems touched on in the above discussion. As researchers we nevertheless remain people (Georges and Jones 1981); and to a very large extent 'research' is simply a conscious focusing on questions and issues ordinarily treated in taken-for-granted ways. However, 'becoming feminist' and 'being feminist' is, for most of us who call ourselves feminists, a transformation of our consciousness of the nature of social reality, including our own participation in it (often, indeed, mainly our own participation). One result is that the 'taken-for-granted' is no longer so, nor is it simply consciously focused on. Instead it is questioned, for example: Is it actually the way it is said to be? Does it mean something different from what we're told? Who tells us the way it is and why?

The specific ontological basis of feminist consciousness is something relatively unexplored within feminism (Bartky 1977; Morgan 1977). But the work that does exist suggests that 'becoming feminist' involves massive and consequential, and frequently sudden shifts in perspective and understanding. Almost literally, 'being feminist' and 'doing feminism' involves 'being different', because you come to see, understand and participate in social life on a different basis.

A feminist researcher, then, already experiences social life in largely uncharted ways which are different from those of non-feminists. Her experience of 'the research process' itself further compounds such differences. Feminist research that involves men, no matter how tangentially, almost inevitably involves the feminist researcher in experiences of sexism, in sometimes gross and sometimes subtle ways.

Feminist research that involves women also involves the question of how feminist researchers should relate to the women included within 'the researched', and thus raises the conundrum of how not to undercut, discredit or write-off women's consciousnesses different from our own while retaining our sense of the preferential nature of feminism. 'False consciousness' is not only not an answer, it also denies something of the essence of feminism, at least feminism in the sense that I understand it. This is a point I return to in the following section; but it might be useful to say here that this is because it embodies the 'one reality' line and portrays researchers/theoreticians as a vanguard in possession of this real reality.

Should feminist researchers manage to explore and make use of all the complexities and possibilities I have referred to, then a further series of issues arises around whether and to what extent these matters should be encompassed in research reports. Research reports are presented to peers, to supervisors, in theses for examiners, for funding bodies and in prospective publications. In other words, they are presented to gatekeepers of various kinds, for these are the people to whom researchers in some sense feel accountable. After all, if such people don't agree with, or approve of, our work then our credibility is diminished. We may be seen as inadequate researchers and thus as professionally incompetent; and this in turn can have further and important consequences for us.

I have suggested, then, that conventional research models are problematically experienced by all newcomers to research, but especially so by feminist researchers. Feminist consciousness itself leads us to question various aspects of the taken-for-granted, which thus becomes problematic to us. Because of this there is an obvious need to attempt to construct feminist alternatives to the conventional models; and it is to a discussion of this that I now turn.

Feminist Consciousness and Feminist Research

In constructing feminist alternatives it is important to do so working from feminist principles and understandings rather than from the existing models and their assumptions. This involves starting from an identification of the most important elements of 'feminism'; and I suggest that there are three of these.

The first is the acceptance that women are indeed oppressed. This is treated as a factual statement, rather than a statement of belief. However, its factual nature derives from an especially feminist reliance on the validity of experience, coupled with the knowledge that all women share important experiences simply because they are 'women in sexist society'. Included here might be, for example, experiences of inferior treatment on grounds of sex, of sexual harassment, of sexual objectification, of fear of rape and other sexual violence.

The second concerns the insistence on the essential validity of experience and the irrevocably political nature of 'the personal'. Here the conventional distinction between personal life (home, family, relationships, emotions) and politics (pressure groups, political parties, unions, elections, the economy, the courts, the armed forces) is rejected. 'Politics' is instead interpreted as the distribution and use of power; and its presence in all aspects of social life is emphasized. One such appearance of power is in situations where women's experiences are invalidated just because they are women; and in contrast feminism argues that women should accept other women's experiences as valid, in the sense of 'valid for them' and without necessarily agreeing with them.

The third is that a uniquely feminist consciousness is produced out of the practice of feminist beliefs in everyday life − 'doing feminism' − in the sense that this sets up a situation in which women 'see reality differently', as I have already outlined.

I doubt that many feminists would dispute the importance of these three elements, although many might disagree about what they mean, in practice as well as in theory. For example, a number of feminist writings reject the earlier feminist treatment of 'the personal' (which is what I have outlined above) in fairly explicit terms (Mitchell and Oakley 1976; Brunsdon 1978; Sayers 1982), while many more do so implicitly. This of course points up my earlier remarks about different kinds of feminism and that what I'm doing is outlining my kind; and so in this section I am discussing 'my feminist alternative' to conventional research models.

These principles converge in the phrase 'the personal is the political', for this argues that power and its use can be examined and analysed within personal life and, indeed, that in some sense the political must be examined here. It also emphasizes that structures and systems are experienced in everyday life and aren't separate from it in the way that many structuralist approaches suggest. And so feminism also argues that social structures can and must be understood through a rigorous exploration of relationships, experiences and interactions within the realm of social life. Thus feminism sees 'the personal' as deeply and irrevocably social and political in nature and eschews those approaches which locate the dynamic of social life in either psychological reductionism or decorticated structuralism.

For feminists the axiom 'the personal is the political' is then no mere slogan. Instead it reflects and gives expression to the kind of changes in experience and consciousness which occur in the processes of 'becoming feminist'. That is, feminist consciousness both derives from, and permits seeing the everyday in sexual political terms. Through this developing consciousness women's understandings of their lives are transformed so that they see and understand them in a new and different way, at the same time continuing to experience them in the old familiar way. This 'new way' involves a situation in which women come to understand the (seemingly endless) contradictions present within social life. Reality is much more complex and multifaceted than we ordinarily admit it to be, and it is contradictory.

Feminist research derived from 'feminism' in this way takes as its task the exploration of our everyday knowledge and behaviour as women, as feminists and as social scientists. It goes about this by starting from the experiences of the researcher as a person in a situation. Researchers, like all new members of situations, have to find out what's going on and how to behave appropriately. How we find out, how we come to know what it is that members know, is a basic concern here. And in doing so, we must make available to others the reasoning procedures which underlie the knowledge produced from research – we must make available what I earlier called 'intellectual experience'. Thus we necessarily explore our experience of 'being a researcher', and by such exploration we discover how to find out what constitutes 'social reality' in any particular setting.

There are similarities here with the basic arguments of interactional and phenomenological sociologies, and with symbolic interactionism and ethnomethodology in particular. However, there is one crucial difference. It has often been said that women have a 'dual vision' of social life because they can see the world as men see it, for they have been brought up to search out and accommodate to their view, but they also see it as women and thus as members of an oppressed group. For feminists, a third 'vision' also exists, in the form of 'seeing differently'. Ideas about different 'visions' are neither new nor exclusive to feminism of course; and one could say similar things, for example, about the experience of being black. However, the point is that this particular configuration of 'visions' is exclusive to feminism, for only feminist researchers are both women and feminists.

This kind of feminist research seems to me necessary and even crucial to the feminist enterprise. It is crucial because my understanding of feminism identifies the realm of the personal, women's experiences of our everyday lives and the things that occur in them as basic in women's oppression. But there is another and more mundane reason for our concern. 'Everyday life' is what we spend our lives doing. What all people spend their lives doing must obviously be the subject of research. What all women spend our lives doing must equally obviously be a legitimate subject for feminist research.

Rather than examining this kind of feminist research in any more detail here (although I have done so elsewhere, in Stanley and Wise 1979, 1981, 1983), it seems more appropriate to examine some of its implications. I do so around three objections which have been made to it.

These are: that it is concerned merely with a sample of one; that it is concerned with a far too limited range of research; and that what it produces is merely literature. I discuss these because it seems to me that they reflect conventional (including conventional academic feminist) assumptions about 'right' and 'wrong' ways of doing research; and they thus reveal the grounds on which discrimination against 'feminist research' so-constituted may take place.

The researcher is usually only one person; and an obvious objection to research directed towards 'intellectual experience', thus using only a sample of one, is that it uses a very small and unrepresentative sample indeed. Such a 'sample' would tend to come from a small and extremely privileged section of society. The objection is, therefore, that this kind of feminist research wouldn't permit us to say anything about the experiences of the vast majority of people. However interesting or uninteresting it might be, this kind of research wouldn't permit generalization from the person doing it to conventional 'research populations'. An associated problem is seen to be that this kind of research couldn't be replicated because it would be quite unique to the original researcher.

It is most certainly true that social scientists tend to come from a very limited section of society. However, the kind of research I'm advocating would at least make that explicit, while conventional research approaches try to legitimate the pretence of representativeness. They do so by claiming that adherence to various practices and techniques enables the true and adequate representation of the understandings and experiences of 'research populations', even where the people concerned reject these as neither true nor adequate. All research inevitably involves a power relationship between researcher and researched. Conventional social science justifies this in various ways that I've already outlined, both above and earlier. The kind of feminist research I'm advocating approaches this power relationship in a different way. Its 'different way' is to make the researcher vulnerable, in the sense of presenting their reasonings, deductions and evidence to others.

I'm not suggesting that this provides us with any magic key that enables us to enter other people's experiences and emotions. However, we all of us construct a view of other people's understandings and intentions from their behaviours, appearance and so on. It is this construction which is made accessible through presentation in intellectual experience. And, of course, such a presentation makes it quite apparent that researchers not only 'present' and 'interpret' but also 'construct' as an essential element of what we do. Events, behaviours and situations can only be constructed and then interpreted by the person who is presenting their experience of them; obviously all members of a setting do this, but it is only researchers who do so in 'scientific publications' of one kind or another. All this would be made explicit in the kind of feminist research described here, which might not be 'representative' in conventional ways but does at the least provide basic information about the research process as an intellectual as well as a practical phenomenon.

This kind of research focuses on 'experience'; and it is sometimes objected that it will thereby focus only on what is immediately and directly experienced by researchers, because this wouldn't enable us to find out the kinds of things that feminism needs to know. We don't need an exploration of the everyday, this objection suggests, because we already know about it. Experience is already known to us; we need answers to basic problems of far greater concern to feminism than the exploration of 'experience'.

This objection, as far as I'm concerned, turns on unrelated misconceptions. No one has access to 'direct experience', for all experience is always mediated by mind, by consciousness and by the constructions we each put upon it. And we all of us articulate and use information and understandings drawn from quite different settings. In this sense what is often referred to as 'direct experience' is a ragbag of events and persons and speech-acts in which many 'indirect experiences' are centrally involved. There is thus absolutely no reason why 'intellectual experience' should not include ideas about race, capitalism, the structure of the unconscious, rates of recidivism or anything else not directly represented within particular settings. Indeed, it nearly always does, for people are social beings with a vast stock of social knowledge which we make use of in all kinds of ways. Moreover, without properly understanding what is going on, without subjecting experience to analysis, then 'experience' – even our own – is not something we already know about. Most of what we do is done in routine ways; we treat it as unproblematic and uninteresting, and we don't consciously analyse it.

In addition, this kind of objection derives from the belief that we already have adequate feminist understanding and analysis of women's oppression and that we need to move on from such basic analytic work. I don't accept this. Although I accept that all women are oppressed, I don't accept that all women share exactly the same range of experiences. I think that the material forms of our oppressions differ; and that an enormous amount of very basic research needs to be done in exploring them.

The kind of feminist research I'm advocating here rejects the idea that there is only one social reality and only one 'women's oppression'. For me this flows directly from the axiom 'the personal is the political' and the belief that other women's experiences and understandings are to be seen as valid and real, for them if not for me. At the same time, however, I also recognize that everyone sees and experiences the world in 'positivist' ways; and we rank peoples' experience, but give our own pride of place. But feminist research as I envisage it has at its heart the insistence that many 'objective realities' coexist and compete; and it takes as its task the exploration of these, not their obliteration and dismissal as 'false' or 'inadequate'.

That may sound odd in a paper advocating that 'the researcher's experience' is what research should be 'about'. My response is that research is like this anyway, but it is disguised or denied; and that by 'undisguising' it and making it obviously central a more exciting and rigorous style of analysis is made available, one concerned with intellectual processes and not just their product. It has the additional benefit, for feminists at least, of making researchers more 'vulnerable' because more accountable; and that, in turn, affects the distribution of power in research situations and outcomes.

However, it has been said that such an approach is merely the production of literature, for it is 'fiction' in the sense that it provides one person's attempt to describe and account for 'society' in one of its aspects. That it is the stuff of novels and poetry, but not of science, seems to be the crux of the argument here.

I reject the point, for I cannot accept that 'science' exists in quite the way that some people still claim it does. 'Truth' is a social construct, in the same way that 'objectivity' is; and both are constructed out of experiences which are, for all practical purposes, the same as 'lies' and 'subjectivity'. These are names only, which embody sets of meanings given to particular behaviours; and feminism chooses to give them different names and different meanings. Moreover, all research is 'fiction' in the sense that it views and constructs 'reality' through one person – the researcher.

However, there is a sense in which I would accept the point in so far as much literature is concerned with 'society' through particular characters and incidents but ultimately through the author; and at least some literature has influenced and changed people and their lives in a way that little conventional research has done. If that is the kind of literature that this form of feminist research is being compared to then who would not accept the comparison and feel immensely flattered, for is that not high praise indeed?

Feminism, Research and Discrimination

The analysis of 'discrimination' against women in higher education usually focuses on either the constitution of occupational or student groups or the products of theory and research. The feminist critique, examining these products, has demonstrated their sexism and argued for future corrective research on and for women while making a distinction between some research methods as sexist and others as non-sexist.

However, this chapter has been concerned with a changing attitude among academic feminists, in which the whole 'research process' comes under scrutiny. In the discussion attention has moved away from particular 'methods' towards a broader examination of the entire process and of the feminist experience of research. For feminists a particularly crucial gap exists between the theory of research, in the form of conventional models of research, and its reality in the form of practical experiences of research. This 'gap' is widely acknowledged among feminists and increasingly well documented. There is a consequent and growing awareness that the kinds of contradictions that exist are an inevitable by-product of trying to accommodate to conventional social science practices; practices at odds with the essence of feminism.

There is thus a need to construct a model/s of feminist research beginning from feminism, from its constituent principles and practices. Doing so will, I believe, produce a very different style of feminist research from that which we are used to and will bring academic feminism into more obvious confrontation with conventional social science; and I say 'more obvious' because it already exists. Confrontation is never pleasant; but then neither is covert, disguised and politically-motivated discrimination against women and against feminism nor incorporation and accommodation among erstwhile revolutionaries.

Academic feminism, it seems to me, is at a particularly important juncture in its history. Those of us involved in it can either become the new experts on women and more or less indistinguishable, except in our topic area, from our non-feminist colleagues; or we can reassert our commitment to feminism and explore it in new ways. 'Feminist research', as I see it, exists in a symbiotic relationship with an exploration and analysis of feminist consciousness. Doing this kind of feminist research opens up for feminist analysis interesting, exciting and intellectually stimulating possibilities for future work. We can and must make full use of such possibilities, whatever the consequences, or we do not deserve to be called feminists.

References

Barker,D. and Allen,A. (Eds)(1976a) *Sexual Divisions and Society* London: Tavistock

Barker,D. and Allen,A. (Eds)(1976b) *Dependence and Exploitation in Work and Marriage* London: Longman

Bartky,S. (1977) Towards a phenomenology of feminist consciousness.

In Vetterling-Barggin,M. et al.(Eds) *Feminism and Philosophy* New Jersey: Littlefield, Adams & Co, pp.22-34

Bernard,J. (1973) My four revolutions *American Journal of Sociology* 78, 773-91

Brunsdon,C. (1978) It is well known that by nature women are inclined to be rather personal. In Women's Studies Group (Eds) *Women Take Issue* London: Hutchinson, pp.18-34

Cuff,E. (1980) *The Problem of Versions in Everyday Life* Occasional Paper 3, University of Manchester

Duelli Klein,R. (1980) How to do what we want to do. In Bowles,G. and Duelli Klein,R. (Eds) *Theories of Women's Studies I* Berkeley: University of California, pp.48-64

Ehrlich,C. (1976) *The Conditions of Feminist Research* Baltimore: Research Group One

Friedan,B. (1963) *The Feminine Mystique* Harmondsworth: Penguin

Garfinkel,H. (1967) *Studies in Ethnomethodology* New Jersey: Prentice Hall

Georges,R. and Jones,M. (1980) *People Studying People* University of California Press

Glaser,B. and Strauss,A. (1968) *The Discovery of Grounded Theory* London: Weidenfield and Nicholson

Halfpenny,P. (1982) *Positivism and Sociology* London: Allen and Unwin

Hochschild,A. (1975) The sociology of feeling and emotion. In Millman,M. and Kanter,R. (Eds) *Another Voice* New York: Doubleday, pp.280-307

Jayaratne,T. (1981) The value of quantitative methodology for feminist research. In Bowles,G. and Duelli Klein,R. (Eds) *Theories of Women's Studies II* Berkeley: University of California, pp.47-67

Johnson,J. (1977) *Doing Field Research* New York: Free Press

Kelly,A. (1978) Feminism and research *Women's Studies International Quarterly* 1, 225-32

Kleiber,L. and Light,L. (1978) *Caring for Ourselves* University of British Columbia

Kuhn,T. (1962) *The Structure of Scientific Revolutions* University of Chicago Press

Lofland,J. (1971) *Analysing Social Settings* California: Wadsworth

Lury,C. (1982) *An Ethnography of an Ethnography: Reading Sociology* Occasional Paper 9, University of Manchester

Millman,M. and Kanter,R. (Eds) (1975) *Another Voice* New York: Doubleday

Mitchell,J. and Oakley,A. (Eds) (1976) *The Rights and Wrongs of Women* Harmondsworth: Penguin, pp.7-15

Morgan,D. (1981) Men, masculinity and the process of sociological enquiry. In Roberts,H. (Ed.) *Doing Feminist Research* London: Routledge and Kegan Paul, pp.83-113

Morgan,R. (1977) *Going Too Far* New York: Vintage Books

Oakley,A. (1974) *The Sociology of Housework* London: Martin Robertson

Outhwaite W. (1972) *Understanding Social Life* London: Allen and Unwin

Reinharz,S. (1981) Experiential analysis: a contribution to feminist research. In Bowles,G. and Duelli Klein,R. (Eds) *Theories of Women's Studies II* Berkeley: University of California, pp.68-97

Roberts,J. (Ed.) (1976) *Beyond Intellectual Sexism* New York: David McKay

Roberts,H. (1978) *Women and their Doctors* Unpublished SSRC Workshop on Qualitative Methodology

Roberts,H. (Ed.) (1981) *Doing Feminist Research* London: Routledge and Kegan Paul

Sayers,J. (1982) *Psychoanalysis and Feminism Revisited* Unpublished, British Sociological Association Annual Conference on Gender

Smart,C. (1976) *Women, Crime and Criminology* London: Routledge and Kegan Paul

Smith,D. (1974) Women's perspective as a radical critique of sociology *Sociological Quarterly* 44,7-13

Smith,D. (1978) A peculiar eclipsing *Women's Studies International Quarterly* 1,1-17

Spender,D. (1978) *Educational Research and the Feminist Perspective* Unpublished, British Educational Research Association Annual Conference on Women, Education and Research

Spender,D. (Ed.) (1981a) *Men's Studies Modified* Oxford: Pergamon

Spender,D. (1981b) The gatekeepers: a feminist critique of academic publishing. In Roberts,H. (Ed.) *Doing Feminist Research* London: Routledge and Kegan Paul, pp.186-202

Stanley,L. and Wise,S. (1979) Feminist research, feminist consciousness and experiences of sexism *Women's Studies International Quarterly* 2, 359-74

Stanley,L. and Wise,S. (1981) 'Back into the personal' or our attempt to construct 'feminist research'. In Bowles,G. and Duelli Klein,R. (Eds) *Theories of Women's Studies II* Berkeley: University of California, pp.98-118

Stanley,L. and Wise,S. (1983) *Breaking Out: Feminist Consciousness and Feminist Research* London: Routledge and Kegan Paul

Tobias,S. (1978) Women's studies, its origins, its organisation and its prospects *Women's Studies International Quarterly* 1, 85-97

Wieder,D. (1974) *Language and Social Reality* The Hague: Mouton

12 A feminist perspective on affirmative action

Helen Roberts

The purpose of this chapter is to look at affirmative action as a principle of fairness, not as 'giving' something extra to women in higher education, but as attempting to right past wrongs, some of which are described in detail in other contributions to this volume.[1] The chapter begins with a brief overview of the way in which affirmative action policies have operated in the United States, and problems which have been associated with the policy there. Notwithstanding these problems, suggestions are made for two avenues of affirmative action here, which even given the political, economic and financial climate could make an immediate difference to women in higher education. Since the Sex Discrimination Act came into force in 1975, much has been claimed for the British record, and indeed some progress has been made, but at the end of 1979, women still formed less than 16 per cent of total full-time academic staff in universities, and even then tend to be concentrated in the lower ranges (Women in Universities 1982).

Of course progress has been made in some areas, but what is being done, and what has been done is not enough. Such progress as has been achieved is only a beginning, and there is some evidence that that beginning may be eroded, or is being eroded. We cannot congratulate ourselves on the particular course designed for women here, the special recruitment campaign there, the good publicity campaign aimed at mature women returners at this college, and the flourishing crêche or nursery at that one. Of course these represent enormous efforts, often on the part of individual women or groups of women, but goodwill is inadequate where financial cuts are being sought.

A policy is needed to change the status quo, and it is arguable that the affirmative action campaign in the United States, for all its faults and failures is a very considerable advance on the sort of positive discrimination we have in Britain.[2] For the 'policy' we have here is a form of positive discrimination we have always had, and one which does not draw

210

howls of protest; it is positive discrimination in favour of men. The ways in which our college and university systems operate, the amount of attention given to men and women students (and at an earlier stage, to boys and girls in schools), the ways in which the domestic lives of men and women academics are organized (and are perceived by appointing committees to be organized) may not be a form of direct discrimination against women, but they certainly discriminate in favour of men.

The term 'positive discrimination' has certain negative connotations, although it is the term frequently used in Britain to refer to what is known in the States as 'affirmative action' or 'positive action'. These latter terms will be used in this chapter, not only because they are more accurate in describing the policies outlined, but because discrimination, positive or otherwise, is against the law in the sorts of areas discussed below.

Affirmative Action in Principle

'Affirmative action refers to those steps taken to remedy the grossly disparate staffing and recruitment patterns that are the present consequences of past discriminations and to prevent the occurrence of employment discrimination in the future.' (US Commission on Civil Rights 1973)

The principle of affirmative action and the rationale behind it imply a particular way of looking at the world. If it were believed that women 'under-achieved' because of genetic make-up there would be no point in affirmative action; no effort to give women a chance would make any difference to brain capacity or ability. But there is no evidence that the problem is a genetic one, and indeed, far from being under-achievers, given the constraints under which women work with the care of children, the elderly and men, they might well be characterized as over-achievers.

To believe in a policy of affirmative action is to believe that there is something wrong with the way in which goods are distributed in society and that there needs to be some form of re-allocation. To have an affirmative action policy identifies a problem, and I would argue that this is not the problem of female under-achievement. Within this context (as in so many others) it is a problem of male (white, middle class) power. In looking at the distribution of power and privilege, we can, crudely speaking, suggest two principles to guide redress. First, that there are certain areas of privilege and everyone should have access to them, and secondly that there are certain areas of privilege and they should be abolished.

The first principle, that of equal access, is normally more acceptable than the second. That all people should have equal access to privilege is not normally contentious, but once you start taking away what some people believe to be their inalienable right to privilege, their heritage to privilege, then problems arise. If the power or privilege certain individuals or groups have come to expect is distributed elsewhere, it tends to cause resentment. What is more, principles need to be established for the redistribution of power which may be resented by those who are not, as well as those who are, in powerful positions.

In some respects, this identifies a factor which can be a problem with affirmative action: that in elevating one or two women to the ranks of the privileged no significant change is made. In order to examine this further, it is worth looking at some of the ways in which affirmative action has been operating in the United States.

Affirmative Action in Practice: the Example of the United States

Affirmative action in the United States has been about equal access, about women having a larger slice of the cake, and about women having access to male privilege in the same way as men have access to male privilege. Such a philosophy is not inconsistent with a particular American way of life, and represents one model of social mobility. Sociologists suggest that Americans have a system of 'contest mobility', in which the best man (sic) wins, while the British go for a system of 'sponsored mobility' in which the already privileged are privileged further, or, to be a little more generous, an improved chance is given to those who show some ability (and in certain cases to those who do not).

How then does affirmative action operate? What follows does not describe the legal intricacies and complexities of the operation of affirmative action programmes, but gives a broad overview. It is worth noting that affirmative action and the role of affirmative action officers (whose work is to implement affirmative action programmes), is one which causes an enormous amount of antagonism, confusion, and suspicion. Lora Liss, who has herself worked as an affirmative action officer, writes:

'Few ideas in academe have emerged amid so much controversy, have so much potential for social change, and have proved to be so misunderstood as that of affirmative action officer.' (Liss 1977, p.418)

How then, does affirmative action operate? The guidelines adopted by the Department of Health Education and Welfare in 1972 state:

'*Affirmative Action* requires the contractor to do more than ensure employment neutrality with regard to race, colour, religion, sex and national origin. As the phrase implies, affirmative action requires the employer to make additional efforts to recruit, employ and promote qualified members of groups formerly excluded, even if that exclusion cannot be traced to particular discriminatory actions on the part of the employer. The premise of the affirmative action concept of the Executive Order is that unless positive action is undertaken to overcome the effects of systemic institutional forms of exclusion and discrimination, a benign neutrality in employment practices will tend to perpetuate the *status quo ante* indefinitely.' (Higher Education Guidelines 1972)

Affirmative action policies are those based on the premise that intentional discrimination is merely the tip of the iceberg, and that the most persuasive form of discrimination is built into the systems which control access to employment and opportunity.

It is easier to do something about blatant and crude intentional discrimination than it is to cope with discrimination which is built into a system, and the purpose of affirmative action is to undo a preferential system of positive discrimination not to create a preferential system of positive discrimination.

In the United States the law requires that institutions with 50,000 or more dollars worth of federal contracts and fifty or more employees have their plans for affirmative action approved by the Office of Civil Rights. Such plans are based on the undoubtedly correct view that ending overt and intentional discrimination is not sufficient to end years of prejudice. Because of women's experiences in the past, it is not enough merely to offer 'equal opportunity'.

Steven Miller (1979), a Boston sociologist, distinguishes three basic affirmative action strategies employed in the United States: preferences, targets and quotas; allocational priorities; and incentives.

To begin with preferences, targets and quotas: a quota, as one might suppose, requires that a specific number of jobs be filled by, for instance, women (or blacks or minorities). In some cases, instead of filling a specific quota, a target approach is utilized so that no specific numerical commitment need be made. The preference approach involves giving certain categories preferential treatment or extra 'points'. This practice was used in Britain to give preference to returning soldiers taking the Civil Service examination after World War II. So far as I know, no such preference has ever been given to individuals involved in other pursuits of national importance such as staying at home to bring up the nation's children.

Miller points out three dangers in undertaking these forms of affirmative action. First, there is the danger of tokenism, although it can be argued that even a token woman is better than no woman at all. Symbolic actions are critically important and the presence of so called 'token' women can have an enormous consciousness-raising effect. The danger is, however, that tokens will not be followed by large-scale changes, and that in fact tokenism may be used actually to avoid change, as in: 'We have a woman Prime Minister so women must be equal'. Secondly, Miller sees in the quota target and preference scheme the danger of 'creaming off' the least disadvantaged of the disadvantaged group, so that those left behind may actually be relatively worse off. Thirdly, he sees the danger that progress may actually be slowed down once a few rapid changes have occurred in the spotlight of attention. The dangers of the preference approach are clear: what sort of activities 'deserve' preferential treatment?

The second major strategy for affirmative action, allocational priorities, is concerned with the use of government funds for certain groups of people who are particularly disadvantaged.

The third major strategy is that of incentives, where firms and organizations are offered financial incentives to offer posts to disadvantaged workers. Clearly a scheme such as this is most likely to be successful in an expanding economy, although it has been suggested that incentives can operate more effectively in a climate of cuts and limited resources.

In relation to higher education, the preferred form of affirmative action, for those who prefer it at all, is similar to Miller's category of 'targets' and is that of goals and timetables. This form of action involves a statistical analysis of the composition of the workforce, identifying the extent of the problem within a particular institution and putting forward a plan for increased recruitment of the under-represented groups over the next few years. To take one example, the Affirmative Action Plan of Lehigh University in 1976 revealed:

'No women or minorities among the top administrators, ... 6% women, 2% minority men at the next highest administrative level, ... 10% women, 6% minority men, no minority women among faculty, ... in professional, non instructional positions, 27% are women and 2% are minority men. There are no minority women.' (Liss 1978)

This is not dissimilar to Britain where, although women are well represented on the 'shop floor' as primary school teachers, they are virtually absent from top levels of educational policy and decision-making.

The 'identification of the problem' section of Lehigh University's Affirmative Action Plan showed:

'the greatest under-utilisation to be of white women and black and Hispanic origin men and women in the higher executive, managerial and administrative classifications as well as in faculty positions. Black and Hispanic origin clerical workers are underutilised; white women are concentrated in clerical positions. There are no concentrations of black men and women.' (Liss, 1978, p.32)

'As a result,' writes Liss (the Affirmative Action Officer), 'goals and timetables were established, through which a total of 58 women and 70 minority men and women at all levels were projected to be hired over the next 6 years. If attained, this would mean that the faculty would include 28% women and 12% minorities' (and the proportions of minorities and women in other grades would also be increased). Such plans sound very attractive. What have the problems been?

Problems

There have been two major difficulties with affirmative action in higher education. First, gains in concrete terms appear to have been extremely limited, and secondly, some (normally those who feel threatened) feel that standards are being eroded and that 'reverse discrimination' is taking place. It is worth tackling the second misapprehension first: the fear of 'reverse discrimination'. The evidence hardly sustains such a view. Ray and Johnson (1974) have suggested that unjustified cries of 'reverse discrimination' are an indirect result of 'past vigorous efforts to locate and place white males'. Within the context of affirmative action, preference for a less qualified person on grounds of race or sex remains illegal.

'Universities are not "above the law", therefore external constraints applied to hiring practices which are illegal are to be expected. Some may see this as a violation of "academic freedom". However, there has been for years a more fundamental violation of human rights in terms of admittance to academia of women and minority group members and this is what affirmative action guidelines are meant to redress.' (p.44)

As Joan Huber has pointed out in relation to reverse discrimination, what people perceive about discrimination is an important datum in itself but it does not constitute a description of the actual state of affairs:

'The fascination with the possibility of reverse discrimination seems strange, in view of the systematic discrimination against better qualified women candidates for admission to colleges, universities and graduate schools'. (Huber 1974, p.44)

The accusation of reverse discrimination may be irritating and tedious, but there is no evidence to support the view that it is a problem. More disturbing is the view held by some (and not without reason) that affirmative action plans have been ineffective. Certainly there are indications that results of affirmative action plans have often been dismal. Loeb, Ferber and Lowry (1978), working as feminist economists, suggested that the cost to institutions has far exceeded the benefit to the affected group and that although the programmes seem to have had some effect on the recruitment of women (though even here, the results are equivocal) salary and rank are still unequally rewarded. Governmental regulation, they conclude, has been largely ineffective. It has created costs and backlash but has been too weakly enforced to bring about significant results. Therefore, more positive alternatives (in the form of financial incentives for achieving the desired goals) should be put into effect in order adequately to address the problems that still exist.

Such then, is the somewhat gloomy picture of affirmative action in the United States. It is still better, in my view, than nothing, but by no means as successful as one might hope.

And Britain?

What is the relevance to Britain of a discussion of the North American experience? Rather little, one might conclude, as one hears of the closure of another college nursery, of cuts in teacher training places (always a traditional avenue for women), of the lack of availability of discretionary grants for married women returners to certain courses, and of the general dismantling of higher education. Certainly, one can hardly envisage any of the major political parties giving priority to significant expenditure to encourage affirmative action plans in the immediate future.

Given the financial, cultural and political constraints, what sort of positive recommendations could be made for a form of affirmative action that would work financially, would be possible in terms of human and material resources, and would not be beyond the pale in practical terms?

Two relatively easily attainable positive recommendations can be suggested as a starting point. A first prerequisite of any programme of affirmative action is the establishment of crèches and nurseries on a scale which will realistically allow parents (and in most cases for parents read mothers) to participate in higher education. We cannot talk of equal access to higher education while one section of the community is systematically excluded by its need to care for young children.

To require adequate care for one's children while one works is not a radical demand. Men have this assurance; they do not have to think 'A career or a child?' They know that both are possible, and for them childcare arrangements are built into the system. In demanding childcare facilities as a prerequisite to affirmative action, we would only be redressing the balance of past discrimination. It may be of some comfort to see that falling rolls may actually induce institutions to re-consider the provision of crêche and nursery facilities and use them as bait to catch the market of young mothers. While present cuts may make provision of this kind from extra funds, unlikely cogent arguments may be put forward for it to be made through re-allocation within existing budgets. Childcare may not be close to the heart of all educational administrators, but keeping up admissions certainly is.

A second form of affirmative action open to us, even within the current climate, is, like the first, nothing to do with the American model of goals and timetables. It involves making better use of colleges of education and colleges of higher education. Since the seventies, smaller colleges have progressively been closed and staff made redundant. Many young academics currently cannot find work.

These closures have been a serious blow to women students and potential women students. As Peter Scott (1979) has pointed out, colleges represent a valuable tradition that places emphasis on intimacy and general education – qualities important for a more accessible and more popular system of education in the 1980s and 1990s.

We have the plant and resources available to mount affirmative action courses for women students in colleges all over the country. To some extent this is already being done in New Opportunities for Women courses, and in pioneering courses for women in accountancy and other non-traditional areas (for women), but we need to expand what is available and one way of responding to both the cuts and the need for affirmative action is to see such expansion as a way forward.

It has been suggested that one of the reasons why we have no coherent policy for higher education in this country is that it affects such a relatively small proportion of the population that no government wants to over-commit or over-emphasize the area. Perhaps if we were to adopt forms of education which affected a larger proportion of the population, rather than a tiny élite, it would make sense in political as well as 'fairness' terms.

What is more, there is no reason why 'positive discrimination' of this type could not be accomplished under the provisions of existing legislation. Section 47 of the Sex Discrimination Act does permit certain sorts of 'positive action' by training bodies, by employers and by trade unions, employers' organizations, etc. For instance:

> 'Nothing in the Act makes unlawful any discriminatory act done by one of the eligible training bodies in or in connection with affording access to training to people who in the view of the training body are in special need of it because of the period for which they have been discharging domestic or family responsibilities to the exclusion of regular full-time employment (for example, married women who have given up work to bring up a family and now wish to return.' (Sex Discrimination, 1975, p.34)

Up until now, achievement in the area of sex discrimination and higher education has been dismal. But the experience of other countries such as the USA suggests that something can be done. We now face the danger of cuts whose effects are discriminatory being added to the existing structures of discrimination. The need to learn practical lessons from achievements elsewhere is even more urgent.

Notes

1   An earlier version of this paper was given at a conference on Equal Opportunities in Higher Education organized by the Equal Opportunities Commission and the Society for Research into Higher Education in March 1980. A short article based on this appeared in the *Times Higher Education Supplement* (Roberts and Spender 1980).

2   For an excellent pamphlet on positive action, see Robarts (1981). As well as discussing the situation in Britain this draws on work done by Sadie Robarts in the United States.

References

Higher Education Guidelines (1972) Executive order 11246, US Department of Health Education and Welfare, Office for Civil Rights, Washington DC

Huber,Joan (1974) Reverse discrimination: structure or attitudes *The American Sociologist* 9, pp.43-47

Liss,L. (1977) Affirmative action officers: are they change agents? *Educational Record* 58 (4) 418-428

Liss,L. (1978) *Impact of an Affirmative Action Crisis on Campus Women* Paper presented to the Research Committee on Sex Roles, International Sociological Association, Uppsala, Sweden

Loeb,Jane, Ferber,Marianne and Lowry,Helen (1978) The effectiveness of affirmative action for women *Journal of Higher Education* 49 (3)

Miller,S.M. (1979) A critique of US experience. In Glennester,Howard and Hatch,S. (Eds) *Positive Discrimination and Inequality* Fabian Research Series, No.314

Ray,N.T. and Johnson, U.S. (1974) Comment on reverse discrimination *The American Sociologist* 9, pp.43-47

Robarts,Sadie (with Anna Coote and Elizabeth Ball) (1981) *Positive Action for Women The Next Step* London: NCCL

Roberts,Helen and Spender,Dale (1980) Casting the old boys network aside *Times Higher Education Supplement* 19 September

Scott,Peter (1979) *What Future for Higher Education?* Fabian Tract 465

Sex Discrimination (1975) *A Guide to the Sex Discrimination Act* London Home Office

Statement of Affirmative Action for Equal Employment Opportunities (1973) United States Commission on Civil Rights, Clearing House Publication No.41

Women in Universities (1982) Statistics Unit, Equal Opportunities Commission

13 The intellectual necessity for Women's Studies

Renate Duelli Klein

> No one ever told us we had to study our lives
> Make of our lives a study, as if learning natural history
> (Adrienne Rich)[1]

Why Women's Studies?

While I have been asked the question 'Why Women's Studies?' many times, I want to begin by asking 'Why would someone ask "Why Women's Studies"?' for it seems to me to represent the crux of the issue and to point both to the necessity for Women's Studies and to the resistance that it encounters. In this first section I am going to look at the assumptions behind the question 'Why Women's Studies?' and indicate why these assumptions need to change and why Women's Studies exists to change them.

I want to start by saying that for me — my assumptions, my particular female experience, and my perspective on the world — the evidence that women as a group continue to be oppressed, subordinated and discriminated against everywhere is overwhelming. I think that we women are oppressed because of our sex, and as a woman I am motivated to describe, analyse and change this oppression which impinges on my life.

Because of the tradition in which I have been reared, which tells me that knowledge is produced and distributed in institutions of higher education, I will look to these institutions for space to pursue my analysis of human issues that are of great significance to the biggest single population group in the world. However, for reasons I will discuss later, I find that none of the established disciplines are suitable for my purpose as their very development and present practice does not represent 'A Group Called Women' (Cassell 1977) of which I am a member and whose conditions I wish to explore and change. So I, like many other women, have looked towards the construction of a new basis in academia for the generation of knowledge of this particular aspect of human existence, which has led us in the last decade to the development of Women's Studies, or, as it is sometimes called, Feminist Studies or Female Studies (Groag Bell and Schwartz Rosenhan 1981).

There are precedents for this procedure. The disciplines which exist today have not always been there – on the contrary they have not been there very long at all. They are less than 100 years old in their present compartmentalized form. It was the newly developing sciences that attacked the previous 'holistic' (from an androcentric perspective) theological curriculum and replaced it with the present system for categorizing and classifying knowledge (Howe 1979).

A century ago when new perspectives on humanity presented themselves, they were encoded into a host of new disciplines (the various branches in natural science and later in social science), so today, when new perspectives emerge on the way women are part of and contribute to humanity, the establishment of one new discipline seems but a reasonable step.

But there is a lot of resistance – and I attribute much of that resistance and the particular forms it takes (from ridicule to sheer incomprehension) to the fact that the new discipline centres around women. And that brings me back to where I first started – one of the reasons for the question 'Why Women's Studies?' is that we live in a society where women are not taken into account and so the idea of an academic discipline about and for women is in itself a contradiction.

A look at the socio-economic position of women confirms that our priorities are not men's priorities. Whether we live in western capitalist or socialist countries or elsewhere in the world it can be seen that women's status is not only not improving but in fact in many instances deteriorating. Gains that women have made are insignificant compared with gains some men have made during the same time; and losses are much greater.[2] Why is it that the uncontested United Nations figures (1980) are not the basis for world-wide scandal and immediate action? They show that:

'Women constitute half the world's population, perform nearly two-thirds of its work hours, receive one-tenth of the world's income and own less than one-hundredth of the world's property.'

When women in Britain constitute forty per cent of the workforce yet, as Wendy Owen reports, earn only seventy-two per cent of men's wages, when since 1975 women's unemployment has increased by 207 per cent compared with sixty-one per cent for men (Owen 1981), when women continue to perform vast amounts of unpaid emotional and material work — the labour of love at home — which is not just unpaid but is invisible in government statistics on employment — then my question is, WHY is Women's Studies not a priority, a necessity?

Women's position in education mirrors precisely their socio-economic status at large: they are present in large numbers as primary and secondary school teachers and increasingly as university students and teachers in the lower echelons,[3] but according to Eileen Byrne (1978, p.15), men constitute ninety-seven per cent of the government of education. The British university statistics for 1980 (DES 1982, p.53) state that women are 2.7 per cent of full professors and 6.4 per cent of senior lecturers and readers in Great Britain. In some instances women's position is not improving but deteriorating. Despite the increase in numbers of women academics on lower echelons in the last decade, the percentage of women in influential positions in education has actually declined (Byrne 1978, p.218; Rendel, this volume). In brief, women are absent from top positions of power in the policy and decision-making apparatus of the educational system. As Dorothy Smith has said 'power and authority in the educational process are the prerogatives of men' (1978, p.289).

This information is incontestable — yet there is still a considerable segment of society asserting that women are better off now than they have ever been (pointing to the few token women as presidents of banks or motor companies or as heads of states). Understandably for people who hold such beliefs, the issue of women's oppression is either solved or almost solved but in either case no longer relevant, and a field of study that concentrates on 'women only' is not only unnecessary but a luxury not to be afforded in these dire days of economic recession. There are, we are told, more important issues to be dealt with than whatever is left of 'the women question'.

'Important for whom?' is the question to be asked next. Who decides what a significant issue is? Who makes the rules and who profits? Who controls? Those who deny women's economic plight are also denying the systematic violence practised by one sex against the other and they accuse women of 'over-reacting' and 'generalizing' when we point to men's roles in incest, child abuse, prostitution, battering, clitoridectomy, sexual harassment, pornography and rape (Brownmiller 1975; Dworkin 1979; Barry 1979; Farley 1978; MacKinnon 1979; Griffin 1981). Who are they and on what do they base their judgement? What are the assumptions, values, standards, ways of collating and interpreting evidence that enable them not only to oppress women but to remain oblivious to the very fact that they oppress us?

It might be argued that we all have our biases and assumptions and tend to think that we are 'right' and the others are 'wrong'. And there is no doubt that one of the unquestioned assumptions in our society is that the prevailing sexist (and racist and classist) ideology is not just a particular way of organizing the world but the <u>only</u> way. Looking at this issue in a detached manner one might come to the conclusion that 'truth' and 'objectivity' do not exist anyway and that it is all a matter of degree. ...However, 'detachment' leaves out the fact that it is live women of all ethnicities, ages and social groups who are beaten up and raped, that it is live women who lose their jobs and are humiliated and declared inferior, that it is live women who are portrayed as sex objects in the media. And it is these value judgements which lead me to think I am 'right' to want change: change in the theories that bolster such despicable treatment and in the praxis that effects it.

And here is the crux of Women's Studies: Women's Studies is not 'just' about facts and figures, it is not 'just' another academic discipline – it involves a different way of viewing the world. It is about change: in consciousness; in material and psychological circumstances; in power and control. It was developed in academia by feminists active in the Women's Liberation Movement and therefore has been called 'the educational arm of the feminist movement'.[4] What Women's Studies grapples with is the premise that if women's oppression remains deniable and women's lives – work, art, culture – invisible, then there must be something in the values, standards, reasons and logic of society which needs to be changed.

The absence of women from positions of power is reflected in the curriculum at all educational levels as well as in the research that is being pursued and is thought important and worthwhile in all the academic disciplines (Spender 1981a). As has been stated for psychology (Parlee 1979), for theology (Radford Ruether 1976), for biology (Hubbard 1979), for the social sciences (Westkott 1979; Roberts 1981), for education (Spender 1981) and for literature (Kolodny 1981) – to name only a few of the critiques of the present state of the academic disciplines – it is MEN – in particular white, middle-class men – who continue to control the production, the assessment and the distribution of knowledge. Consequently, females who have succeeded in getting access to education get a male-dominated, male-oriented and male-defined education: they are guests in Men's Studies (Spender 1981a). In this male-as-the-norm ideology (Acker 1980a) there is more material about men (Acker 1980b) and it is accorded more significance. It is knowledge produced, distributed and owned by men (Spender 1981c) and because it focuses on men and their 'achievements' such as wars and revolutions, when women want to be successful in a man's world what else can they do but copy men's styles and become 'social males'?

However, we feminists have continued to assert that we need not accept as 'natural' or 'sacred' what denies women their experiences. By exposing what it is that we oppose, by unveiling the all-pervasive (often hidden) presence of androcentricity, we are already on our way to work for a different future, in which women's perspectives are as important and powerful as men's. Says Marcia Westkott (1981, p.125):

> '...to assert that "it need not be" presumes both the ability to take the oppression of women as an object of understanding as well as (the ability) to feel the oppression in a deeply personal way. Moreover, this refusal to tolerate the conditions that we discover proceeds from the historical consciousness that the world could be different. It assumes that alternatives are possible to the historically created male-dominated structures that presently oppose the freedom of women.' (underlining mine)

The women who are in Women's Studies – students and teachers – both recognize and feel women's oppression from personal experience. By bringing these abilities to our attempts to understand it in an academic scholarly way not only do we 'deconstruct' and 'reconstruct' previous knowledge (Stimpson 1978) but we also construct new knowledge that includes women as self-determining human beings, that empowers women to explore ways to end their status as underpaid and overworked, abused and exploited second-class citizens.

Women's Studies is an intellectual necessity if we are to avail ourselves of 'equal opportunities in education'. It provides us with a self-enhancing, 'positive' education because it acknowledges as real and important not only the similar experiences, needs and interests of women as a group but equally their differences of ethnicity, cultural background, age, sexual orientation, social status,[5] religion. It puts women's perspectives at the centre of our intellectual quest for knowledge – a marked shift from the perspective in Men's Studies that, as an example, asks the question 'Why Women's Studies?'

What is Women's Studies?

Defined by the founders of the US National Women's Studies Association as 'an educational strategy for change' owing its existence to the Women's Liberation Movement (1977),[6] it is important to stress that Women's Studies consists of both teaching and research. It is the interaction between feminist scholarship and learning that takes place in the classroom which respectively inspires, probes, reinforces, expands and develops them. Rather than transmitting knowledge as 'the truth' from 'the expert' to 'the ignorant', students and teachers in Women's Studies attempt to create knowledge in an environment in which all are learners. Some, usually the teachers, are more familiar with the existing scholarship on a topic and make this resource their contribution to the classroom. Others bring their life experiences as a resource, and, as many of the students (and teachers) in Women's Studies are mature women, their contribution is just as pertinent in gaining an understanding of a phenomenon and developing an analysis. It is here that 'the personal becomes the intellectual and the intellectual the personal' (see Rutenberg 1980 for her account of a student's learning experience in Women's Studies). The enthusiasm that most students and teachers display in Women's Studies courses stems from the attempt to blend theory and praxis, a rare happening in other disciplines. Whether the topic is work, health, politics or literature, discussing it from a perspective that puts women at its centre allows us to compare and contrast our own (and other people's) experiences with the given 'facts and figures'. Thus some of the dichotomies inherent in Men's Studies begin to vanish: the division, for example, between 'public and private', 'intellect and passion', 'theory and praxis'. Women's learning experiences are no longer divorced from their lives. Instead, what emerges is an attempt to understand problems and to develop means of solving them. Pieces come together in the process of discovery, and, for example, the use of language or information on women's job segregation might lead directly to action to change one's life.

As students and teachers working closely together we try to break down hierarchies, interact collectively rather than competitively, take each other seriously and respect each other's different perspectives, particularly relevant among women from different ethnic/cultural backgrounds. In attempting to account for diversity, rather than dismiss it and seek for the one and only 'truth', we are trying out models for different forms of human relationships. In Women's Studies we are 'testing' the very same concept raised by feminists outside academia – to whom we must feed back our analyses and engage with in their actions – which is working towards a world free of power relationships. Trying to engage in such activities within an academic environment that is neither geared to nor inclined to welcome our presence and goals raises a number of serious questions, some of which I will discuss later. However, as stated earlier in this chapter, as a woman and a feminist I need a space to learn about, develop and expand feminist perspectives on the world and I think women have every right to demand more than 'A Room of One's Own' (Woolf 1929) in those institutions which claim to represent an all encompassing universal perspective.[7]

The 'subject matter' of Women's Studies is women, but women's lives do not exist in a vacuum: they are located in a social context which includes the study of men (and children) as well as the natural and the 'man-made' environment. The economic situation of women that I mentioned earlier is as much part of Women's Studies as is violence against women, dangers and possibilities in technological, psychological and biological aspects of life, and the various forms of art that have been created by women. Women's Studies is not limited to specific 'women's issues' such as female biology, health care and reproduction, nor to studies on the sexual division of labour or to women's participation in men's trade unions or men's wars. In fact every human issue is a women's issue and at the core of Women's Studies lies the demand to look critically at every facet of life from interpersonal relationships to politics, from language to law, from the (ab)use of natural resources to the social construction of reality, and to look at it differently, from a woman-centred perspective.

Clearly such a definition shows that Women's Studies cannot remain within the compartmentalization of knowledge as it is established in the present academic disciplines. While some call Women's Studies 'interdisciplinary', I prefer the term 'transdisciplinary', arguing that 'interdisciplinary' still accepts as a given the only recently institutionalized academic disciplines.

Looking at the production of scholarship in Women's Studies — the body of knowledge classes in Women's Studies are based on — various types of research can be differentiated; however, they can all be done simultaneously. What has been called 'compensatory' by Lerner (1979) and 'collecting' by Register (1979) is research that meticulously examines with a women-centred perspective where and how in what we currently call 'knowledge' women are 'omitted, distorted or trivialised' (Stimpson 1973). Freud and Marx get re-visited; we ask 'where were all the women in history?' and we find that they had 'a literature of their own' (Showalter 1978). Such work leads for example to a new periodization in history (Kelly-Gadol 1976) in which it emerges that the 'dark' midde-ages were much lighter for women than the allegedly 'enlightened renaissance'. It also leads to a reconceptualization of the question of 'good' and 'bad' in literature, in art and in research itself.[8]

Compensatory research and the collection of data cannot take place without 'criticizing' which eventually leads to the production of new theories and models which I find the most fascinating aspect of feminist research. *Men's Studies Modifed: The Impact of Feminism on the Academic Disciplines* (Spender 1981a) is a collection of essays that looks closely at thirteen academic disciplines, criticizing and exposing their male bias and — after discussing the impact that feminist scholarship has or has not had on these fields — proceeding to discuss the new questions raised and the new theories that emerge.

The past decade has seen a virtual explosion in feminist scholarship. There is hardly any field that has not been touched (which does not mean that the gatekeepers of these fields — men — notice or value this scholarship). However, much of it is still in line with traditional concepts, be it in asking the questions or in using orthodox methodology. As I have argued elsewhere (Duelli Klein 1980) I think that such research remains research on rather than for women. While there is now a considerable amount of feminist theory written by marxist-feminists, radical-feminists, liberal feminists and other 'kinds' of feminists we need translators to make connections between them, intertwine them, point to similarities and differences and build new theories — Women's Studies Theories. We need to be what Liz Stanley and Sue Wise call 'breaking out' (Stanley and Wise 1983): of our own disciplinary backgrounds, of our own upbringing. As Stanley and Wise say (1981, p.108):

> We're first, foremost, and last feminists; not feminist-phenomenologists, feminist-marxists or feminist hyphen anything else. Our interest and concern is with feminism and feminist revolution.'

We must 'withdraw consent from the patriarchal construction of reality' (Du Bois 1981, p.18). We need more irreverence, more 'disobedience to patriarchy' (Rich 1981). Adrienne Rich herself is a good example for irreverence and her theories on compulsory heterosexuality and lesbian existence genuinely challenge previous notions of sexuality (Rich 1980).

Doing Women's Studies

As we are pursuing our goal for a feminist future we become increasingly interested in 'Trying to find out <u>how</u> to find out what we know' (Bowles and Duelli Klein 1981; see also Roberts 1981).

Space does not allow me to elaborate on the questions 'What is feminist research?' and 'Is there a feminist methodology?' but some salient points can briefly be made. At the heart of feminist research lies the imperative that it should be <u>for</u> women, in order to improve our lives inside and outside academia. As each of us has our own subjective experiences we must bring ourselves and our 'conscious partiality' (Mies 1981, p.29) to our research and become an integral part of the research process. This is in marked contrast to the 'myth of value-free science' and 'objectivity' that still pervades much of traditional research. Being part of one's research demands acknowledging that we are both 'subjects' and 'objects':[9] as women, we are members of an oppressed group, as researchers, we are studying them/us. So when we are engaged in empirical research, we try and replace research hierarchies by collaborative relationships with those we study. Put differently, we try to come to terms with the dichotomy of 'researcher' and 'researched'. These relationships not only influence the research process but the product itself: our own ideas and concepts change through these interactions and we ourselves undergo changes in consciousness.[10] The research process, which it is important to document carefully so that we can learn from one another, is not a linear progression from hypothesis formulation to experiment to verification/refutation. Rather, it is 'interactive, circular and reflexive' (Du Bois 1981, p.14), looking for synthesis rather than analysis, conceptualizing what we see as 'whole, entire, complex ... and in context' (Du Bois 1981, p.17),cyclical, creating theory rather than testing it.

There are a number of research methods (the tools with which we do our research) that seem better suited than others to feminist research (eg qualitative rather than quantitative; personal rather than impersonal; situation embedded rather than context-stripped (Reinharz 1981, p.75/76) But feminist researchers try to adapt and adjust their methods according to the varying circumstances in their work – to be creative and flexible rather than dogmatic and rigid.[11]

As an example: for Stanley and Wise (1981, 1982), research should not differ from what we do in everyday life, meaning that we should use the same approaches and procedures in each. The different strategies with which to survive in a sexist world are our methods and we use this 'documentary method' whether we are doing research, surviving in academia, or sitting in the London tube.

As to the priorities for feminist research: according to Stanley and Wise, 'what feminists spend our lives doing must obviously be the subject of feminist research' (1981, p.102), and 'We need to know how, in minute detail, all facets of the oppression of all women occur, because if we are to resist oppression then we need to understand how it occurs' (p.113).

Stanley and Wise's demand brings me back to 'What is feminist research?': whether we decide to research ourselves, other women, do a historical study or look at the influence of nuclear technology on our lives, it seems to me we have to start with connecting what we study with our experiences as women living in a patriarchal world. The discrepancy between 'what we see' and the responses we get will enable us to understand what exactly it is we oppose and what strategies we might devise to change it. As Maria Mies says (1981, p.32):

'... we have to start fighting against women's exploitation and oppression in order to be able to understand the extent, the dimensions, the forms and the causes of this patriarchal system.'

Implicit in this statement are two messages. One is that it is imperative that in all we do we incorporate an historical perspective: patriarchy was not invented yesterday and we had better learn about our sisters of the seventeenth, eighteenth and nineteenth centuries who had at least as radical ideas as we have, and try to find out why and how they were prevented from having a large impact on society. As Dale Spender puts it so pointedly: 'Men either use or lose women's ideas' (1982), and indeed, we have little reassurance that our new knowledge will meet with a different fate.

The other message is that only in doing (eg doing irreverent research, challenging the traditional norms, living differently, doing Women's Studies, etc.) will we develop a deeper understanding of why, how and where women have to effect change.

Ideally – and I was fortunate to have this experience – 'doing Women's Studies' also provides us with the opportunity to bring our research into our classrooms where it will be discussed and will be criticized if it does not seem 'relevant' to the students who might be more active in one of the many groups of the Women's Liberation Movement than we are. This connection to 'reality' is vital; it should prevent Women's Studies teachers from becoming unimaginative 'ivory-tower feminists'.

Moreover, there is another side to Women's Studies altogether that I admit I have not talked about much here but which is, in my experience, of paramount importance. It is the sheer joy, fascination and energy that usually surfaces in Women's Studies classes.

Such vibrance has two main sources. One is the students (and teachers) themselves: committed, concerned, hard-working, interested, lively and full of energy, engaged in a multitude of extra-curricular professional and voluntary activities as well as in personal relationships with lovers and spouses and as single parents with children whom they support on their own. There can be disagreement and uproar in Women's Studies classes but rarely boredom; the atmosphere is exciting and challenging. We try to take care of each other (although sometimes the practice doesn't quite match the theory!), we know there aren't too many of us and we know that all of us are overworked and over-committed. We acknowledge that we are privileged in having the opportunity to get a feminist education.

The other energizing source lies in the content of the material we cover in Women's Studies classes. In our attempt to study/research our lives and those of other women, we engage in re-claiming the word 'power' for women: not to dominate others, but to keep empowering ourselves (Howe 1975). We also give it a new context. Re-discovered through feminist research emerge all those women who, even in spite of their ongoing oppression, have chosen not to be victims. They were strong, imaginative and for centuries have been developing an independent woman-centred understanding of the world (Spender 1982). They asserted their power of choice and survived by creating what Lynn

Herring (1980) has described as the force in Adrienne Rich's poetry: 'the power of the ordinary – a universe of humble things'.

Role models can be useful. The re-discovery of these women is reason for joy and it is in Women's Studies that we can legitimately pursue the discovery and perpetration of our heritage: a validation both of the extraordinary resilience of women struggling in isolation and obscurity – ' "gaslighted" for centuries' (Rich 1979b, p.190) – and of 'the power of the ordinary' – of women's lives, past and present.

Obstacles to Overcome

I started by saying that women need not accept the continuing domination of women's education by men (nor men's domination of our lives) and I suggested that Women's Studies was a way of ending this domination, by shifting the male perspectives of Men's Studies and putting women's perspectives at the centre of our inquiries. However, as the issue is about power, it remains to be seen whether we will succeed in making Women's Studies strong enough to shift the power balance effectively.

We face quite a few external and internal obstacles. The external ones are clear: there are men (and women) who do not understand, and/or are threatened and thus oppose us. Lack of money, menacing cuts, discussions about whether we are really legitimate and truly academic are one form or another of saying that they think we are not important (or are a threat). Then there is the 'Men Problem' in Women's Studies: is there any room for men as teachers and students (see Duelli Klein (1983) for an elaboration on this thorny theme). However, although our present marginal status is clearly not a comfortable position to be in, why should it astonish us? We are up against enormous odds, for, as I have argued earlier in this chapter, many do not even recognize our need and right to exist.

The internal obstacles, I think, are more difficult to outline, face and overcome. First, there is the problem that all of us have been impregnated (sic) and damaged by the values of the misogynist society we live in. As members of a colonized sex we have been socialized to be women and even if we rebel – and being feminists in Women's Studies means that this is precisely what we do – we constantly have to fight our own ingrained prejudices. One of them is the fear of working with other women without the customary rivalry and competition we were trained in, but with collaboration, support and respect. Moreover, as we do not want simply to exchange knowledge by and for white, heterosexual middle-class men for knowledge by and for white, heterosexual middle-class women, we have a lot of work to do before we come to terms with racism and homophobia in and among ourselves. Another obstacle, as I have already mentioned, is that we have been trained in a traditional discipline and we have to cope with the necessity of shedding the layers of acquired 'dos' and 'don'ts'. Bringing ourselves and our experiences to our research and teaching is difficult; as I tried to point out, our experiences have not been validated: 'women have been barred from experiencing our experience' (Bowles and Duelli Klein 1981, p.3). This difficulty may help account for the fact that in my view not every course which includes material 'on women' is a Women's Studies course. 'Adding-women-on' to an existing framework, having the odd lecture on 'great women poets' without actually attempting to extend and trans-form the framework of Men's Studies by shifting the centre of the perspective from men to women for me remains 'the study of women' rather than 'Women's Studies': a beginning perhaps, but ultimately, I feel, unlikely to contribute significantly to women's liberation.

However, as Sandra Coyner has said (1980), with the real possibility of becoming a 'genuine Women's Studies person' by getting an education from BA to PhD in Women's Studies (as yet more feasible in the USA than in Britain; see Appendix), future Women's Studies scholars might be able to develop an 'autonomous identity' rather than the present schizoid state that often demands oscillation between two fields – Women's Studies and the 'ex' – pledging loyalties to both, feeling torn by the contradictions, being overworked by taking on this 'double burden'.

The combination of internal and external obstacles makes it difficult indeed to survive within the restricting male-centred structure of academia and continue our work for social change. As Marcia Westkott says about Women's Studies (1981, p.172):

'To criticize the culture, history and procedures that undergird the institution through whose ranks we seek to advance, and to expect that our criticism will be accepted as a valid means to that advancement, is to face a tough problem indeed.'

And Elizabeth Minnich highlights the revolutionary nature of Women's Studies (1982, p.9):

'What we (feminists) are doing, is comparable to Copernicus shatter-ing our geo-centricity, Darwin shattering our species-centricity. We are shattering <u>andro-centricity</u>, and the change is as fundamental, as dangerous, as exciting.'

Some of us will leave the institutions and give up hoping that the move towards a 'woman-centred university' (Rich 1979a) can be achieved within the academic gatekeeping of the present institutions of higher education. Others will stay in the institution but will do 'projects of reform and repair' (Frye 1980) rather than work for fundamental shifts in consciousness and perspectives. This is Marilyn Frye's concern when she writes (1980, p.38):

> 'We suffered a single flash of vision ... and set about to institutionalize it; but the project has not liberated us or our students in a way which would make the unfurling of new vision a way of life.'

Hopefully there are enough of us who will insist on the intellectual necessity of Women's Studies in higher education and continue to struggle imaginatively, innovatively and with much physical stamina for a model of education that negates and transcends categories and concepts which do not hold for women. And I believe strongly that Women's Studies does make a difference: just as we are inspired and get strength from the women of our past who were intellectual thinkers and survivors in the most difficult material and emotional circumstances, so students and teachers in Women's Studies have a chance to get experiences validated and to participate in an alternative education to develop new theories on and for women's lives. Independent of which of the avenues we choose, we should not forget the purpose of our work. To quote Marcia Westkott again (1981, p.127):

> '... whether we leave the academy or attempt to survive within it, the goal of creating change for women guides us in our struggle.'

If higher education purports to be 'fair' then we cannot afford to ignore the feminist presence. Women's Studies exists and the proponents of Men's Studies should note that their work will not remain unchallenged. To quote Mary Evans (1982, p.73):

> 'Women's Studies has a most important part to play in ensuring that knowledge, itself a form of social power, is not produced solely in the interests of the powerful and the influential, to the detriment of the powerless and weak.'

By changing the rules, we work towards changing power relationships and the exclusion of women from the production of knowledge. Maybe indeed change will occur!

Appendix: the Current State of Women's Studies in Institutions of Higher Education in the USA and Great Britain[12]

For detailed information on the state of Women's Studies in the USA see: Howe 1977; the Monograph Series on Women's Studies (eight volumes) of the National Institute of Education (US Department of Health Education and Welfare, HEW) 1980; and *Women's Studies Quarterly*. For overview articles on Women's Studies in the US see: Schöpp-Schilling 1979; Tobias 1978, and Evans 1981. For Women's Studies in Great Britain see: Hartnett and Rendel 1975; Spender 1978; Bradshaw, Davies and De Wolfe 1981.

Since the first individual courses in 1969 and two US Studies Programmes at Cornell University and San Diego State University, (Howe and Ahlum 1973, p.393) the Women's Studies movement in the US has grown considerably: the 1981 figures list over 20,000 individual courses, and over 350 Women's Studies Programmes, more than a hundred of which grant a BA, thirty-nine an MA, and eleven a PhD degree. In addition, twenty-two research centres for women exist.[13] While the first programmes were established in less prestigious public (= state funded) and a few private colleges and universities, by 1981 even the prestigious 'top universities' such as Princeton and Berkeley and Stanford had programmes or at least a 'concentration' in Women's Studies (Yale and Harvard). (Berkeley has offered a BA degree in Women's Studies since 1977.) The first clusters of courses were offered in the humanities, gradually spreading to the social sciences, while the number of Women's Studies courses in natural science continues to be low. Most of the programmes are interdisciplinary, ie the students choose an emphasis in social science, the humanities (rarely the sciences), and combine Women's Studies courses from various departments to meet their degree requirements.

The budgets of Women's Studies Programmes range from a few dollars to approximately $150,000.00 and usually pay for a full-(or part-) time co-ordinator, the core courses and (a) lecturer(s) who may or may not have joint appointments in other departments.

Since 1977 Women's Studies has had its own professional organization (the National Women's Studies Organisation, NWSA) which serves as a network, has its own journal (*Women's Studies Quarterly*), organizes annual national and regional conferences and undertakes research projects in the field of Women's Studies. In 1981 (repeated in 1982) the first National Institute in Women's Studies took place at the University of Michigan in Ann Arbor and brought together seventy scholars, teachers and administrators in Women's Studies to discuss developments in theory and praxis.

A number of scholarly American journals spread the growing body of feminist scholarship in Women's Studies; among them are: *Signs; Feminist Studies; Frontiers; Women's Studies*; and *Quest*. On the international scene there are among others: *Women's Studies International Forum* (Britain/USA); *Feminist Review* (Britain); *Resources for Feminist Research* (Canada); *The International Journal of Women's Studies* (Canada); *Feministische Studien* (Germany); and *Memoria* (Italy).

The current political climate in the US and the enormous budget cuts in higher education, are likely to influence the further growth of Women's Studies. However, as it continues to draw large numbers of students into its classrooms (an important factor in US institutions of higher education) its existence is not jeopardized. Two main developments are taking place in many institutions simultaneously: first, a trend towards more autonomy in terms of budget and faculty hiring procedures, the nature of course offerings, the position of Women's Studies as a discipline of its own (often in connection with the establishment of MA and PhD programmes); and secondly, a trend towards the 'transformation of the curriculum of the traditional disciplines' (also called 'main-streaming'), often promoted by offering so-called 'Faculty Development Seminars' that are organized by the Women's Studies Programme: seminars and workshops for interested faculty about feminist scholarship and teaching and how to integrate these appraches into the various disciplines.

In Britain also, Women's Studies as a field of its own in institutions of higher education is growing.[14] However, at the level of degree-granting courses it has taken a different path from US Women's Studies: it is on the level of postgraduate education only that official degrees in Women's Studies are offered. These include an MA course in Women's Studies at the University of Kent at Canterbury (since 1980); an MA in Women's Studies at Bradford University (since 1982) and an MA in Women's Studies at Sheffield Polytechnic (starting in 1983). An increasing number of MA courses offer an option in Women's Studies (eg at the University of London as part of the Human Rights in Education course; at Essex University as part of the MA in Social History) and so do many postgraduate courses in education (PGCE) (eg at Bristol, London and Dundee Universities). The polytechnic of Central London offers a Diploma in Women's Studies (since 1977) and a new Diploma course is to start at Goldsmiths' College London in Autumn 1983.

So far, there are no degree-granting undergraduate courses, although since the early 1970s many courses have been offered, such as 'Women in Society' (eg at Cambridge, Manchester, Bradford, Hull, Lancaster and Warwick Universities) and 'Sexual Divisions in Society' (eg at Essex, Lancaster, Leeds, Liverpool and London Universities, at Thames Polytechnic and at the City University, London). From 1983, the Open University is offering students in any faculty of the OU a 2nd-year option (half-unit) called 'The Changing Experience of Women.'[15]

The need for a national network in Women's Studies is acknowledged and the first two national conferences in Women's Studies took place in London (December 1981/October 1982). Participating teachers and students from Women's Studies in higher, adult and further education discussed possibilities for a Women's Studies organization to provide contacts and further co-operation between students and staff interested in doing feminist teaching and research in Women's Studies, and the formation of a National Women's Studies Association is underway.

In addition, it is possible to do research degrees (MPhil and PhD), which, although not officially conferring degrees in 'Women's Studies', provide, as the first National Conference in 1981 at Bradford University on 'Women Postgraduates Doing Feminist Research' revealed, the chance for feminists in Britain to do feminist research in institutions of higher education.

Events such as these, together with the 1982 conference of the British Sociological Association on the theme 'Gender and Society', that drew a large number of feminist academics, demonstrate the ongoing interest in Women's Studies and the increasing visibility of Women's Studies in Britain.

Acknowledgements

My warm thanks to Dale Spender and Elizabeth Sarah for reading and commenting on an earlier draft of this paper and to Sandra Acker for her valuable editorial suggestions on the final version.

Notes

1 Adrienne Rich (1978) Transcendental étude. In *The Dream of a Common Language* New York: Norton, p.73.

2 For a useful overview on the alleged 'progress' that women have made, see Ann Oakley (1981) *Subject Women* Oxford: Martin Robertson. As an example, between 1960 and 1970 the number of illiterate men rose by eight million, while the number of illiterate women rose by forty million (UNESCO Report 1978).

3 Women comprise 6.4 per cent of readers and senior lecturers, 14.5 per cent of lecturer and assistant lecturers and 33.8 per cent of all other teaching posts. In total, women comprise 13 per cent of the academic staff. In terms of student numbers women comprise 36.8 per cent of undergraduates in British universities and 28.6 per cent of postgraduates (all figures from the 1981 DES statistics).

4 For a detailed account of the early development of Women's Studies in the US see Howe and Ahlum (1973) and Tobias (1978).

5 I prefer 'social status' instead of 'class' which (at least in its usual androcentric definition) does not account for the fact that women may switch 'classes' in their lives depending on the man they happen to be attached to at a particular time; see Comer (1978) for further elaboration on this issue.

6 Constitution of the NWSA (1977) *Women's Studies Newsletter* 5 (1/2) 6.

7 Today's feminists are not the first to demand a woman-centred education. As Spender (1982) has indicated, since Mary Astell (1694) made her 'Serious Proposal to the Ladies' — which was a demand for a woman's college free from the influence and domination of men — through to Virginia Woolf (*A Room of One's Own* 1928), women have been arguing consistently for an education over which they have control instead of an education controlled — as it is still today — by men.

8 Ironically, while feminist scholarship proceeds with its analysis, it is itself declared by many to be 'bad scholarship' and is still considered an illegitimate child in the realms of academe ... which confirms what I said in the first pages of this chapter that it all depends on where you come from, what your assumptions are and whom your work is for.

9 Both terms have bad connotations: 'subjects' are used by psychologists and kings, and the term 'object' conjures up particularly unpleasant images for women who are objectified as 'the other' (Simone de Beauvoir's term), the deviant, the sex object. To talk about 'members' in Women's Studies and feminist research (which is borrowing a term from ethnomethodology) seems more appropriate.

10 That the research process serves as a means to raise consciousness is Paulo Freire's idea of 'conscientizacao'. His theories and methods as well as those of the Critical Theory of the Frankfurt School, of ethnomethodology and phenomenology are useful for feminist theory as a point of reference but have now to be modified, changed, enlarged to account for woman-centred perspectives.

11 For a detailed discussion of feminist research and 'appropriate' research methodologies see Bowles and Duelli Klein (Eds) (1981) *Theories of Women's Studies II*; in particular Maria Mies' account of feminist action research, Toby Jayaratne's defence of quantitative methodology, Shulamit Reinharz' 'Experiential Analysis', Barbara Du Bois' appeal to 'Passionate Scholarship' and Liz Stanley's and Sue Wise's 'Back into the Personal' — their attempt to construct

feminist research. Stanley and Wise go furthest in their claim that feminists should appropriate any methodology: '...feminism should borrow, steal, change, modify and use for its own purpose any and everything from anywhere that looks of interest and of use to it, but we must do this critically' (p.108).

12 This is a selection grounded in my own involvement in teaching and studying Women's Studies at the University of California at Berkeley as well as in my current research on the development of Women's Studies in Great Britain. Although it is fair to say that the Women's Studies movement is best developed in the US, followed by developments in Britain, Germany, Holland, Italy and other European countries, a recent UNESCO survey does show (Rendel, in press) that Women's Studies appear in Japan, Korea, the Philippines, South America and various parts of Africa, as well as many other places. Another self-imposed restriction in this paper is the discussion of Women's Studies within institutions of higher education only. In both the US and Britain the concept of Women's Studies is incorporated in many classes at primary and secondary school level. Women's Studies courses are also offered within further and adult education. To be noted in Britain are the many WEA Women's Studies courses; in the US those in 'Community Colleges' and 'University Extension Programmes'. Furthermore, some of the most innovative learning/teaching goes on in 'autonomous Women's Studies' – so-called 'Street Women's Studies' (Tobias 1978): events that range from theory groups to workshops on topics from writing, affirmative action, and the lesbian novel to how to organize women's groups, houses for battered women, a crisis-line, etc. In addition, there are already a number of autonomous feminist institutes (eg the Berkeley Feminist Institute) which offer Women's Studies classes.

13 Listed in *Women's Studies Quarterly* (1981) 9 (2) 25-35.

14 By far the greatest proliferation of Women's Studies courses has been at the level of adult and further education, where the degree of institutionalized sponsorship varies and the courses exist independently of an institutional academic structure and do not grant official qualifications.

15 For the most recent listings of Women's Studies courses in Britain see Bradshaw, Davies and De Wolfe (Eds) (1981) *Women's Studies Courses in the UK* Women's Research and Resource Centre.

References

Acker,Sandra (1980a) Women, the other academics *British Journal of Sociology of Education* 1 (1) 81-91

Acker,Sandra (1980b) *Feminist Perspectives and British Sociology of Education* Paper presented at BSA Annual Conference Lancaster 8 April

Barry, Kathleen (1979) *Female Sexual Slavery* Englewood-Cliffs: Prentice Hall.

Bowles,Gloria and Duelli Klein,Renate (Eds) (1981) *Theories of Women's Studies II* Berkeley: University of California Women's Studies Program

Bowles,Gloria and Duelli Klein,Renate (1981) Trying to find out how to find out what we know. In Bowles and Duelli Klein (Eds) *Theories of Women's Studies II* Berkeley: University of California Women's Studies Program 1-10

Bradshaw,Jan, Davies,Wendy and De Wolfe,Patricia (1981) *Women's Studies Courses in the UK* London: Women's Research and Resources Centre

Brownmiller,Susan (1975) *Against our Will: Men, Women and Rape* New York: Simon and Schuster

Byrne,Eileen (1978) *Women and Education* London: Tavistock

Cassell,Joan (1977) *A Group Called Women: Sisterhood and Symbolism in the Feminist Movement* New York: David McKay

Comer,Lee (1978) The question of women and class *Women's Studies International Quarterly* 1 (2) 165-174

Coyner,Sandra (1980) Women's Studies as an academic discipline: why and how to do it. In Bowles and Duelli Klein (Eds) *Theories of Women's Studies I* Berkeley: University of California Women's Studies Program 18-40

Department of Education and Science (DES) (1982) *Statistics of Education Vol.6: Universities* London: HMSO

Du Bois,Barbara (1981) Passionate scholarship. Notes on values, knowing and method in feminist social science. In Bowles and Duelli Klein (Eds) *Theories of Women's Studies II* Berkeley: University of California Women's Studies 11-24

Duelli Klein,Renate (1980) How to do what we want to do: Thoughts about feminist methodology. In Bowles and Duelli Klein (Eds) *Theories of Women's Studies I* Berkeley: University of California Women's Studies Program 48-64

Duelli Klein,Renate (1983) The 'men problem' in Women's Studies: experts, ignorants and poor dears *Women's Studies International Forum* 6 (4)

Dworkin,Andrea (1979) *Pornography, Men Possessing Women* New York: Putnam's Sons

Evans,Mary (1981) Women's Studies research in the United States: a review and discussion *Women's Studies International Quarterly* 4 (2) 221-224

Evans,Mary (1982) In praise of theory: The case for Women's Studies *Feminist Review* 10 (Spring 1982) 61-74

Farley,Lin (1978) *Sexual Shakedown: the Sexual Harassment of Women on the Job* New York: McGraw Hill

Frye,Marilyn (1980) On second thought... *The Radical Teacher* 17 November, 37-39

Griffin,Susan (1981) *Pornorgraphy and Silence Culture's Revenge Against Nature* New York: Harper & Row

Groag Bell,Susan and Rosenhan,Mollie Schwartz (1981) A problem in naming: Women's Studies – Women Studies? *Signs* 6 (3) 540-542

Hartnett,Oonagh and Rendel,Margherita (Eds) (1975) *Women's Studies in the UK* London: London Seminars

Herring,Lynn (1980) *Feminist Critical Consciousness* Paper given (with Marcia Westkott) at NWSA Conference at the University of Indiana Bloomington 16-20 May

Howe, Florence (1975) Women and the power to change. In Howe,Florence (Ed.) *Women and the Power to Change* Report of the Carnegie Commission. New York and San Francisco: McGraw-Hill, 127-171

Howe,Florence (1977) *Seven Years Later: Women's Studies Programs in 1976* Report of the National Advisory Council on Women's Educational Programs, Washington

Howe,Florence (1979) Breaking the disciplines. In Reed,Beth (Ed.) *The Structure of Knowledge: A Feminist Perspective* Proceedings of the 7th Annual Great Lakes College Association Conference November, 1-10

Howe,Florence and Ahlum,Carol (1973) Women's Studies and social change. In Rossi,Alice S. and Calderwood,Ann (Eds) *Academic Women on the Move* New York: Russell Sage, 393-423

Hubbard,Ruth (1979) Have only men evolved? *Women Look at Biology Looking at Women* New York: Schenkman

Jayaratne,Toby (1981) The value of quantitative methodology for feminist research. In Bowles and Duelli Klein (Eds) *Theories of Women's Studies II* Berkeley: University of California Women's Studies Program 47-67

Kelly-Gadol,Joan (1976) The social relations of the sexes *Signs* 1 (4) 810-811

MacKinnon, Catharine (1979) *Sexual Harassment of Working Women* New Haven: Yale University

Kolodny,Annette (1981) Dancing through the minefield: some observations on the theory, practice and politics of a feminist literary criticism *Men's Studies Modified* Oxford: Pergamon, 23-42

Lerner,Gerda (1979) Placing women in history (1975) *The Majority Finds its Past* Oxford: University Press

Mies,Maria (1981) Towards a methodology for feminist research. In Bowles and Duelli Klein (Eds) *Theories of Women's Studies II* Berkeley: University of California Women's Studies 25-46

Minnich,Elizabeth (1982) A devastating conceptual error: how can we *not* be feminist scholars? *Change Magazine* 14(3) (April) 7-9

NIE Monographs in Women's Studies (1980) *The Effectiveness of Women's Studies Teaching; The Impact of Women's Studies on the Campus and the Disciplines; The Involvement of Minority Women in Women's Studies; The Relationship Between Women's Studies, Career Development, and Vocational Choice; Re-Entry Women involved in Women's Studies; Women's Studies as a Catalyst for Faculty Development; Women's Studies Graduates; Women's Studies in the Community College* Washington: US Department of Health, Education and Welfare

Oakley,Ann (1981) *Subject Women* Oxford: Martin Robertson

Owen, Wendy (1981) Women hit back on jobs *The Observer* 10 May

Parlee,Mary Brown (1979) Psychology and women *Signs* 5 (1) 121-133

Radford Ruether,Rosemary (1976) Sexism and god talk *Women and Men: The Consequence of Power* The University of Cincinnati: Women's Studies Program

Register,Cheri (1979) Brief a-mazing movements *Women's Studies* Newsletter 7 (4) 7-10

Reinharz,Shulamit (1981) Experiential analysis: a contribution to feminist research. In Bowles and Duelli Klein (Eds) *Theories of Women's Studies II* Berkeley: University of California Women's Studies 68-97

Rendel,Margherita (1980) How many women academics 1912-1976? In Deem,Rosemary (Ed.) *Schooling for Women's Work* London: Routledge Kegan Paul, 142-161

Rendel,Margherita (1982) *Women's Studies — The Study of Women* UNESCO Survey, in press

Rich,Adrienne (1979a) Towards a woman-centred university *On Lies, Secrets and Silence. Selected prose 1966-1978* New York: Norton, 125-155

Rich,Adrienne (1979b) Women and honor: some notes on lying *On Lies, Secrets and Silence. Selected Prose 1966-1978* New York: Norton

Rich,Adrienne (1980) Compulsory heterosexuality and lesbian existence *Signs* 5 (4) 631-660

Rich,Adrienne (1981) *Racism, Homophobia and the Power of Women* Keynote address (with Audre Lorde) given at the NSWA conference University of Storrs, Connecticut 31 May — 4 June

Roberts,Helen (Ed.) (1981) *Doing Feminist Research* London and Boston: Routledge and Kegan Paul

Rutenberg, Taly (1980) Learning Women's Studies. In Bowles and Duelli Klein (Eds) *Theories of Women's Studies I* Berkeley: University of California Women's Studies Program 12-17

Schöpp-Schilling,Hanna Beate (1979) Women's Studies, Women's Research and Women's Research Centres: recent developments in the USA and the FRG *Women's Studies International Quarterly* 2(1) 103-116

Showalter,Elaine (1978) *A Literature of Their Own, British Women Novelists from Brontë to Lessing* London: Virago

Smith,Dorothy (1978) A peculiar eclipsing: women's exclusion from men's culture *Women's Studies International Quarterly* 1 (4) 281-296

Spender,Dale (1978) Notes on the organisation of Women's Studies *Women's Studies International Quarterly* 1 (3) 255-276

Spender,Dale (Ed.) (1981a) *Men's Studies Modified The Impact of Feminism on the Academic Disciplines* Oxford: Pergamon

Spender,Dale (1981b) Education: the patriarchal paradigm and the response to feminism *Men's Studies Modified* Oxford: Pergamon, 155-174

Spender,Dale (1981c) Boys own education. In *Is Higher Education Fair?* Proceedings of the 1981 Annual Conference of the Society for Research into Higher Education Manchester 16-17 December. Guildford: SRHE

Spender,Dale (1982) *Women of Ideas and What Men Have Done to Them: From Aphra Behn to Adrienne Rich* London and Boston: Routledge and Kegan Paul

Stanley,Liz and Sue Wise (1981) 'Back into the Personal' or: our attempt to construct 'Feminist Research'. In Bowles and Duelli Klein (Eds) *Theories of Women's Studies II* Berkeley: University of California Women's Studies Program 98-118

Stanley,Liz and Sue Wise (1983) *Breaking Out: Feminist Research and Feminist Consciousness* London and Boston: Routledge and Kegan Paul

Stimpson,Catharine (1973) What matter mind: a theory about the practice of Women's Studies *Women's Studies* 1, 293-314

Stimpson,Catharine (1978) Women's Studies: an overview *Papers in Women's Studies* Ann Arbor: University of Michigan Women's Studies Program 14-26

Tobias,Sheila (1978) Women's Studies: its origins, its organisation, and its prospects *Women's Studies International Quarterly* 1(1) 85-97

Universities Statistical Record (USR) (1982) *University Statistics 1980 Vol.I: Students and Staff* University Grants Committee

Westkott,Marcia (1979) Feminist criticism of the social sciences *Harvard Educational Review* 49 (4) 422-430

Westkott,Marcia (1981) Women's Studies as a strategy for change: between criticism and vision. In Bowles and Duelli Klein (Eds) *Theories of Women's Studies II* Berkeley: University of California Women's Studies Program 123-130

Woolf,Virginia (1929) *A Room of One's Own* London: The Hogarth Press

Women's Studies International Forum (1983) Battell, Duelli Klein, Moorhouse and Zvirozcek (Eds) *Women's Studies in Britain* 6(4)

Conclusion

Sandra Acker and David Warren Piper

Certain themes emerge not from any single chapter in this book but from a reading of them all. First, there is the notion of women-as-a-group. As Joan Burstyn shows, this has frequently been the opponent's approach, this denial of diversity and difference. Most of our research reports find differences <u>among</u> women, especially differences linked with the disciplines into which they have been (imperfectly?) socialized. Women's career and value orientations, as Peter Burnhill and Andrew McPherson remind us, do change as society changes. On the other hand, many feminist arguments, including several in this book, while acknowledging diversity, put a much greater emphasis on commonalities among women. How can we reconcile our distaste for discrimination, which in the past has frequently implied separation of the sexes, with the (often self-chosen) separation implicit in some concepts of Women's Studies and feminist research? Can we speak comfortably of 'women as a group' when it suits our purposes and oppose such talk when it doesn't?

Second, there is the dialectical relationship between identity and structure. Women in higher education must negotiate their relationships with peers and superiors and decide upon their plans and priorities in an institutional context governed according to the male life-cycle (see Hochschild 1975) within which women are inevitably alien. The institution itself exists in a larger social setting with particular economic structures and ideological climates. Women's 'aspirations' and 'opportunities' are only partly of their own making. Yet the structures will not change without individuals changing them.

Third, there is the link between marginality and creativity. We see this in the Sue Scott/Mary Porter tale of two researchers, in Liz Stanley's analysis of newcomers' perceptions of social science, and in Renate Duelli Klein's account of innovation in Women's Studies. We learn that while women are frequently subordinate within and marginal to the academic establishment, they may be in a unique position to see through

242

and break away from outdated assumptions and create something new and better. Women are victims, in one sense, but they are neither powerless nor defeated.

Fourth, and finally, there is the theme of continuity and change. The historical papers describe an era not unrecognizable to today's women in higher education.Things have changed – for example the proportion of women undergraduates has risen steadily in the past few years – but many of the dilemmas echo those of the pioneers. Are women in higher education better off as 'separatists', creating their own knowledge, institutions and research methods, or should they be 'uncompromising', insisting women can compete and win equally with men even on men's terms? Are these the only alternatives? There are further conundrums bound up with continuity and change that are of special concern to educators. How can women use the resources and knowledge of the present to prepare for an unknown future? Are we justified in trying to convince people to do what we think is good and right for them even when experience and intuition tells them otherwise? If not, how can we influence the next generation?

Is Higher Education Fair to Women? has its gaps and omissions, as with all edited collections: one is the lack of an explicit socialist-feminist perspective, another is the concentration on universities with rather less attention paid to colleges of higher education and polytechnics. A third is the minimizing of other social divisions such as ethnicity and social class that interact with gender in determining educational outcomes. The omissions reflect the state of the art: as we commented earlier, very little work on women in higher education has been undertaken in Britain. We hope this book will be a stimulus toward further efforts to fill the gap.

There is every sign that in the coming years women will have to fight to stand still. Dramatic cuts have been made in the resources for British higher education, and new hiring has come to a halt in some disciplines. Teacher-training and adult education are two sectors that have been dramatically slashed, to the especial disadvantage of women (Bone 1980; Deem 1981). In the university sector resources have been shifted from 'arts' to 'sciences' (both broadly defined). Yet women students and staff are for the most part arts-based. Among full-time non-clinical university academic staff, 44 per cent of men but 68 per cent of women teach education, social science, or arts subjects. In contrast, 53 per cent of men and 29 per cent of women teach science, engineering or medicine (EOC 1982). The 1983/84 'new blood posts' go for the most part to those scientific and technological fields where men predominate and are restricted to the age range (under thirty-five) when women are most likely to be involved with children (THES 1983-4). What then is the prognosis for women in higher education? Can it be more than 'fair'?

References

Bone,A. (1980) *The Effect on Women's Opportunities of Teacher Training Cuts* Manchester: Equal Opportunities Commission

Deem,R. (1981) State policy and ideology in the education of women 1944-1980 *British Journal of Sociology of Education* 2 (2) 131-143

Equal Opportunities Commission (1982) *Women in Universities 1982: A Statistical Description* Manchester: Equal Opportunities Commission

Hochschild,A.R. (1975) Inside the clockwork of male careers. In Howe,F. (Ed.) *Women and the Power to Change* New York: McGraw-Hill

THES (1983-4) See for instance 29.4.83, p.4. See also 13.1.84, p.3: Report on Daphne Jackson addressing a conference on women in technology